The publisher gratefully acknowledges the generous support of the Simpson Humanities Endowment Fund of the University of California Press Foundation.

Breaking Bread

CALIFORNIA STUDIES IN FOOD AND CULTURE

Darra Goldstein, Editor

Breaking Bread

RECIPES AND STORIES FROM
IMMIGRANT KITCHENS

Lynne Christy Anderson

Foreword by Corby Kummer
Photographs by Robin Radin

UNIVERSITY OF CALIFORNIA PRESS

BERKELEY   LOS ANGELES   LONDON

University of California Press, one of the most
distinguished university presses in the United States,
enriches lives around the world by advancing scholarship
in the humanities, social sciences, and natural sciences. Its
activities are supported by the UC Press Foundation and
by philanthropic contributions from individuals and
institutions. For more information, visit www.ucpress.edu.

University of California Press
Berkeley and Los Angeles, California

University of California Press, Ltd.
London, England

Library of Congress Cataloging-in-Publication Data
Anderson, Lynne Christy.
    Breaking bread : recipes and stories from immigrant
kitchens / Lynne Christy Anderson ; foreword by Corby
Kummer ; photographs by Robin Radin.
        p.   cm—(California studies in food and culture ; 29)
    ISBN-13: 978-0-520-26257-7 (cloth : alk. paper)
    1. Cookery, International.   2. Food habits—United
States.   3. Immigrants—United States—Anecdotes.
I. Title.
TX725.A1A564   2010
394.1'20973—dc22   2009043911

Manufactured in the United States of America
19   18   17   16   15   14   13   12   11   10
10   9   8   7   6   5   4   3   2   1

The paper used in this publication meets the minimum
requirements of ANSI/NISO Z39.48-1992 (R 1997)
(Permanence of Paper).

For my mother, who instilled in me the pleasures of cooking and eating, and for my father, who taught me to listen to my students

There is a communion of more than our bodies when bread is broken and wine drunk.

M.F.K. FISHER, *The Gastronomical Me, 1943*

CONTENTS

FOREWORD

CORBY KUMMER

LYNNE ANDERSON LIVES IN MY neighborhood—Jamaica Plain, a part of Boston—and is as proud of its diversity as I and the rest of us who choose to live here because of it. But my, what she found in our shared streets! A whole world of cooks, mostly women, living the cultures they came from at the markets I shop in and the kitchens I never see or even imagined were here.

But Anderson, a former professional cook turned teacher of immigrant communities, found them. Families recently arrived from Ireland, Greece, and Italy, traditional Jamaica Plain mainstays, and from countries that have a more recent but strong presence here, like Haiti, Cape Verde, Costa Rica, El Salvador, Guatemala, and Brazil. And families from countries I had no idea were so close by: Sudan, Latvia, Morocco, Venezuela, Chile, Vietnam. Yes, she went looking. But I don't think her tour would be so difficult to take in most other large American cities.

Even if other cities might have international riches, though, they likely don't have any listeners and writers as gently sympathetic as Anderson. She went looking for more than interesting dishes most anyone can cook, though she gives us abundant, tempting, and accessible recipes. She also went looking for the meaning of home.

In her warm, subtly attentive interviews—though she never mentions herself or her way of interviewing, you can sense her tact and acceptance of people just as they are—Anderson listens for what is most important to a cook far from the place she grew up. That can be the way to knead pasta dough, the choice of curry stirred into a stew, the friendships formed with the only people who sell ground okra or the vegetables, fish, and cuts of meat that can best reproduce a memory.

And she listens for the language of the women (and a few men) who cook, usually with children or friends, to understand and show us how cooking and food form and forge lasting connections. As they tell Anderson about the lands they left and the lives they led then and lead now, the cooks become lost in their memories, as if the smell of a certain stew is the royal route to the kitchens and the people they most loved there. The actual circumstances that brought them to leave can be too painful to recount directly. It is hunting for mushrooms like they did in Latvia, or stuffing pork into soaked corn husks for Christmas tamales as in Costa Rica, or boiling beef and beets for a health-transmitting broth as in Vietnam, that lets them live again their childhoods.

Not that most of the cooks Anderson found left terribly painful pasts. Some did, and suffered for their beliefs or family circumstances they could not change. But most came here for opportunity, for education, for better lives for their children: the goals that have always driven people to emigrate. And most seem content with the new lives they have made—or, rather, they seem adaptable and resourceful, the necessary calling cards of the immigrant. Finding or improvising the tools and ingredients to reproduce remembered dishes, knowing how to handle food and the way to move in the kitchen—subtleties and graces Anderson is alive to—will endure displacement and disruptions, will literally keep families together.

This book of vivid, living memories can help you make memories of your own. Through the cooks Anderson presents, you can reproduce some of the elegance of a cinnamon-flecked Persian green herb omelet, the earthiness of Venezuelan roast beef with baked plantain and corn cakes, the surprising satisfaction of Irish baked sole with mashed potatoes ("Be sure to use enough butter," a mother admonishes her tech-minded son via a video camera on his laptop screen—naturally, given that the best butter in the world is Irish) and a carrot-parsnip mash. Best of all, you can—whatever your own family background, wherever you are now—live a part of the American immigrant experience through Anderson's words and the lives and food she celebrates.

ACKNOWLEDGMENTS

I WOULD LIKE TO THANK all of the people who invited me into their homes and so generously shared their stories and foods; I am greatly indebted to all of you. To Robin Radin, who accompanied me with her camera into kitchens, markets, gardens, and far-flung foraging sites, your photos add a depth to this book I could never have achieved with words alone. Special thanks go to my editor, Jenny Wapner, whose gentle guidance throughout the writing of the book has made it much stronger. I am hugely indebted to Cristina Rathbone, who first told me what I needed to do when I didn't have a clue. To Chuck Collins, who read numerous drafts of proposals and early chapters and came up with the book's title, thank you. Thanks also to Elsa Auerbach, who has always been there as I tried to teach my way through Boston's immigrant communities, and to Vivian Zamel, who first made me think I could write. My dear friends Dana Burnell, Anna Brackett, and Tracy Strauss read drafts, gave me invaluable feedback, and never got frustrated with my endless editorial concerns. Alice Waters, Corby Kummer, Nikki Silva, Anna Lappé, and Nazli Kibria provided early encouragement for the book and helped to shore up my sometimes wavering optimism. Eva Katz, thank you for showing me how to write a recipe.

Many people and organizations helped in my search to find immigrant cooks, and, even though I wasn't able to include everyone in the book, thank you for your persistence: my sister, Betsy Anderson, Viki Bok and

Dick Jones, Tyler Haaren and Daniel Moss, Kristina Hals, Andy Reyes, Chee Tran, Stella Fateh, Roula Kappas, Eva Katz, Raquel Cardoso, Meenakshi Khanna, Eileen McMahon, Breige Kerr, Bob Magane, Wandee Mayer, Sarah Slavick, Sue Kalt, Michelle Cheeseman, Kaye Stroshine, and the wonderful teachers and staff at Neighborhood House Charter School in Dorchester. To Bill Baxter, a.k.a. Officer Donut, from the Boston Police Youth Service and Community Outreach Department, thanks for bringing Boston teenagers to cook with me; some of their families contributed to this book. Thanks to Debbie Sercombe and the Title VII gang and Gretchen Lahey and GEAR UP; the ESL classes are where I first began to have conversations about the power of food. And thanks to Bunker Hill Community College and Boston College, where I have had the privilege of teaching a wonderfully diverse group of nonnative English speakers, some of whom appear in this book.

So many people and organizations helped to guide my research and answer questions about writing and publishing, including the Fine Arts Work Center in Provincetown, Massachusetts, Jane Brox, Anne Stuart, and the members in our seminar, Jim Grace, Sheri Mason and the other volunteer lawyers at VLAMA, Devin Anderson, Katia Edwards, Sandra Darling at the Adult Literacy Resource Institute, Whole Foods Market in Brighton, Massachusetts, the Photographic Resource Center in Boston, Michael Jacobsen-Hardy, Danielle Durkin, Peter Thomson, Ruth Adams, Eve Tai, Patty Moosebrugger, Lou Howland, and Joe Skokowski.

There are people who helped me maintain my sanity through the very long process of writing a book. Linda Heald, thanks for taking the kids. Jim Dube always had a full pantry when I was testing recipes. I am, however, most indebted to my family, without whose support this book could never have been written: to my father, Jay Anderson, for teaching me how to listen to other people's stories and giving me the time to write them down; to my mother, Patricia, for reading early drafts and offering encouragement; and to my sister and brother, Betsy and Justus, for always being there when I needed you. And to my little prep cooks, Lilly, Sam, Callie, JD, and Lissa, thanks for helping me test recipes and for your continued enthusiasm.

Finally, to Erik, for always believing in me.

Introduction

I HAVE A DISTINCT MEMORY of my favorite food. In my mind, it sits on the sideboard in my grandmother's dining room in Connecticut, where so many of her delicious desserts made their appearance. Its meringue peaks curl toward the ceiling and are a light golden brown, as if the tips had been glazed with a brush. The granules of sugar sprinkled over the top of the pie before it went into the oven reflect the afternoon sun streaming in through the nearby window, and the memory of the pale yellow custard, just a hint of which reveals itself between the meringue and crust, teases me to this day with its citrusy zing.

The lemon meringue pie is my madeleine, and, like Proust's narrator, whenever I am offered a piece now, I find myself plunged into that long-ago place where several generations of us would gather for dinner, my grand-mother at the head of the table. Her voice is a distant echo now, but it lingers nevertheless. She makes her apologies: she could have added another drop of lemon to the custard; the crust is slightly underdone this time; the meringue, too sweet. The rest of my family—my grandfather, parents, brother and sister, aunts, uncles, and cousins—are there, too. Their younger selves call out from around the table in protest, telling her the pie is just as wonderful as ever. I can even see a glimmer of blue, the small pale sapphire that she wore on her hand, its gold band twisted slightly on her thin fingers as she hands me my piece, slightly larger than the others, on one of the crystal dessert plates she used on Sundays.

We all have one particular food so wedded to our sensibilities that it has the power to resurrect the past. During the years I worked in professional kitchens, the foods many of the other cooks and I really longed for weren't the risottos scented with saffron or the rabbit braised with fresh truffles we were preparing for the award-winning menus. Rather, they were someone's grandmother's potato salad, an aunt's famous gingerbread, a mother's meatloaf. A piece of the past is what we really wanted to eat.

When I hung up my chef's jacket, I turned to a career in teaching, one I believed would be more conducive to raising a family. That first year, staring out at a roomful of immigrant adults—mothers and grandmothers from places like Guatemala, Pakistan, and Haiti, fathers from Sudan, Cape Verde, and Brazil—many of whom hadn't stepped into a school for decades, I knew I had to find a way to build their trust. We needed a common language. That language turned out to be food. So I asked them what they cooked over the weekend, where they liked to shop, what they wanted to eat most. Soon they were telling me about their own madeleines: the *sancocho* someone's mother made every Sunday back in Santo Domingo, the Haitian *piclise* that's good when you can find the right peppers, the arepas that just don't taste the same in America.

The great food writer M. F. K. Fisher knew only too well that talk of food leads to other things when she said, "It seems to me that our three basic needs, for food and security and love, are so mixed and mingled and entwined that we cannot straightly think of one without the others." Inevitably, this twining happened in my classroom, and I found myself listening to stories about life back home, the decisions that had to be made in coming to America, the hope now for something more. As the semesters passed by, I watched my students' English improve, their lives become a little easier, their longing for home, somewhat less apparent. But still they cooked—the same *sancochos, piclise,* and arepas—the things they had always eaten, only now they were cooking them in their kitchens in Boston.

Breaking Bread builds on the kinds of stories I first began hearing in the classroom over a decade ago. A few of the people featured in the book are former students from the adult literacy programs and colleges where I have taught. Others I've met in Boston, where I've lived for over twenty years and which, like most cities in America today, is a diverse place. I've tried to include cooks that represent some of the immigrant groups that have made their home in and around the city; however, the book is not meant to be a definitive breakdown in demographics, and I've certainly missed some groups. I have, however, searched for women and men who love to cook and eat, people passionate about food, someone with a story to tell.

For the last few years, I have had the great privilege of hearing these stories and learning about the roles that food plays in the lives of those who have left almost everything behind. The families I've met have been generous, sharing their stories, foods, and culinary traditions that have been passed down through the generations, for example, rolling phyllo dough with a *plastis* for spanakopita, pureeing vegetables with a wooden *mufraka* for Sudanese lamb stew, and rolling fettuccini on a hand-crank pasta machine. These wonderful meals came out of kitchens that, for the most part, were devoid of high-end stoves and fancy appliances. Rarely was there a cookbook or measuring cup in sight. Here, the cooking was done by feel. In backyard gardens, vegetables were harvested for dinner, or grape leaves and mushrooms were collected at coveted foraging sites. At ethnic food markets across the city, families shopped for the ingredients needed to make authentic Filipino adobo, Panamanian sorrel drink, and Chinese stir-fry with fresh bamboo. And finally, when the harvesting, shopping, and cooking were done, there was the breaking of bread at kitchen tables.

When I'm asked whether it was difficult to find people to interview for this book, the answer has always been no. Simply put, people like to talk about food. For the most part, the immigrant cooks featured here enjoyed reminiscing about their favorite meals and the people and places connected to those times as they eagerly welcomed me into their kitchens, along with Robin Radin, whose photographs appear in these pages.

Food is our common language, and we connect to it in our own way. Zady, from a small village in Côte d'Ivoire, who ate mostly rice growing up, feels as strongly about that rice as Fausta does about the multicourse meals she was served at her grandparent's house in Italy. The recipes included here, like Zady's rice and Fausta's fettuccini, represent the dishes that are most meaningful to a particular cook or family. My goal was not to assemble a cookbook with a balance between soups and salads, meats and fish. Rather, the recipes have been chosen by the cooks themselves and function as a commemoration of the past, a celebration of their lives in America.

Although my grandmother is gone, her lemon meringue pie lives on. I can go back home and sit at the same dining room table—in my mother's house now—and share it with many of the family members who always enjoyed it. For the people featured in *Breaking Bread,* however, it's different: there might be desperately needed money to be made, a new language to be learned, children to be taken care of, political regimes to be avoided. For them, going back isn't always so simple.

But they can cook. And that brings home a little closer.

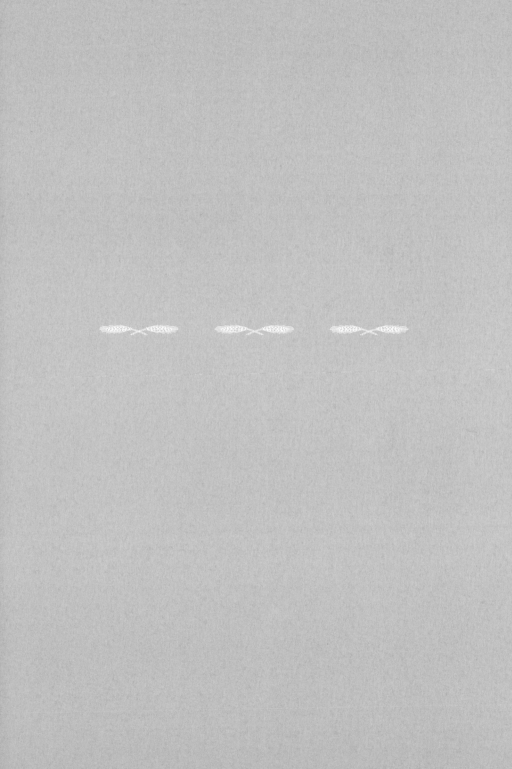

Scooping the Memories

Dmitra Khoury, fifty, is originally from Lebanon. She lives in
Roslindale, Massachusetts, with her husband and two children. The
family makes frequent trips to the nearby Arnold Arboretum to
collect grape leaves during the months of June and July every year.

WHILE DMITRA, HER MOTHER, AND her husband, Farid, pick grape leaves
off vines that grow along this stone wall enclosing the southern portion of the
Arnold Arboretum, her children play on the sidewalk nearby. Nine-year-old
George chases his twin sister, Jessica, and when they get too close to the street,
Dmitra tells them to stop. It is an exquisite Friday evening in June, and the
late-afternoon sun casts a pale orange light on the wall, the grapevines, and
this family of five. They arrived several minutes earlier, each carrying a canvas
bag, and Dmitra and Farid, who is also from Lebanon, are now stuffing theirs
with leaves they've gently torn from the vines. They speak to each other quietly in Lebanese, pointing to spots where the vines look particularly prolific,
while the sounds of George and Jessica shouting to each other in English are
heard from afar. Seventy-nine-year-old Najla, Dmitra's mother, stands several
feet away and pushes at the undergrowth with her cane, checking the vines
that run along the ground. She doesn't pick anything but surveys the area quietly with large, discerning eyes that seem unsatisfied with the prospects.
When George and Jessica finally come after Dmitra has called for them several
times, they grab their bags they'd left in the grass and begin to pick, too.

Opposite: Dmitra and her son, George, pick grape leaves in Jamaica Plain, Massachusetts.

"Georgie, please. It looks like a goat was here!" Dmitra reprimands, showing him how to pull the leaves more gently from their vines while his sister stands next to him, intently picking away. Several ancient oak trees tower above us, their branches swaying in the gentle spring breeze and shading this section of the wall. Dmitra tells me she prefers grape leaves that grow in the shade, because they tend to be thinner and therefore more delicate to the bite when they are blanched and stuffed. They will be filled with a mixture of rice, mint, parsley, tomato, and lemon, a combination of light, refreshing flavors that plunged me immediately into summer when I first tried them on a damp, gray afternoon this past winter.

Each year, she and the family come here to collect the leaves she'll need to fill the thirty or so jars she puts up every summer. It will take several outings, but she guesses that they'll eventually pick three or four thousand among them. When they get home, these will be organized by size and texture, the larger, thicker leaves reserved for her brother in Pennsylvania, who needs them for his restaurant, and the others, divided between those that she'll blanch and store in jars in her pantry and the ones that will be directly frozen after she's rinsed them in water and vinegar.

The leaves are used for other dishes, too, Dmitra explains, including the sandwiches Jessica likes for school, made with homemade pita bread, lettuce, and the grape leaves. We begin to move along the sidewalk searching for another area where the vines grow thick. As we walk, Dmitra and Farid pinch leaves from the vines on the wall, as if it's impossible for them to pass anything that might be suitable for cooking. When Dmitra turns around, she says something quickly to her husband and points in the opposite direction. We all turn and watch Najla scramble across the road. She leans heavily into her cane as she waits for a truck to go by before crossing with determination to the northern side of the arboretum. She doesn't look back when Dmitra shouts after her.

"She's going to give me a heart attack!" Dmitra cries, shaking her head at me. "I swear to God, that lady, she's going to run the marathon one day!" She calls to her mother again, and this time Najla looks over for a moment and then continues on her way.

"When we look, she says, 'I'm tired,'" Farid explains, nodding toward the receding back of his mother-in-law. "When we don't look, she's gone," he shrugs. Dmitra beckons for her mother one last time—with a loud whistle now—and then turns toward Farid and says, "Okay, let her go."

I first witnessed Najla's independent streak earlier this year when she and Dmitra were preparing a Lebanese dinner of stuffed grape leaves, hommus, tabbouleh, homemade pita, and *riz bie dhjage,* a rice dish made with chicken, lamb, beef, and pine nuts. We were in Dmitra's kitchen, and she occasionally asked her mother to do something a certain way or to wait, perhaps, before filling the leaves with the rice and vegetable mixture until more spice had been added. Sometimes, Najla would acquiesce, leaning back in her chair with a shrug. At others, however, she'd continue rolling, mixing, or chopping as if she hadn't heard.

It is Najla, after all, who first taught Dmitra to cook back in Lebanon, where they'd pick the grape leaves that grew on the arbor in the yard. There, Dmitra would help her mother make the 150 pitas they needed each week to feed their family of six. After making the dough at home, they would carry it to Dmitra's aunt's, who had the only oven in the village. When Dmitra first told me this story, she stopped to ask her mother something to make sure she'd gotten it right. Behind her, twelve pitas—far fewer than the 150 of years past—sat on trays that had been placed on the kitchen heater to rise.

Rolling the grape leaves in Dmitra's kitchen that afternoon, the women fell into a comfortable rhythm, sipping their tea as they spooned the rice mixture onto flattened leaves to form the thin cylinders that would later be steamed in a pot and seasoned with garlic, mint, oil, and fresh tomatoes. This is something they do together quite often, in order to keep up with demand. Dmitra brings her grape leaves to family weddings, baby showers, and even to events at George's and Jessica's schools. Usually a plate is made up for the neighbors, too. In Lebanon, she explained to me, more people were always around to help. "You'd call the nieces or aunts, and they would come," she said. "But here, women don't have the time."

Now, as we walk back to the family's minivan, having collected enough grape leaves for the evening, Dmitra stops at one last vine cascading down from the large iron gate by the entrance. She pops a small leaf into her mouth and says, "I love it!" explaining that they have a slight lemon flavor when eaten off the vine. She and Farid begin to unload their sacks, making piles on the hood of the van and discarding any leaves that have been chewed by caterpillars or sprayed by cars passing on the road. George and Jessica run through the parking area, laughing and tossing a stuffed animal they found into the air and pretending not to hear their parents' calls that it's time to go. In a moment, Najla, who disappeared more than an hour ago, comes from around the corner, walking resolutely with her own bag filled with leaves harvested from somewhere else. She slips into the passenger seat and waits quietly for the others.

⟫⟨⟩⟪

That's how we communicate back home—with food. I cook for everyone now: my husband, my kids, my brothers and their families. Sometimes I cook for my cousin and his family. Oh, my goodness, their boy, Patrick, loves it when I come. Everything I have left over, I leave it with him. I feel like that is life's secret. My friend tells me I have the ability to make friends through my table, that I make them happy with my food. I've always said that if you want to discuss something with your husband, don't ever do it on an empty stomach. There is power in eating together, in sharing. So I cook for everyone about once a month. I tell my cousin's wife, my brothers' wives, "Your mother-in-law is not here, so I'm your mother-in-law," and we'll all spend a day together in the kitchen.

We're a food family. My brother owns a business in Boston called Sami's. He started it as a food van, and he sold all the specialties—the hommus, the *baba.* It was the first in Boston to serve Lebanese food. When he first opened, in 1977, we'd have customers coming from New York, Rhode Island, you name it. I worked there for about seventeen years, and we used to have regulars that came every day. We'd always know their order; they'd never even have to tell us what they wanted. We'd prepare their coffee the way they liked it and say, "Good morning, sir. How are you this morning?" or "Have a lovely day, sir." I remember some of the customers wouldn't even answer us. One day, I asked one of the guys in the van, "Why do you bother saying 'good morning' and 'have a lovely day' if he doesn't even look at you?" And he told me, "We are here in America, and they are coming to us. They don't know us. You have to teach them how to be nice and let them get used to it. If you bring it out, one day they'll say something." And, you know, he was right: after three or four months, that guy was smiling and talking with us.

Everybody's so busy here. It's weird. I'm not blaming them, but it's something about American culture. Nowadays in Lebanon it's the same, but when I grew up, it was different. When I was little, my mom used to take care of everything—our school, washing, everything. When we'd come home, she'd always be cooking. "Okay, go wash your hands," she'd say, and then she'd feed us. Always there were people over, always someone to share the food. My father's family would come. Friends would

Dmitra (right) and her mother, Najla, rolling the grape leaves.

come, neighbors would come, and my mother would cook. She cooked from her heart. And me, too, not just [from] my heart, but from the bottom of my feet! And my family loves it now, my neighbors, too. I do it because sometimes it seems like no one has time to cook.

When I first came this was confusing to me. I'd see people eating on the street, getting take-out, and I'd think, oh, she doesn't have time to make a chicken sandwich for herself at home, or a man would come to the van and I'd wonder, why didn't his wife make him something to eat? But my brother would always say, "That's why we have a good business; don't complain!" I was a lot younger then—only twenty-four when I first came—and everything was different: no communication, no social life. The language was not easy. We learned Shakespeare English in my country. It's not like spoken language. I remember one time when I was working and one of the guys came to the window and said, "What's up?" I looked up and saw the cigarettes and said, "Cigarettes!" He was laughing. But you know, Shakespeare never said, "What's up?" So I started to talk like them on the street.

It's easier now. I still have memories of Lebanon—especially when I eat certain things, like the breads, the *manoushe,* the *knefeh.* When I was living in Beirut, I used to sneak out of school to get the bread for breakfast. And after all these years, I still crave the same foods. I think it's in your genes. The other night we were out to dinner with my friend, and guess what she ordered? Kale and cornbread. She's from the South. When she was eating, I thought, she's not scooping the food, she's scooping the memories. I was watching her, and I felt like she wasn't with us. It was like she was thinking about how her mom used to cook. It's just like the bread for me. It still reminds me of the time I lived in Beirut.

That was during the war. Just before it started, I went there to finish school. My mom and dad were in the northern part of the country then. It was very dangerous. When they started bombing, there were a few months when my family didn't know if I was alive or not. At my parents', people would come to the door and ask questions all the time. "Where are your kids? Where is your daughter? Do you have a gun?" they'd say. So we were really tired. I didn't know anything about my parents, and they didn't know anything about me. We were not like a family. A family is together. Sometimes, though, we had contact through my uncle. He had a taxi and drove from Tripoli to Beirut, so my mother would send food for me when he came. But it was a frightening time: you didn't know when you were going to die. One day my father said, "Would you like to go to America?" And I said, "Yeah."

Now, I'm cooking for my mother. It's not always easy when we're in the kitchen together. "No, we do it this way," she'll say. Like if I add something to the food, she'll ask, "Since when do we put cumin in the *kibbeh?*" I tell her, "If you don't like it, Mama, send it back!" "No, no, I ate it," she'll say. But I appreciate her. She's never told us no. And I appreciate the time she spends with my kids. She's almost eighty years old and she's healthy. Well, when she wants to be.

And my kids, they cook with me, too. My daughter, Jessica, she loves to eat. I always tell her she's a little girl with a big stomach. I make anything she and her brother want. If they want meatballs, I make meatballs. The other day they wanted pizza, so I made pizza. They helped with the dough. They do other things, too. I always take them to the park so they can help pick the grape leaves. They know I'm going to save them for the winter instead of having to pay four or five dollars for the ones in the store. And I'll make them for their teachers and friends at school. I know they like the grape leaves. The hommus, too. I send it in as a treat sometimes, and then, when I go to the school, all their friends will say, "Miss Khoury, I love your hommus! Miss Khoury, I love your grape leaves!"

My dream is to write a book about the food with recipes like the hommus and *baba,* even the grape leaves, things that won't be too difficult to make. Women won't have to say that they don't have time to cook, because I'll explain how they can plan ahead to make it easier. And it will have healthy recipes, recipes that they can prepare for their families. I'm not going to say I don't let my kids eat other things—they do like McDonald's as a treat sometimes—but they really love my cooking. They'll say, "Mommy, you are the best chef!"

Dmitra's Lebanese Stuffed Grape Leaves, Hommus, Tabbouleh, and Pita

Each recipe serves 6 to 8 as appetizers.

If you are going to preserve your own grape leaves, it's best to pick them in the spring and early summer, when the leaves are still tender. Medium-large leaves make rolling easier, but if they are too large, they can be tough. Avoid picking leaves that may have been sprayed with pesticides or salt from the road. Dmitra, her mother, and sometimes her children roll these together in front of the TV at night or in the afternoon, around the kitchen table with cups of tea. Stuffed grape leaves and hommus can be made several days ahead and served at room temperature. Tabbouleh and pita bread, however, are best prepared on the day they'll be served.

PREPARING YOUR OWN GRAPE LEAVES

8 cups water

1 cup salt

60 fresh grapevine leaves, rinsed and stems snipped

In a large pot, bring the water and salt to a boil. Working in batches of 12 to 15 leaves each, blanch for 1 minute. Remove from water with a slotted spoon and immediately plunge into a cold-water bath. Drain and spread on paper towels to dry.

Use the leaves immediately. Or, to freeze for later use, stack them in rolls of 6, with the fronts of the leaves facing upward, and roll from the side to form tight cylinders. Seal tightly in plastic wrap. To use, defrost and use immediately. These keep in the freezer for up to 6 months.

STUFFED GRAPE LEAVES

Makes 40 to 50

   1   cup uncooked long-grain white rice

   2   cups water

40 to 50   preserved grape leaves (about 1 large jar, if using
         store-bought leaves), drained and stems removed

   2   teaspoons Lebanese seven-spice powder*

   ⅓   cup plus 2 tablespoons vegetable oil, divided

   ⅓   cup lemon juice

   ½   small white onion, finely chopped (about ¼ cup)

   8   cloves garlic (6 minced and 2 thinly sliced)

   ⅔   cup flat-leaf parsley leaves, finely chopped

   ⅓   cup plus 2 tablespoons fresh mint leaves, finely
         chopped and divided

   4   plum tomatoes (2 cut into ¼-inch dice and 2 sliced)

   2   cups cooked, drained chickpeas, mashed

   1   large potato, cut into ½-inch slices
         Salt and freshly ground pepper

Soak the rice in 2 cups of water for 1 hour. Drain.

Meanwhile, if using store-bought leaves in a jar, you will need to blanch
them. In a large pot, over high heat, bring 2 quarts of water to a boil. Add
the grape leaves and turn off the heat. Let the leaves soak in the hot water
for 1 minute. Drain. Place the leaves in a large bowl of cold water to cool.
Drain. Gently separate the leaves and spread them, shiny sides down, on paper towels to drain.

In a large bowl, combine the drained rice, Lebanese seven-spice powder,
⅓ cup of the vegetable oil, lemon juice, onion, the 6 cloves of minced garlic, parsley, ⅓ cup of the mint, 2 diced tomatoes, and the mashed chickpeas.
Season with ½ teaspoon of salt.

To roll the grape leaves, spread a leaf flat, shiny side down, on a clean
work surface. Place 1 tablespoon of the rice mixture on the center of the leaf.
Turn up the stem end of the leaf and then, one at a time, each of the sides

---

* Found in markets specializing in Middle Eastern products. A mixture of equal amounts
  of ground allspice, black pepper, cinnamon, clove, fenugreek, nutmeg, and ginger can be
  substituted.

to enclose the stuffing. Beginning at the stem end, gently roll the grape leaf into a cylinder.

Layer the bottom of a heavy 2- to 3-quart casserole with the sliced potatoes to prevent the leaves from sticking to the pot when cooking. Stack the stuffed grape leaves, side by side with seams down, in layers in the casserole. Cover this with the remaining 2 tablespoons of mint, the 2 cloves of sliced garlic, 2 tablespoons of vegetable oil, tomato slices, and several pinches of salt. Add enough water to just cover the grape leaves. To prevent the leaves from unrolling while cooking, place a heavy plate on top of the stacked leaves.

Place the casserole over high heat and bring to a boil. Immediately reduce the heat to low and simmer gently, tightly covered, until the water has been absorbed and the rice in the grape leaves is fully cooked, about 40 minutes. Carefully remove the stuffed grape leaves from the pot and arrange them on a serving dish. Cool to room temperature before serving. (These may be made 1 to 2 days ahead and stored in a sealed container in the refrigerator.)

TABBOULEH

½ cup fine bulgur

4 medium tomatoes, finely chopped

2 cups parsley leaves (flat-leaf or curly), finely chopped (approximately 2 bunches)

⅓ cup mint leaves, finely chopped

⅓ cup scallions, finely chopped

⅓ cup fresh lemon juice

½ cup olive oil

Salt and freshly ground pepper

8 to 10 romaine lettuce leaves, washed and dried

In a small bowl, soak the bulgur in enough water to cover it completely. Allow it to soak for about 10 minutes. Drain well.

In a mixing bowl, combine the bulgur, tomatoes, parsley, mint, scallions, lemon juice, and olive oil. Season with salt and pepper.

To serve, arrange the lettuce leaves around the edges of a serving bowl or platter, with the stem end toward the center. Mound the tabbouleh in the center so that the top ends of the leaves are still visible. To eat, spoon a small amount of tabbouleh onto one of the lettuce leaves.

HOMMUS

1½ cups cooked chickpeas, drained and cooking liquid
  reserved (a 15-ounce can, drained and rinsed, can be
  substituted)

1 clove garlic, minced

⅓ cup tahini paste

¼ cup lemon juice

½ teaspoon salt

In a blender or food processor, puree the chickpeas, garlic, tahini, lemon juice, salt, and approximately ½ cup of the reserved cooking liquid from the chickpeas. (If you used canned chickpeas, substitute water.) More liquid can be added if mixture is too thick. Blend until smooth.

Can be made 1 to 2 days ahead. Serve with pita bread. (Recipe follows.)

PITA BREAD

Makes 6 rounds

- 1 package active dry yeast (2¼ teaspoons)
- 1 tablespoon honey
- ½ cup plus 1 cup warm water, divided
- 3 cups all-purpose flour
- 1½ teaspoons salt
- 1 tablespoon olive oil

In a large mixing bowl, dissolve the yeast and honey in ½ cup of the warm water and allow to proof. (The yeast should begin to froth, indicating it is converting sugar into carbon dioxide bubbles.) Add the remaining 1 cup of water, flour, and salt. Mix until combined. (The dough will be sticky.)

Turn onto a floured surface and knead until the dough is smooth and elastic, about 10 minutes. (An electric mixer with a dough hook attachment can be used instead. The kneading time will be less.)

Shape the dough into a ball and place it in a large bowl that has been brushed with the olive oil. Turn the dough in the bowl to coat its entire surface with oil. Cover and let rise in a warm, draft-free spot until it has doubled in size, about 1½ to 2 hours.

Punch down the dough and turn it onto a floured surface. Divide it into 6 equal pieces and shape each into a ball. Roll each ball into an 8-inch circle, approximately ¼ inch thick. Lay the circles on baking sheets that have been lightly dusted with cornmeal. Let rest in a warm spot for 30 minutes.

Meanwhile, preheat the oven to 500°F. Bake the pita loaves until they begin to puff up, approximately 3 to 4 minutes. (Do not allow pitas to brown.) Turn them over and bake for an additional 3 to 4 minutes. Stack them on a plate and cover with a clean, dry cloth. Allow the loaves to deflate slightly before serving.

It's Like a Continuum

Ines Brito, fifty-five, lives in Hanson, Massachusetts, with her family. Nezi, as she prefers to be called, came to the United States from Cape Verde in 1996 and teaches English as a Second Language at the Jeremiah E. Burke High School in Boston.

⚜

THERE IS NOTHING QUIET ABOUT Nezi's kitchen. In the midst of four chattering parakeets in a cage by the window and the whimpering of Kiki the dog begging for scraps, Nezi's nine-year-old grandson, RJ, break-dances past the stove. His older sister, Maura, calls out over the onions frying and the coffee brewing that she'll answer the phone. When Layla, Nezi's daughter, opens the fridge to show us some of the ingredients they use in their cooking, RJ warns, "Whatever you do, don't eat that blood sausage. You'll end up in the hospital!" His eyes are smiling as he awaits our reaction before he runs into another room. It's a warm, friendly place, and Nezi and Layla offer food to us throughout the morning while they prepare *katxupa,* the classic Cape Verdean stew, which needs to simmer for hours before it's ready to be eaten. The women relay some of their favorite family memories while they chop vegetables, stir the pot, and keep up with the dishes. Maura, who eats her breakfast at the kitchen table, occasionally interrupts with her own take on a particular story.

The myriad scents of pork, corn, and yucca boiling away on the stove begin to fill this kitchen, which looks out onto pine woods that were once farmland. Nezi's husband grew up here; his parents emigrated from Cape

Opposite: Nezi and George with *katxupa* for Mother's Day.

Verde years ago and worked the land for decades, selling vegetables at a little stand down on the main road. Although she's lived here for only a short time, the house very much seems like Nezi's now, the kitchen filled with the pots and plates she's brought with her from Cape Verde and Portugal, her books that line the walls, and all her family members who have made an appearance this morning.

Just when it seems we must have met everyone, a young man in jeans and a blue bandana slips quietly through the door. It's George, her nephew, who lives downstairs. He's carrying a bouquet of flowers for Mother's Day and passes it to his aunt with a shy smile. He slips quickly out of the room before she can say anything. "The first time we clone something, it's going to be George," Layla tells us when he's gone.

Nezi nods, explaining that nothing ever bothers him. "He helps me calm down when I'm stressed about things," she adds, and then turns toward her daughter and says, "I'm all done. You can finish it," pointing toward the stove. The *katxupa* is a combined effort: Nezi started cooking the cracked corn at six this morning, added the beans at around eight, and chopped some of the vegetables—sweet potatoes, butternut squash, and yucca—and marinated the pork so that Layla could add everything later.

"Me finish? No way!" Layla jokes, walking toward the refrigerator to get the *linguica* and chorizo sausage that she will brown and add just before serving. Layla is good with a knife and quickly chops the sausage while she talks about her part-time catering job, her love of cooking, and the many different ways *katxupa* is prepared in Cape Verde. "We have an open door policy when we make it," she tells us. "Whoever stops by gets some." When I look into the two huge pots cooking on the stove and ask her how long they'll be eating leftovers this week, she laughs, "You don't make plans for *katxupa*. It will be gone by tomorrow."

Kiki the dog, drawn to the sausage Layla is chopping, begins to jump in the air, trying to reach the counter. Nezi claps at her to stop from across the room. "She's Creole, like me—part chihuahua and who knows what else," she smiles as she gathers scraps of sweet potato skins to add to the compost bin. Outside, she shows us around her yard, pointing out the gardens she's been working on since she moved in with her husband and the small pool for fish George has been helping her build. "I'm trying to give life to something abandoned," she explains, gesturing around the place. She bends down to pull some weeds by her feet, and the hem of her multicolored African dress flutters in the cool breeze. "Every single day this spring I came to check on these," she tells us, pointing proudly to all of the tulips blooming around her.

We linger in the May sunshine and talk about her mother's beautiful gardens in Cape Verde, while inside, Nezi and Layla's version of *katxupa* simmers. It proves to be delicious when we sit down to eat it later, and in the end Layla was right: the pot was nearly empty by the time we left, after Nezi's friends from down the street stopped in when they heard what was on the menu today.

⤛✕⤜

When I was young, I didn't pay much attention to cooking. I was very outgoing, wanted to be independent, and was more interested in politics. It wasn't until I came to America that I had a desire to learn. And that was because I had to. I think I surprised my friends when they found out I was doing all this cooking. They'd say, "Who made this food? Wow, finally you learned to cook!"

My intention wasn't to immigrate here but to help my son. He was in eleventh grade then and came to live with my ex-husband. I wanted to give him some support during my vacation, but, when I was getting ready to [return to Cape Verde], I saw that he was not settled, and that was heartbreaking to me. I decided to stay right then, and I've been here ever since. I had a nice, settled life in Cape Verde, with a very good job: I was running an institute that worked with unions to train workers. I had never considered leaving. For me, the U.S. was a place to visit, not to live. Yes, some people from my country immigrated here, but that was not in my plan.

So I stayed. I didn't tell my son I was here for him, because he wouldn't want me to do that, but I felt that if I did stay, he'd always have someone. And he's doing well now: he went to college and got his master's. He's in California, but everyone else lives with me: my daughter, who came after I did, and her family, my husband, my niece and nephew. We all cook together, especially on Sundays, and that's when we make the *katxupa*. We can put it on the stove and then do the cleaning and errands, because it takes a long time to cook. My grandkids don't like all the Cape Verdean dishes, but they do love this, especially the *katxupa rafugadu*—or *katxupa gizode;* that's what they call it on another island, but it's the same thing—when you take the leftover *katxupa* from the night before and cook it in butter or oil so that it gets thick and really dry. You serve it with *linguica* and fried eggs. It's delicious. They love to do this with me. We put on the aprons, and they help on Sunday mornings.

Nezi (seated on the left) enjoys *katxupa* with George, Layla, and Maura (seated on the right).

But when I was growing up, this was something I ate every single day. And you know, I didn't get sick of it!

So we love the food, and I find when we don't have it, we miss it. At one family gathering, I think it was last Thanksgiving, I didn't bring the *doce de leite*—that's a custard I do that I learned from my mother—and everybody was feeling like they didn't have dessert. And there were many things there! It's like there still was a space that was waiting to be filled.

I think I learned things from my mother when I was a kid that, at the time, I didn't even realize I was absorbing, like this desire to have certain foods. It's the same with my garden. My mother had the most beautiful garden on my island, Fogo. When I was young, I didn't think much about the garden; I just enjoyed it. Now, I am gardening. I read everything I can and talk to people. When I garden, I feel as though I am celebrating my parents' lives. You know when you are young and your parents tell you something, it's like you are not really listening. But everything stays! I know that, because I can hear my mother when I'm gardening. People used to ask her, "Why are your plants so beautiful?" And she used to say, "I talk to them. I look at them. They are like friends." Now I'm the same. When I'm in my yard here, there's a movie running in my head of my mother's garden in Cape Verde. It's like a continuum. The food, too. Because now I'm cooking what my mother cooked, like the *doce de leite* and the *katxupa*.

If you go to Cape Verde, you can find *katxupa* in all the restaurants. It's a dish that everyone eats, but in the past, it was traditionally something that only poor people made. We have poor *katxupa* and rich *katxupa*. Poor *katxupa* is the real *katxupa*—no meat, just the corn and beans. You can find both kinds everywhere now, but this is not the way it used to be. Before, we would never think of serving something like *katxupa* to guests, and you'd never find it in restaurants. You'd only see European—especially Portuguese—food. That has all changed: independence taught us to value what is ours, but before, many of us only valued the Portuguese culture. Now, I see there is a great pride in things that are Cape Verdean.

And I feel this, too, although I try not to think of my culture as a special culture. There is no such thing as a special culture. Cape Verdean culture is just special to me maybe. But actually, if you look closely, a lot of things about different cultures are actually similar. For instance, I find when I talk with Caribbeans or Latinos, they make the same food we make—maybe slightly different—but it's still beans and rice. I remember when I went to Cuba I was telling some people I met there how to make *katxupa*, and they told me, "That's our Cuban *sancocho* you're describing." So there are things that are similar. I guess I like to find the things we share, not how we're different.

I have had conversations with women in Cape Verde, and I have had the same conversations with women in other places. Our problems are universal. I've found in traveling and meeting people that it shouldn't be difficult to go from one culture to the next, that things aren't that different, and that really, we all share many things. People in Cape Verde make such a big deal about how things are so different from one island to the next, but they're really not. And if I start to think about putting down roots—staying here or going back—I've decided that it doesn't necessarily have to be in any one place, because your world is everywhere you go; it's all the places you've been. Sometimes I think you are small when you just live in one place. You have to be big, so spread yourself, because you are connected to everybody.

I like to say that when I look at my life, it's like a circle: I was born in Fogo, then I went to San Vicente—another island—and then I went to Portugal to study. Finally, at forty-three, I came here and found my childhood friends, because they ended up here, too. And not just my childhood friends, but my whole island! Sometimes I think America is more Fogo than other parts of Cape Verde, like San Vicente or Santiago. So, coming here has been a very spiritual experience. Yes, I have lost some things, but when I stop and see what I've gained in living here, I think, no, I haven't lost anything. Of course I miss it at times—my mother is there, my sisters, too. But I know if I went back, I'd miss the things here: my students, my friends, all the new experiences. I love what I do now. My life is full. I've had wonderful experiences and met so many wonderful people involved in so many interesting projects, people who share similar views as I do. I feel like I'm lucky: this is not my country, but I'm very happy here.

I guess the only thing that's really been a challenge has been the language. I am always thinking more than I am able to express in English, and it's frustrating. So I sometimes feel, oh, I'm not going to do this because I can't express myself very well. Let's say I'm going to talk about Cape Verdean culture. I know so many things about this subject, but I'm not able to operate on the level I'd like to in English. I try not to let these thoughts take over, but sometimes it's hard. You know, when I first considered talking about the food from my country for this book, I thought, oh, Nezi, you cannot do this; you will not be able to do this. Then out comes all the pain. I think, why am I doing this? I don't know how to express myself. But my husband encourages me a lot. He says, "Do it! Just do it! Don't stop!"

So, I'm trying. And I share my experiences with my students. I tell them how I've struggled. I tell them that I am still learning English. And, you know, they feel relieved. I think if someone older, someone with more experience, tells you that they've been through the same thing that you have, it's like, wow! She's had a hard time, too! So I share my experiences with them. I think we should talk about our weaknesses; it makes us stronger.

NEZI'S CAPE VERDEAN *KATXUPA* (*CACHUPA*)

Corn, Bean, and Pork Stew

Serves 6 to 8

Because katxupa (cachupa *is the Portuguese spelling, while the other is the preferred Creole) takes several hours to cook, Nezi wakes up at 5 A.M. to begin cooking the hominy on the days the family plans to serve it for dinner. Although you could reduce the cooking time by soaking the hominy overnight, Nezi says traditional* katxupa *is not prepared this way.*

- 2 pork feet (1 pound boneless pork shoulder, trimmed and cut into 1½-inch pieces, can be substituted)
- 2 cloves garlic, minced
- 1 teaspoon paprika
- 1 tablespoon white vinegar
- 1 cup dried hominy corn
- 3 bay leaves
- 12 cups water
- 1 cup dried lima beans
- 1 smoked pork hock
- 1 sweet potato, peeled and cut into 1½-inch pieces
- 1 small onion, chopped
- 1 small butternut squash (about 1 pound), peeled, seeded, fibers removed, and cut into 1½-inch pieces
- 1 yucca, cut into 1-inch pieces*
- 1 pound collard greens, stems removed and chopped into 1-inch strips
- 1 tablespoon vegetable oil
- 1 pound *linguica* and/or chorizo sausage, chopped*

Marinate the pork feet or pieces of pork shoulder in the garlic, paprika, and vinegar in the refrigerator overnight.

Rinse the hominy. In a large pot, bring the hominy, bay leaves, and 12 cups of water to a boil. Reduce heat and simmer, uncovered, until the corn is cooked halfway, about 2 hours.

---

* Found in markets specializing in Latino, Caribbean, and Portuguese products.

Rinse the lima beans. Add the beans, pork feet or pieces of pork shoulder, and smoked pork hock to the pot of hominy. (The hock is added for flavor and can be removed before serving.) The liquid should cover everything by several inches. Add more water if necessary.

Continue to simmer until the beans are soft, about 2 hours. Add the sweet potato, onion, squash, and yucca. The liquid should just cover the vegetables. Again, add more water if necessary. Continue to simmer, uncovered, until the vegetables are nearly soft, about 20 minutes. Add the collard greens and continue to simmer until soft, about 20 minutes.

In a small pan over medium heat, heat the oil until shimmering. Working in batches, add small amounts of the chopped *linguica* and/or chorizo sausage to the pan and cook until lightly browned on all surfaces, about 3 minutes. Add the cooked sausage to the pot of soup and simmer for 10 additional minutes. If desired, remove the hock before serving. Season with salt and pepper.

Add a Place at the Table

Fausta Scarano Finkemeyer, thirty-eight, left Italy for the United
States in 1986. She lives in the Jamaica Plain section of Boston with
her husband, Berndt, originally from Germany, and their six-year-
old son, Matthias. She teaches Italian cooking to children in a local
after-school program. Her mother, Rosalba, visits yearly from
Gaeta, Italy.

FAUSTA LOOKS ACROSS THE KITCHEN table at me, her large brown eyes
both curious and melancholy as she considers the direction her life has
taken. Although she's been in the United States since she was a teenager,
she still struggles to feel comfortable in a place so different from her native
Italy, with its focus on food and family. She recalls memories from her
childhood spent in a small coastal town outside Rome, where she'd help
her grandmother, mother, and aunts during the summers to prepare food
both for the store they owned and for the multicourse meals they all shared
daily in her grandparents' large dining room. "It was incredible. I had an
incredible childhood," she says as she describes the local specialties they
prepared, including *tiella,* a savory pie made of yeast dough and filled with
seafood they would buy directly from the local fishermen, and *limoncello,*
a liqueur made with lemons from the yard.

As I listen to Fausta speak, I'm mesmerized by the lyrical rolling *l*'s and
melodic vowel sounds of Italian being spoken by a native. I feel that I could
listen to her all day as she peppers her sentences with the Italian names for

Opposite: Rosalba adjusts for seasoning.

33

particular dishes and other words she is unable to find the English equivalent for quickly. Her eyes become misty when she talks about her family's passion for food and the long lunches they'd share every afternoon, something she is unable to re-create here. She describes a place she wants to take her son one day when they go to Italy: "It's a little restaurant on a hill surrounded by fields and horses, not even a restaurant really, but a house. The whole family cooks together in the kitchen, and the mother brings out a plate of beautiful food. You have a glass of wine and you think, ah, I'm in Italy."

Today Fausta's mother, Rosalba, who is visiting for several weeks, is hand-rolling pasta with her grandson, Matthias, in the kitchen. Fausta defers to her mother when it comes to the cooking and steps aside to allow Rosalba to crack eggs into a pile of flour on the counter for the pasta dough she is making for the midday meal. Six-year-old Matthias plays with the pasta machine nearby, grabbing bits of dough from his grandmother and sending them through the rollers by quickly cranking the handle to make vermicelli. Rosalba admonishes him good-naturedly in Italian, telling him they're not making vermicelli, but fettuccini today, as she gently moves him aside to begin to roll the pasta herself. She feeds long sheets of dough through the machine, turning the handle steadily with her free hand to pass it through the rollers to be cut. Matthias stands next to her, his chin just reaching the counter and his arms outstretched, ready to catch the long strands of golden fettuccini coming out of the machine. When his grandmother turns away, he grabs another handful of dough, sending it through the machine to make one last portion of vermicelli, which he hides under the pile of his grandmother's fettuccini. He smiles mischievously at me and then runs off into the living room.

A sauce made with tomato, onion, and olive oil simmers on the stove, filling the small kitchen with its sweet scent. In Italy, the pasta itself is the main event, and sauces are usually simple, like the one Rosalba has made today. As she prepares to serve the meal, she pulls several strands of cooked fettuccini from the boiling water to check for doneness. She drops these into a small bowl with a spoonful of sauce, mixing it with a fork before passing it to me. The sauce is straightforward in its simplicity, allowing the subtle egg flavor of the fettuccini to come through. Rosalba takes a bite to check for taste and waves a hand in the hair. "Good," she tells her daughter and turns back to the stove.

The women serve the pasta in large bowls, sprinkling freshly grated parmesan on each. The first goes to Matthias, who sits on a stool in the corner of the kitchen. He pulls another over as a makeshift table and hunches over it to eat his fettuccini. Fausta smiles and runs her fingers gently through his hair, saying, "Matthias, you know you're going to have to roll the pasta every day this summer when we go to Italy to visit Nonna." He glances up for a moment and nods before quickly returning to his dinner.

⁂

When I cook with my son, we like to make believe that we're on TV. So he's chef Matthias, and I say, "Okay, Matthias, do this," and he whispers, "Mommy, we're on the cooking show." It's this little game that we play. I remember my dad doing that with me when we cooked. When we used to have people over, he and I would do the decorating. We'd roll up the prosciutto on the *grissini,* the long bread sticks, and arrange them on a plate with melon.

My mom was the cook in the family. She made *tiella.* It's a specialty from our hometown, Gaeta. Basically it's a type of pizza with a dough base, but you can put anything inside it like *frutti di mare* with mussels and octopus, or you can make it with escarole, or with ricotta and eggs. There are many, many different versions, and they're all so delicious. My mom was so good at it that she used to sell them out of the house to restaurants and other places. She's such an incredible cook that it really took me a while to feel that I could try a particular dish and it would be okay. When I was young, I mostly helped her out in the kitchen, meaning, she was the chef. She'd say, "Can you get me a spoon? Can you get me this? Can you do that?" I watched her though, so now when I make something I know how it should be.

It took me a while to pick up those recipes and think, oh, wow, I can do this, too! A couple of years ago, I gave my mother this book and told her to write everything down. Now I'm practicing. For example, for New Year's Eve I've been making this specialty called *cotechino* with lentils. It's an Italian pork sausage, and, in Italy, *cotechino* is only for New Year's. The lentils represent money. The more lentils you eat, the more money you'll have. So I continue this tradition here, because we all do that in Italy. Matthias loves it. He loves all the foods: the pastas, the soups, and the cookies. He calls them Nonna's cookies, because those are the cookies that my mother always makes.

I don't always have time to really cook because I'm so busy, but sometimes when I really crave something, like the lasagna, I'll make it. But it's never the same as my mother's, because I don't always hand-roll the

Rolling pasta.

pasta, and the *besciamella* isn't the same. Matthias loves it, though. He'll say that it's just like Nonna's, and I'm like, come on, really?

When my mother comes, I usually cook for the first day, just to give her an update on how I'm doing. She'll say it's good, but that's it, because when she comes, she takes over the kitchen. And you know what? I don't mind! Some other people might, but I know that's her way of saying that she's here and wants to help. She's wonderful! My friends always ask when she's coming so they can have her food. She has a passion for cooking, and that's the way she shows her love.

I haven't been to Italy in four years. The last time I was there, my mom made *friarielli* for me, the little green peppers that you eat with the sauce. I remember when I first put those peppers in my mouth—you know what?—I started to cry. I cried because of the taste! Here, things don't have that flavor. I thought, oh, my God, what a taste! It reminded me of growing up in Italy.

My grandmother used to make them, too. We lived in this big house by the sea, and she had a food store on the first level and my grandfather ran a café upstairs. So I would spend my summer going up and down the stairs, from the café to the store and back again. My cousins were there, too, with my grandparents and aunts. During lunchtime, they'd close the store, and then we'd lower the shades to eat. You know, you have to know Italy in summertime, that silence when everything closes down. The sun, it's so hot, but it's cool inside where we'd sit down all together to eat. It was beautiful! It was a long meal—pasta, salad, and meat. The salad was so simple but incredible, because everything was fresh: the olive oil, *aceto* (the vinegar), the fresh tomatoes from the garden.

And the *contadini,* the farmers, I remember them, too. There was one that I loved, an old man named Santino. My grandfather used to joke with him. *"Capa d'auciello!* Hey, Bird Head!" he'd call to him. That was his nickname. He'd come with a big basket of fresh vegetables every day. I still can see the soil all over his shoes and hands. He would bring everything to my mom in the store and sit down and have a little coffee. I would love to see him again.

We always had people stopping by for coffee or something to eat. There's a song in Italian that goes, "Aggiungi un posto a tavola," which means add a place at the table because we have one more friend. That's our culture. Here, I don't have the friends that stop by without calling first. It's not the same. I live with this big expectation that I have to cook, but to sit down and have a nice dinner together just doesn't always happen.

I don't think it's possible to re-create my childhood for my son. Things are just so different here, but maybe by doing the food and getting him to recognize those different flavors and tastes, I can pass it along somehow. I really want to bring him to Italy again, because he loved it. He knows when he goes, the first thing he'll get are the little ice creams. For me, it's the coffee. As soon as I get to the airport, I get an espresso. Then, when I get out into the airport, I hear the noise, the language, and I think, ah, it's Italian. These are my people!

When I first got here it was really hard. It was terrible! My father came over with an American company. I didn't want to go. I went to school here for a while. It was so different, with those big hallways and everything so structured. If the crowd goes this way, you go this way. If the crowd goes that way, you go that way. There's this sense of organization here, even in the way you move. In Italy, you just move. It's chaotic! I think there's a certain amount of freedom in the disorder and chaos. Now, when I go back to Italy, I find that I sometimes get annoyed because of the disorganization, but there's a beauty about it. There's something real.

I want Matthias to experience that. Things don't always have to be this way. You can also go the side way. And that is the Italian way.

Lately, I've been feeling a loss of identity. I feel that one part of me is gone. There's a lot that I've been given in this country, but I always feel like a foreigner still, and even though I speak and write well, I still feel that people consider me differently. It's like I'm missing something, like I'm not a whole person, not the whole Fausta that I could be or should be. In Italy, I feel whole. I know who I am, even though I've been gone for so long. Coming here has changed me. I'm a little bit scattered, and I have a tough time connecting a lot of memories, because it was a big trauma for me to come. I was upset at my parents at first. Now I know that they just didn't understand the impact it had on me. I remember telling my mother that I wanted to go back, that I could go to university in Italy and stay with Nonna. I was in my twenties then. Here, when you're twenty, you're considered an adult, but in Italy you're not seen as independent, so I was not strong enough to take a step like that by myself. I regret that now.

My husband and I have been planning to go back, maybe to Germany, where he's from, because one of the things about our choice is linked to my son's health. He's been sick with bone cancer, and for the longest time I haven't wanted to leave because we've been so attached to the doctors here. Now, though, who knows? That's another big story. You're talking to me today, and I'm a different person. Matthias is doing so well now. Maybe we could go back to Europe. Maybe there's a possibility.

I know I don't want to wait until he's a lot older so that he has to deal with the things I went through when I came. I want him to experience his own culture while he's young. So for now, I try to give him everything I can. I don't know what he'll pick up. I guess, practically, I want him to remember that this is how you make this particular dish and we eat it at this time of year, but in terms of really remembering, I just hope that he thinks that I was a fun mum to be with. I hope he remembers that I was playful and listened to him, and that we shared things together. And we do that. We really talk a lot.

FAUSTA'S ITALIAN FETTUCCINI

Fresh Pasta with Tomato Sauce

Serves 4

Fausta and her mother, like most Italian cooks, believe pasta dishes should be served with a small amount of sauce so that the flavors of the fresh pasta are not lost.

PASTA

2¾ to 3 cups flour

1 teaspoon salt

4 large eggs, beaten

1 tablespoon extra virgin olive oil

Freshly grated parmesan cheese for serving

Special equipment: hand-cranked or electric pasta machine*

SAUCE

2 tablespoons olive oil

2 tablespoons onion, finely chopped

One 28-ounce can Italian plum tomatoes, finely chopped and liquid reserved

Salt and pepper to taste

Combine 2¾ cups of the flour and the salt in a large bowl. Form a cuplike well in the flour and add the eggs and oil. Work the mixture with a fork until the dough begins to come together.

Gather the dough and turn it onto a floured surface, beginning to knead it. (If the dough sticks to the surface, work in the remaining flour. If it is too crumbly and hard to work, several drops of water can be added.) Knead until the dough becomes smooth, shiny, and elastic, about 10 minutes.

Follow the instructions on your pasta machine to roll fettuccini. If using a rolling pin, split the dough into quarters and roll each to ¹⁄₁₆-inch thickness on a floured surface. Dust the dough with flour and gently roll it into a jelly-roll shape. With a sharp knife, slice across the roll into thin strips,

* Found in most food supply and some hardware stores.

approximately ¼ inch wide. Unroll the strips and set them aside on a floured plate. (Homemade pasta can be cooked at once or covered tightly with plastic wrap and stored in the refrigerator for up to 2 days.)

For the sauce, heat the oil in a medium saucepan over medium heat until shimmering. Add the onions and cook, stirring frequently, until soft but not brown, about 5 minutes. Add the tomatoes and the reserved liquid, salt, and pepper and simmer, uncovered, for 40 minutes, stirring occasionally. The sauce is done when bubbles no longer form along the edges of the pan and most of the liquid has evaporated.

Bring a large pot of water to a boil over high heat. Add 1 tablespoon of salt and the fresh pasta. Cook until just tender, about 4 minutes. Drain the pasta and transfer it to a serving dish. Serve with the sauce and freshly grated parmesan cheese.

Foraging Together but Alone

Yulia Govorushko, forty, is originally from Latvia. She lives in
Watertown, Massachusetts, with her husband, Bruce Gellerman,
whom she met in the early nineties when he was visiting her country.
They later married and had two children, Andre, twelve, and Anya,
eight, both born in the United States. Yulia's parents, Natasha and
Edward, live in the apartment downstairs. The family travels to
Wellfleet, Massachusetts, on Cape Cod, several times a year to
forage for mushrooms.

———※—✕—※———

THE DAPPLED LIGHT THAT FILTERS through this outer Cape forest of
pine and oak casts irregular patterns on the hill in front of us. As we wander toward it, the ground below shifts in a palette of color: first, the fading
copper of pine needles that have fallen earlier in the year; next, a wispy
mound of pale turquoise and silver that is a patch of moss growing in our
path. "I'm the champion," a voice calls out gleefully from above, inter-
rupting the quiet. Twelve-year-old Andre has just found a big one.

It's the orange-cap boletus mushroom we're in search of on this clear afternoon in early September. The mushroom, one of over a hundred species
of the genus *Boletus,* is easy to identify with its distinct deep orange color
and rounded dome. At the sound of Andre's cry, Yulia, Bruce, and Anya
scurry up the hill to get a better look. Yulia smiles and hands her son a small
steak knife, saying something in Russian when he points to the mushroom by his foot. He responds in the same language and, unlike many

Opposite: The Govorushko-Gellermans forage for mushrooms in Wellfleet, Massachusetts.

American-born children his age, seems comfortable conversing in something other than English. This is Yulia's doing: she insists Andre and Anya speak to her and her parents in Russian, as well as keep up with reading and writing in the language.

"This one's a prince," Andre announces, cutting through the stem and removing it carefully so that more mushrooms will continue to spread here. "It's the best mushroom in the world!" he cries, waving it in the air before handing it to his mother. The large fungus disappears into the cloth shopping bag hanging from her arm.

The family moves on, Yulia and eight-year-old Anya going off in one direction while Andre runs in another. Yulia's husband, Bruce, stays behind, telling us he's surprised they're finding anything today, because it's still early in the season. In a month or so, when the weather on the Cape turns cool and wet, growing conditions for these mushrooms will be ideal. As Bruce wanders along slowly, his eyes scanning the ground, he explains that foraging is one of the aspects of his wife's Russian culture that he relishes. "Look at this," he says, gesturing to Anya and Andre in the distance. "One day they'll be doing this with their kids."

For Russians, mushroom hunting is a deeply rooted tradition that allowed families to supplement in the winter. In Latvia, where Yulia grew up, the family would forage for these same mushrooms as well as wild strawberries, blueberries, and cranberries, which were used to make preserves. With an eye on Andre, who has run ahead, Bruce begins to describe the very matriarchal family that he has married into, one in which his mother-in-law has a strong presence. Adapting to a new culture may not be a challenge only for Yulia. Bruce also seems to struggle with cultural differences in his own home. When he describes the tightly knit structure characteristic of Russian families, he says this is something he appreciates, because activities like foraging are often centered around the children. He admits, however, that it can be confusing at times, because his in-laws are very involved in Anya and Andre's upbringing. "And then, who's the boss?" he asks.

An electronic ring cuts through the sound of twigs snapping under our feet. Several yards ahead, Yulia pulls a cell phone from her pocket and speaks quickly in Russian. "She's calling to say, how could you go mushrooming without us?" Yulia tells Bruce, slipping the phone back into her shorts several minutes later. Her parents, whom I met on another occasion, are unable to make it to the Cape today. "We've never been here without them," Yulia says, explaining that her father, too, was unable to come. Marveling now about his father-in-law, Bruce tells me that, at sixty-nine, Edward is a "gifted" forager. "It's in his blood," he says, and Yulia nods in agreement.

"My father loses himself when he forages. He can become completely disoriented in the woods," she explains, resting a hand on the blond head of Anya, who has come up beside her. "Oh, Anya, that's a beauty," she whispers, taking a small mushroom from her. When Yulia smiles, her serious, sometimes stern expression becomes one of carefree abandon, and she seems much younger than her forty years. She laughs now when Bruce points to something nearby. "Oh, Bruce, that's terrific," she tells him, admiring another boletus mushroom nearly hidden by a layer of damp pine needles on the ground.

This species of *Boletus* tends to grow on high, open, mossy areas, Yulia explains, and back in Latvia, they grew in the forests along the Baltic Sea. Here in Wellfleet, with the damp salt air and woods of pine and oak, the habitat is similar, making it a destination spot for Russian foragers. Unlike the famed *Boletus edulis,* or porcini, mushroom, revered by cooks in many parts of the world, the orange cap isn't widely available here. "I can't find it in any of the markets," Yulia tells me, so if she wants to cook the recipes from home, they must forage.

When I ask what the family will do with the harvest, I get several responses. Bruce raves about the sauce his mother-in-law makes with sour cream, which is traditionally served with black bread, a Latvian specialty made with rye flour. "It's the best recipe in the world!" Andre says of his grandmother's sauce, adding that her mushroom soup, which he has learned to make himself, is also delicious.

It's clear, however, that the purpose in coming here today is more than collecting food for later consumption. What draws Yulia, Bruce, Andre, and Anya to an afternoon in this wooded area, reached only by a narrow dirt road overgrown with beach plum bushes, is the challenge of the hunt. The quest to find the biggest mushroom with the dome closest to perfection— not the delicious soups, sauces, and stews that will be enjoyed later—is what drives this family to forage.

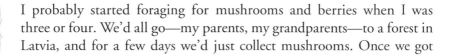

I probably started foraging for mushrooms and berries when I was three or four. We'd all go—my parents, my grandparents—to a forest in Latvia, and for a few days we'd just collect mushrooms. Once we got lost. It's easy to do. I mean, when you go mushroom hunting, you just go crazy! We ended up walking in this huge circle for hours and hours.

Sometimes we'd go to the dacha that my grandparents had. It's like a little hut where we'd stay when we wanted to forage. It was on top of a hill, and, at that time, there were only a few other people there, so it was fairly wild. From the dacha, we could just go into the forest and start walking. When you forage, it's a contemplative state of mind. You're outside with nature, and you have a chance to discover something together unexpectedly. A lot of times you might find something else besides mushrooms, like an animal maybe. Just the other day, when we went with the kids, we found a turtle. But when you do find a mushroom, it's always an exciting discovery. Sometimes they're very beautiful, sometimes just interesting. And it's the fact that you physically can take it from the ground, that you can do something with it later on, that is so meaningful. It's also about being together yet being separate at the same time. You are on your own on the one hand, but on the other you're all together as a small group, and you can share that. And whatever you find, you can share that with the kids. I also find the forest very peaceful. I love the sea, and I love the forest.

From my parents' perspective, foraging was a way to teach us about nature. It's not necessarily a walk in the park, and it's also different from hiking because it has another purpose. I think you become more aware of what's around you, and you have to become attentive to what's on the ground, to be able to distinguish the play of light, to recognize whether something is a leaf or a mushroom or, if the ground has a little bump to it, whether there could be a mushroom there. So we teach the kids to be attentive to all that, but you don't sit there and lecture them. It's really like a game. And for me, it's a way of escaping routine and just kind of forgetting everything and doing something together, just getting lost in the woods together. So, you refresh yourself in many ways.

When we go, there are lots of mushrooms we don't take. There are just certain kinds we're looking for, but you can still appreciate the ones that you can't eat. My father says it's like fishing, which he says is mushrooms with water, because you have no guarantee that you're going to find anything, so the reward is not necessarily in the end result—which can be great if you get some—but in the process as well. Again, it's a way of being more contemplative. You can think about life and talk to each other.

And for me, it's something that isn't American. Maybe it's not only Russian, but it's a part of my heritage. It's something I did with my grandparents. It's very common for families to do it there and uncommon here, so it's one thing that I hope Andre and Anya will take and give to their own kids someday. For them, it's definitely one of the highlights of the year. Even Bruce, my husband, has become a very avid forager.

Another way I try to keep the link is the language. The kids go to Russian school and learn to read and write. They think that because they speak, that's good enough, but that's definitely not the case. You have to really keep up with a language and enrich it, expand the vocabulary. So we try. Just this morning, Andre was complaining, asking me why he needs to read Tolstoy. It can be difficult, because it's definitely an extra effort, but I love to read, and I'd like my kids to inherit that. I think to some extent they already have, but I'd really like them to connect on a deeper level with Russia. When I grew up, I was reading a lot of Russian classical literature, like Tolstoy and Pushkin, and there are certain things that, when you read them translated, don't have the same meaning. You can translate the literal meaning of a word, but you can't translate its context. To know the context, that's what I want for them. When they read those writers, I'd love for them to be able to imagine what it is like to be in that village. In Pushkin, there is a verse where some young girls are picking berries in a garden and singing songs. They were servants collecting berries for their master, a nobleman. They weren't supposed to eat any of them, so they would sing instead. If you don't know something about the culture, it's not clear why they are singing. I want my kids to understand these things.

And of course the food, we pass that along to them, but really it's my mother who bears the bulk of the cooking. We do all kinds of cuisines, because I grew up in the Soviet Union, so Ukrainian, Georgian, it's all part of the mix. That's what we eat here, and we try to do it every day. My father thinks that food is somewhat genetically imprinted on a person. He was born in Belarus, and a lot of foods he loves to cook are from his childhood. He says the food definitely makes it a lot easier for immigrants to get more comfortable here. His two big dishes are cutlets and potato latkes. Sometimes he does a soup with sour cabbage, but my mother says it's just easier if she does the cooking.

I think Russians are much more willing to spend time in the kitchen, not necessarily without cutting corners, but in Russia we easily spend at least an hour every day putting a meal together. And rarely is it a sandwich. When I was growing up, restaurants were a big deal. There really wasn't take-out, so you always cooked. Now people can get food to go, and maybe other things are changing, too. But when I talk to my friends, they still spend a lot of time cooking and do a lot of homemade things, like the preserves. I think that's our big regret here, that the life pace is so frantic we don't have time for things like making preserves. I don't know how we did it back there. I think life was slower. But it's changing there, too. It's becoming very Americanized. And I don't know if it's bad or good; I don't want to make judgments. I think the changes are out of necessity. Life is getting quicker everywhere.

But there are certain things we still make time for. I know my father wants to make sure that Andre and Anya experience certain things, that they learn to welcome people into their lives and to be open-minded. When he first came to this country, he was quite surprised to find that Americans were not all that different from Russians. Maybe he hadn't expected this. He found that over many, many years of propaganda on both sides, people perceive a country as a symbol, not as a collection of people or individuals, but as a symbol. And he says that when he listened to information about the Vietnam War, he learned to see Americans as the enemy, and I think when he came here, all of a sudden that symbol stopped being a symbol. So he was surprised to come here and find there were the same mothers crying for their sons on both sides. He realized more strongly that people were being brainwashed to perceive each other in a certain way, not as a collection of human beings, but something abstract. If you see something on that level, it's easy to manipulate emotions and what you feel toward that country. It becomes much easier to say, "We have to go and kill somebody," if we don't see them as human.

But now my father is smiling. We started out talking about food, and now, it's war.

YULIA'S RUSSIAN MUSHROOM CASSEROLE

Serves 4 to 6 as an appetizer

Yulia and her family forage for their mushrooms and use the orange-cap boletus that they find in the late summer and fall to make this dish. A variety of mushrooms can be substituted, although cooking time may need to be adjusted, depending on the size of the mushrooms.

½ plus 2½ tablespoons butter, divided

1 pound edible wild mushrooms

½ cup onions, finely chopped

1 clove garlic, minced

½ cup milk

4 large eggs, beaten

1 to 2 teaspoons chopped fresh herbs, such as thyme, marjoram, oregano, or parsley

½ teaspoon salt

¼ teaspoon freshly ground pepper

Adjust oven rack to center and preheat the oven to 350°F. Brush the insides of a small casserole or a 9-by-9-inch baking dish with ½ tablespoon of the butter.

Clean the mushrooms by gently brushing any dirt from the caps, undersides, and stems. Chop the caps and stems into ½-inch pieces.

Heat the remaining 2½ tablespoons butter in a large sauté pan until melted. Add the onions and garlic and cook over medium heat, stirring frequently, until they begin to get soft but not brown, about 3 minutes. Add the mushrooms and continue to cook, stirring frequently, until the mushrooms and onions are soft, about 5 minutes. (The time will vary depending on the kinds of mushrooms you are using.) Transfer the mushrooms and onions to the casserole and spread evenly.

In a small bowl, combine the milk, eggs, herbs, and salt and pepper to taste. Pour the egg mixture over the mushrooms and bake, uncovered, until golden, about 20 minutes.

Can be served hot or at room temperature.

A Savage Loves His Own Shore

Barry Nolan, forty, is originally from Ireland. He came here in 1992
and currently lives in the Jamaica Plain section of Boston. He works
as an interactive multimedia graphic designer.

✕

"THERE'S SOMEONE I'D LIKE YOU to meet." I'm surprised at Barry's an-
nouncement when he welcomes us into the apartment. He said he'd be
cooking alone tonight. "This is Mum!" When we enter the kitchen, the
silhouette of seventy-two-year-old Maura Nolan moves in and out of focus on his laptop screen. She smiles back at us from her kitchen table in
Carraig na bhFear, the village in County Cork, Ireland, where Barry grew
up. Barry's computer is outfitted with Skype software, which allows him
to make phone calls and video conference with his family back home. He
brings the laptop toward me, explaining that his mother will see me better if my face is directly in front of the screen. "This is who I owe all my
cooking abilities to," he tells me, and then carries the laptop over to the
counter so she can view the potatoes, carrots, and parsnips he's set aside
for the meal. "Sorry I can't introduce you to Dad," he tells me. "He's out
at cards."

Barry, clearly a techie—his laptop and cell phone are always nearby—
connects with his parents, siblings, and nieces and nephews in Ireland several times each week this way. "It used to be the phone," he's told me, "and
it would cost something like a dollar a minute, and there was always this

Opposite: Fresh parsley.

horrifying thought that as you rattled out what you needed to say, it was costing a fortune." He finds Skype a more natural way to stay in touch. He says good-bye to his mother, explaining he needs to get going on dinner.

"Be sure to put enough butter in the potatoes," she reminds him before the screen flickers off.

Barry turns to the cooking, searching around for a vegetable peeler and heating water for the potatoes in a stainless steel electric pot on the counter. He moves about a bit uncertainly, navigating the kitchen as if he's in it for the first time. (He's staying here temporarily: this is one of the unoccupied rental units in the building he owns, and when he finds renters, he'll return to the much smaller basement apartment downstairs.) He opens a drawer here, a cupboard there, straightens the pots on the stove, all the while narrating his next move. "I'll just peel the potatoes first," he tells me, picking up a large Yukon Gold from the counter. "And then, it'll be the parsnips and carrots." He peels quickly, shooting pieces of potato skin into a pile with a flick of his peeler as he describes his ongoing quest to find the perfect potato. "In Ireland, the favorite would be the British Queen," one with a dry, floury texture, which his mother would use for the dish he's making tonight. He moves on to a discussion about his father, "an expert in spuds," who doesn't believe in removing the dirt before cooking because he thinks it adds flavor. "But then, he's never made a meal on his own," Barry laughs. His mother, who leaves food in the fridge if she won't be home to cook, serves her much-loved Bolognese sauce over potatoes, not pasta, for her husband.

Barry doesn't cook all the foods he grew up eating, because he lives alone and is out all day at work. His friends Angelika and Margaret, who come in to share the meal, insist he makes delicious omelets, usually prepared in a frying pan on the outdoor grill, because the basement kitchen is equipped with a hot plate only. Tonight he's making something his mother always prepared for him and his siblings growing up: baked fish with mashed potatoes, carrots, and parsnips. He spoke with her several times this week so she could remind him of the procedure. When I asked if he's ever made this for his mother, he laughs. "No, but I did cook for Mum once, when her knee locked up. I did the tea, but still, the kitchen was controlled."

A true food lover, Barry lets his nose guide the preparation, sniffing the gray sole he purchased that day: "No smell—it's fresh!" and the parsley, "Spectacular!" which he mixes into the potatoes. When the meal starts to come together but is still at that critical juncture—vegetables waiting to be mashed in the pot, fish baking away in the oven—Barry circles the kitchen quickly. "Under pressure, under pressure!" he chants, looking around for a knife to cut the butter and, when he can't find one, opting for a spatula instead. He plunges it into the block of Irish Kerrygold butter in his hand and tosses a two-inch piece into the potatoes. He looks into the pot, shrugs, and cuts off another, bigger than the last, heeding his mother's instructions with the addition.

The mashing of the potatoes is undertaken in an earnest fashion. Barry breathes heavily as he works the spuds with his metal masher. "A very essential tool in an Irish household!" he laughs, waving it in the air. "Oops, there's a parsnip in there." He stops, quickly lifting out the stray root and putting it where it belongs, in with the bowl of carrots.

Barry is a large man, and when he bends his six-foot frame over the pot of potatoes now, his shoulders hunched and head crooked intently as he mashes and chats away, another tall cook immediately comes to mind. And, like Julia Child, Barry entertains with stories that are delightful, touching on anything from the ideal growing conditions on the west coast of Ireland, which contribute to the delicious flavor of the vegetables, to his father's recent venture as a pig farmer. "Two months of feeding and they're off to market," he says, giving the potatoes one last stir and banging the masher forcefully on the side of the pot. Like Julia, his attitude when he makes a mistake is nonchalant, sometimes irreverent, and he laughs the blunder away with another story or detailed explanation. When his friend Angelika points out that he's forgotten to add salt to the mashed potatoes, he throws his dish towel over his shoulder and looks deep into the pot. "Well, we'll leave them like that," he announces. "I don't want to mix it up any more than it is," and then tells us about colcannon, an Irish dish made similarly with mashed potatoes, onions, cabbage, and bacon.

When it's time for Barry to plate the dinner, he moves at full speed. "This is the important moment," he murmurs distractedly, picking off pieces of parsley to garnish each serving and taking a sip from the glass of wine that Angelika poured for him.

"Shall I bring down placemats?" she asks when she sees Barry tearing paper towels from the roll to set the table. "No, this is fine," he tells her, spreading five of them next to the wine glasses she's set out. We sit down to food that is a beautiful spectrum of colors—the bright orange of mashed carrots and parsnips, the translucent white of the baked sole, the deep green of the fresh parsley garnish, and, most prominent on each plate, a hefty dollop of pale yellow mashed potatoes. "There can be an element of disappointment at times," Barry acknowledges when he pulls his chair in to the table, looking uncertainly from one face to the next.

He needn't have worried. The meal was delicious, and I'm certain his mother would have been pleased. The sole, delicate in flavor and perfectly cooked, combined beautifully with the freshly mashed potatoes (which we all sprinkled with salt) and my favorite, the parsnips and carrots.

⚬

One of the pursuits, and disappointments, I've had here is trying to find a potato that actually tastes like the kinds we have in Ireland. I think what Irish cooking comes down to is very simple: it's the core thing in a particular dish—the potato or parsnip—that gives the actual flavor to the food. It's not about putting stuff on it. I will go to the store here and try all the organic vegetables, but I don't necessarily find the memory in the food. I can try to cook the same things, but, ultimately, when I sit down to eat, it's not the same. To reproduce it is more than just about the same ingredients, the same vegetables. It's about vegetables actually tasting quite different when they're from different regions of the world. You know, people have told me that they hate Irish food, and I wonder, where have they eaten? A colleague once said, "Everything in Ireland is boiled," and I thought, everything is *not* boiled. Then she told me about some farmer who tried to feed her a year-old block of Velveeta cheese. Well, you know, that's not Irish food.

When I go home and eat Mum's cooking, it's phenomenal. There's a comfort there, a familiarity. She just nails it every time. It's spectacular, not because of the spices, but it's really got to do with the vegetables themselves. It's possible that someone would come from a distant land and say, "I don't see what you're talking about. This parsnip just tastes like a different-flavored parsnip." So I don't really know if Mum's parsnips are spectacular—well, I think that they are—but maybe it's just that the flavor is so ingrained because I grew up with it. And after all this time, the food hasn't changed a lot. The roast beef that Mum's been doing all these years is still the same roast beef. It still tastes amazing as ever. I remember when we were kids, at the end of a really good meal we'd all shout, "Best cook in the world! She's a super cook!" We still do that now, but she's funny because she'll try to deny it. She has this thing where she'll make an excuse for any compliment. She'll say it wasn't good enough, or, "Oh, it could have been better." I guess it's kind of a modesty thing. Now we point this out and tell her she should just accept the praise she's due.

We didn't really cook as kids. Mum was so good in the kitchen that she would really take care of everything. But we did pick the berries. One of my earliest memories was going into the local farmers' fields and picking the blackberries off the hedges. We'd bring them back, and she'd make jam. And then in Ross Carberry, where her family is from, we'd get up at the crack of dawn and go out into the fields and pick mushrooms. In fact, I still have problems finding mushrooms that give me that flavor today. I can still remember the big fry-ups we'd have. We'd take the mushrooms back and cook them up with the pork sausages, the rashers, the black pudding. We'd soak our brown bread in the cooked mushroom juice, and it was absolutely fantastic. These days it doesn't really happen that you can get up at six o'clock in the morning and go out and pick mushrooms. One reason is because of all the fertilizers they're using in the fields, and the other is that you're liable to be shot because of trespassing laws. Ireland has become a very litigious country.

When we were growing up, there were certain things that we always got locally, like carrots and potatoes, for instance. You'll still find certain people just selling them on the side of the road. It's certainly true today that there would be [vegetables in] supermarkets, but there are also farmers where you can go for your potatoes, or a friend might even drop off a bag as a thank-you for something. Vegetables will be bought, but they'll also be passed around. When I was growing up, we'd go around to certain farmers with a burlap bag and just buy what we needed. Again, that kind of thing doesn't happen so much now, but you still can get local, basic vegetables. I wish we'd go back to more of that. In fact, I'm beginning to see a movement here back to the farmer's markets, and I think that's fantastic.

When I first came here, though, I realized there's food out there that's flavorless, especially some of the tomatoes in the grocery stores. Sometimes all you can find are those vegetables that have been shipped in by the giant companies catering to the consumer who wants to get that food item grown as fast as possible. But you can't hurry nature, and you can't do better than nature. So if you're going to start messing around with it, you're going to lose the flavors.

I've noticed there's a fear of vegetables here. I don't think people appreciate them the way they ought to. The only time I really see vegetables, except if you're at a fancy restaurant, is at the Thanksgiving and Christmas dinner. The first time I saw a turnip here was at a dinner at my cousin's. It was absolutely delicious, but still, I am looking for those things that will key me into the kind of food that I grew up with. That's the standard I use to judge. If I'm served some Indian food, I'll think about the taste and how beautiful the food is, but if it's presented to me as something that's supposed to be an Irish dish, it's going to have a very high standard against which it will be judged. I certainly have had delicious food here, but there's definitely a difference. If it's mashed potatoes, I'm interested in the texture, the taste, the flavor. And parsnips, that's another one. I think parsnips are very special, an unsung hero of a vegetable. I've met people who don't even know what a parsnip is, but parsnips mixed with carrots, something Mum does, are absolutely spectacular. That's something I'll do sometimes.

When I cook, because I live by myself, I don't do all the things Mum does, like a big roast all the time. I wouldn't be able to cook it like her anyway. I'll make the soda bread, like if it were a special occasion. I have Mum's recipe. In fact, around the time of 9/11, we had a cookie sale in the office to raise money, and I made the soda bread. People were really keen on it. I think I charged twenty dollars [for] each loaf, and they all sold out.

Boston is an amazing city, but I didn't necessarily immigrate here because I wanted to. I needed to find employment. I got out of college in the late eighties, and there was a big recession, so I went to live in London for a while before coming here. What I think I didn't realize after first arriving in Boston is how harsh the winters are. There must have been six feet of snow my first year. Nobody told me about the winters! It's fine now; I get through. I would say I'm still a little bit unsettled, though. I would love to say it feels like home, and in some ways it does, but, in truth, I still feel a draw back to Ireland. It doesn't really have to do with my experiences here; it has more to do with the draw to the country. When I go home to Cork, I always feel like that's the place I need to be. The downtown area, Patrick Street, has tremendous energy. It's different here. To me, Washington Street in downtown Boston doesn't really have that, but Cork does; it has that tremendous social energy, a kind of quirky sense about it.

It's tricky because I've been here for a while now, and I have connections, people that I care for, like my sister and her boys in Connecticut. So to pack up is going to be much more difficult than it was when I was moving around as a much younger person. There's certainly the issue of having a physical connection, too, like the house here. I absolutely love this house. And my job, I have a great job, a very well-paying job. In some ways I think, is this a crazy idea? And people will say, "Oh, Ireland has changed. Why would you even think to go back?" And I've heard cases where people have gone back and they've been horrified, wondering what they were doing. It's wet all the time, there are no jobs, it's not what they thought it would be, not the Ireland they grew up with. So there's this risk that I'd go back and maybe be disillusioned with the place.

But, really, I've just never felt completely settled here. My father has this interesting saying, "A savage loves his own shore," and I think that's all about the tendency, a primitive tendency, that people experience wanting to be back in their place of origin. I definitely feel that.

BARRY'S IRISH DINNER:
BAKED FILLET OF SOLE, MASHED POTATOES,
AND CARROT-PARSNIP MASH

Serves 4

Barry and his mother like to use lots of fresh Irish butter in their cooking. This meal, however, could be made with half the amount and be almost as delicious as it was when Barry prepared it.

BAKED FILLET OF SOLE

1 tablespoon plus 2 tablespoons olive oil, divided

1 small onion, finely chopped (about ⅓ cup)

2 cloves garlic, minced

2 tablespoons unsalted butter, melted

4 fillets of sole, about 6 ounces each

2 tablespoons fresh parsley leaves, chopped

Salt and freshly ground pepper

MASHED POTATOES

3 pounds Yukon Gold, gold, or other small, tender potatoes, peeled

1 to 1½ cups milk, room temperature

6 tablespoons unsalted butter, softened

¼ cup onion, finely chopped

2 tablespoons fresh parsley leaves, chopped

Salt and freshly ground pepper

CARROT-PARSNIP MASH

2 parsnips, peeled

4 carrots, peeled

2 tablespoons unsalted butter, softened

Salt and freshly ground pepper

Adjust oven rack to center and preheat oven to 400°F.

Steam the potatoes, carrots, and parsnips in a large pot until soft, about 20 minutes.

Meanwhile, prepare the topping for the fish: Heat 1 tablespoon of olive oil in a medium-sized skillet over medium heat until shimmering. Add the onion and garlic and cook, stirring occasionally, until soft, about 5 minutes. Set aside.

Use a 9-by-13-inch baking dish to cook the fish. Coat the bottom of it with the 2 tablespoons of melted butter and the remaining 2 tablespoons of olive oil. Arrange the fish in baking dish, top with the sautéed onion and garlic mixture, sprinkle with the chopped parsley, and season with salt and pepper. Bake until the fish is just cooked through, about 8 minutes.

Meanwhile, prepare the mashed potatoes: First, remove the carrots and parsnips from the pot and set them aside. Transfer the potatoes to a large bowl and mash them until no large lumps remain. Add the butter and 1 cup of the milk and mix until smooth and fluffy. (The remaining ½ cup of milk can be added if needed.) Add the chopped onion and parsley and mix. Season with salt and pepper.

Prepare the carrot-parsnip mash by mashing the carrots and parsnips together until no large lumps remain. Add the butter and mix. Season with salt and pepper.

Swapping Food on Sundays

Twenty-five-year-old Johanne Jean Louis left Haiti when she was
nine. She lives with her mother, stepfather, and younger siblings in
the Dorchester neighborhood of Boston. Currently a professional
chef, Johanne is the primary cook in her family, teaching her
younger brother and sisters the Haitian dishes she learned to
prepare with her grandmother.

※✕※

THE LOUIS FAMILY KITCHEN HAS a comfortable, lived-in feel, with several easy chairs pushed against the dark paneled walls and a TV blaring
Friday night sitcoms. The gas range is covered with pots filled with boiling
liquids, their steam filling the room with the rich scent of beef stock and
fresh thyme. Johanne stands over the stove, bringing a large wooden
spoon to her lips before she turns to greet us with an eager smile, introducing two of her younger siblings, Tracy and Emmanuel, who, at twelve
and thirteen, are more than a decade younger than Johanne. They stand at
opposite ends of the counter, peeling the vegetables that are stacked in
neat piles on the two small cutting boards before them. This kitchen has
an air of efficiency and professionalism, with Johanne in her crisp black
apron overseeing both the pots on the stove and her sister and brother,
who are intently focused on the tasks she has assigned to them. Johanne is
a natural teacher and explains each step of the food preparation process,
from the proper technique for flattening the plantain for *plantane fri,* or
fried plantain, to the consistency that is most desirable for the *soup*

Opposite: Johanne cooking *soup joumou.*

joumou, a squash soup traditionally prepared every January 1 for Haitian independence day.

When the simmering and chopping seem to be under control, Johanne recalls the enchanted Haiti of her childhood, with vendors carrying fresh passion fruit, mangoes, and sugarcane in baskets on their heads as they passed daily through her Port Salud neighborhood. Only when she recalls some of the hostilities toward Haitians that she has witnessed here does her smile fade and her speech become muted. She seems intent on debunking the misconceptions she believes some Americans have about Haiti, a place she is fiercely proud of, with its natural beauty, unique traditions, and strong sense of family and community.

⚬

I took over our kitchen in ninth grade, and now I do most of the cooking. My brother, Emmanuel, likes to help me, and he's a good cook. We make all the traditional dishes: the *soup joumou,* the fried plantain, the rice. Sometimes my sisters, Tracy and Phayol, help us too. My mother works a lot, but she cooks on her day off. I'll still help her though, like if Monday is her day off, on Sunday, I'll get things ready for her. I like to do it. I really love to cook!

I learned so much from my grandmother. When she was living here with us, and I was about thirteen or fourteen, she would cook Haitian food, and I would watch her. We had a lot of fun cooking together. When I'd come home from school, she'd be making dinner, and I'd help her out. If she were doing plantains, I would peel and cut them, or if she needed the rice, I'd grab it for her. I'd help her out with everything. I loved to come home and cook with her, to just be with her, because sometimes things at school were difficult.

When I was in middle school, things were really bad. The bus drivers went on strike for a while, so we had to walk home. Every afternoon on our way home there was a fight between the American kids—the black kids—and the Haitian kids. The Americans hated us, and they'd go after us. I don't know why. A lot of the Haitian kids who knew how to speak English pretended they weren't Haitian, but the ones that didn't know English were just stuck. One day, this one Haitian student was walking down the hill to get home and a bunch of kids grabbed him and poured gasoline on him. They poured it all over him! Everyone was screaming. We were screaming our lungs out for help. This older white guy who lived nearby saw them and said he was going to call the police, so they all ran away. Then he called the school, and they sent security to help the one who got attacked and to escort the rest of us to the subway station. It was scary. Really, really terrible! Every day there was a fight. They didn't want us here. They'd say, "Go back to your country! Take the boat back where you came from!" They called us boat people. I didn't come on a boat; I came here on an airplane! They think all Haitian people are poor. It was bad. You always had to have your guard up. I still don't understand why it happened. I'm just glad it's over and that my younger brother and sisters didn't have to go through it.

So I'd come home in the afternoons and cook with my grandmother. She'd remind me of things in Haiti and we'd laugh. A lot of people don't realize that Haiti is really a beautiful place. I know there are a lot of problems, but there are good things, too. I think people have such a bad impression of it because they only see the bad things on TV. But when you actually go there, there are some parts that are beautiful. They never show you that part on TV, though. They always show you the part when people are burning stuff and kids are in dirty clothes. I'm not saying it doesn't exist—it does—but the whole country is not like that.

We try to go back every few years. It's so beautiful there, and the food, it's delicious. Everything tastes better, maybe because it's all fresh. You go to the marketplace every morning to get what you need that day. Like the chicken—over there, you buy the chicken live and bring it home and kill it for dinner. The flavor is so good. Vegetables too—if I were going to make *soup joumou* over there, the squash would taste sweeter, because it would come directly from a farmer. You can tell the difference. We do our best here, though.

Sometimes we all cook together now, but it's hard because everyone is working. I remember in Haiti, on Sunday, you always had a big, fancy meal. We always swapped food with our neighbors on Sundays. Like my grandmother, if she made chicken, and if you were my neighbor and you had fish, you would send us a plate of your food and I would send you a plate of our food. It was a special thing we did every week.

Now we try to cook a nice Haitian meal on Sundays or for holidays, but it's not as big as it is over there. We do make some of the dishes though, like the *soup joumou* on January 1st, but we never swap food here. It's hard because everyone is so busy in America. We don't really know our neighbors. The most I would say to the people on our street is "Good morning. How are you today?" This is the longest conversation I've had with [neighbors on] either side [of us], but in Haiti you know everyone.

When I first came, I was only nine, and everything seemed different. I couldn't speak English then. It was embarrassing! I was so shy, and when I used to go out with my mother, I wouldn't talk to anyone. I remember one time I really felt humiliated: We were at the medical clinic, and my mother had to leave me in the waiting room. One of the nurses came up to me and said, "Hi, what's your name?" I didn't know what she was saying, so I said, "Yes." She asked me again, and I said, "No." There was a Haitian guy there, and he said to me in Creole, "She's asking you for your name." It was so embarrassing because I didn't know anything then.

I can understand now, though. I wanted to know English so bad, and I was like a sponge, soaking everything in just so I could learn to speak. I hate failing, and I hate not knowing. I'm a very curious person, so I want to talk with everyone. When someone's having a conversation, I like to be where the conversation is. I think it's beautiful when someone speaks more than one language, and I don't like it when Haitian people have kids and they don't teach them their language. It's part of you, and I think the more languages you speak, the better it is. We always speak Creole with my mother, but a lot of the Haitian kids I know don't know Creole, and they only speak English with their parents. It's so strange, because their parents really don't know very much English. I don't know how they can communicate together. What do they do if they need to say something important? I think it's sad.

A lot of times, when people hear me speaking Creole and find out I'm from Haiti, they say, "Wow! It's really crazy over there!" Sometimes I get tired and I just say, "Yeah, it is crazy over there," but sometimes I try to explain, and sometimes they understand. Some people are very ignorant, though, and they don't want to hear anything positive; they don't want to listen to what I have to say about my country. There really are so many good things, like the people, the food—stuff that you can't even get here, like the sugarcane. The sugarcane is delicious. It's not like the sugarcane here; it's a purple color, and when you peel it, it's white and juicy. I'd buy it every day from the people who came through our neighborhood to sell it. So I try to tell them the good things, and sometimes they listen.

I think about doing some of the Haitian recipes where I'm cooking now. They love it when I make new things, and I think they might like some of our dishes. When I open my restaurant some day, I know I'm going to serve Haitian food. It's delicious! I think people would love it. Once, when I was looking at all the businesses around here, I didn't see any nice Haitian places. A nice Haitian restaurant would be great, with tablecloths and candles and delicious food. It would be a place where you could come and listen to music and talk with your friends, a cozy place that both Haitians and Americans would come to.

JOHANNE'S HAITIAN *SOUP JOUMOU*

Squash Soup with Beef and Noodles

Serves 4 to 6

Johanne, like many Haitians, serves this soup on January 1 to celebrate Haitian independence. It's a hearty soup that would be perfect on a cold winter day.

1½	pounds beef stewing meat, trimmed and cut into 1-inch pieces
2	large cloves garlic, minced
	Juice of 1 lime (about ¼ cup)
1	tablespoon adobo seasoning*
	Salt and freshly ground black pepper
2	tablespoons vegetable oil
1	medium butternut squash (about 2 pounds), peeled, seeded, fibers removed, and cut into 1½-inch pieces
7 or 8	sprigs fresh thyme
7 or 8	sprigs fresh *recao*** (fresh cilantro can be substituted)
1	stalk celery, coarsely chopped
3	carrots, peeled and coarsely chopped
1	cup dried pasta, such as rotini, spirelli, or vermicelli broken into 1-inch pieces

Marinate the meat in the garlic, lime, and adobo seasoning overnight.

Season the meat with salt and pepper. In a large pot, heat the oil over medium-high heat until shimmering. Working in batches, add a few pieces of beef at a time to the pot and cook until lightly browned on all sides, about 5 minutes. Add more oil between batches if necessary.

Return all of the beef to the pot and add enough water to cover by 2 inches. Bring to a slow simmer.

Cover and cook until the beef is tender, about 1½ hours. Add the butternut squash, thyme, *recao* (a green leaf that has a slightly tangy flavor, simi-

---

* A mixture of 2 teaspoons of ground cumin, ½ teaspoon of black pepper, and ¼ teaspoon of cayenne can be substituted.
** Found in markets specializing in Latino and Caribbean products.

lar to cilantro, and is used in the West Indies, Central America, and parts of Africa), celery, and carrots. The liquid should cover everything. Add more water if necessary. Continue to simmer, uncovered, until the vegetables are soft, about 30 minutes. Remove the pieces of squash from the pot and puree in batches, with a small amount of broth from the soup, until smooth.

Pour the batches of squash puree back into the pot of soup. Simmer, uncovered, for another 30 minutes. Just before serving, add the pasta and cook according to the instructions on the package or until the pasta is firm to the bite.

Remove the *recao* and thyme sprigs and serve.

Living the Culture Every Day

Xotchil Gaarn, forty-one, is originally from Venezuela and first came
to the United States in 1988. She lives in Roslindale, Massachusetts,
with her husband, Christian, originally from Chile, and her three
children, Diego, fifteen, Elsa, twelve, and the youngest, Sebastian,
who was born here and is now six.

⚒

SPENDING TIME WITH XOTCHIL FEELS like reconnecting with an old
friend. She loves to laugh, and entertains me with stories about her family
back home as we linger in her kitchen or, on other occasions, stroll through
the garden in her backyard. The lines in Xotchil's face are set from her
broad smile, and her pale blue eyes glimmer mischievously when she recalls
her experiences both in the United States and Venezuela. At times, however, her face may unexpectedly take on a serious expression, and then her
eyes look gray, not blue.

She laughs now about *"las muchachitas,"* the girls, referring to her mother
and aunts back in Venezuela, who are all in their seventies and still cook together. She tells me that for years they have been getting together on January
1 to make *olleta coriana,* a special soup from the city of Coro, near her hometown. "Wow, it's good!" she says, her thick Venezuelan accent tingeing her
low, raspy voice. When she goes on to describe the impromptu musical per-
formances that have often followed the cooking and eating in her family, she
tells me about her six siblings, some of them professional musicians now,
and her smile subsides. "Those were fun times," she says softly. Xotchil is

Opposite: Xotchil in her garden.

the only member of her family who has left Venezuela. She admits it's been hard, especially for her mother, who has never really understood her daughter's decision to leave.

Today Xotchil is in high spirits because nineteen-year-old Juan, her brother's son, visiting from Venezuela, is here to cook with her. As she pulls carrots and cabbage from the refrigerator, they laugh about something Xotchil's mother, Abuelita ("little grandmother"), did the last time Juan was visiting with her. As he begins to chop the vegetables Xotchil has laid out on the counter, she grabs a CD from her collection—a recording of songs done several years back by her brothers, including Juan's father—and begins to sing along to the music in her deep, throaty voice. She explains that this is *gaita,* a style of music she grew up listening to. The sound of horns playing a fast-paced rhythm is catchy, and soon Juan and Xotchil are moving to the beat.

Asado negro is on the menu today; it's a braised beef dish, which Xotchil tells me her brother Kike is the master of. Her twelve-year-old daughter, Elsa, comes into the kitchen to help and begins to make the arepas, fried corn cakes, which are a staple of Venezuelan cuisine. Elsa works quietly next to her mother, patting the balls of dough between her small hands and neatly laying out a pile of perfectly round arepas on the tray next to her. She is shy and doesn't engage in the joking between her cousin and mother but focuses instead on the food preparation, stopping only occasionally to reply politely to a question or request.

While the beef braises on the stove, Xotchil bends down to open the oven door, releasing the sweet, earthy smell of plantains that are roasting on a tray. Poking them with a fork to check for doneness, she jokes that in Venezuela she could have bought ten pounds for the price she paid for this small bunch.

When the cooking is nearly complete, Xotchil takes a seat at the counter and tells me about some of her more difficult experiences here over the years. She expresses frustration at what she sees as a racially and ethnically divided society, in which differences in skin color, language, and dress can lead to alienation. "I'm lucky," she tells me. "I'm not poor. I could go back home if I wanted to. Other people, they have to come; they have no choice. Maybe, in their country, they had no bread on their table. If you don't have bread, you cannot eat. That means your children will have no food. I don't think a lot of Americans understand this about immigrants. They might say they are interested in their folklore, but they do not really want to get to know them, to really understand them."

Xotchil takes a long drink from the glass of water next to her, and Juan, standing at the sink, looks quietly out the window.

⊱⋅☼⋅⊰

In my home, everything was related to food—sad times and good times. So if you want to celebrate something, you cook and eat. We all love to cook in my family, and everyone has a different specialty. If you want to eat very good soup, you have to call Kike, my brother. Back in Venezuela, my specialty used to be *carne fría.* It's a cold meat you serve with mustard. I still make a lot of the foods now, like *chicha,* a drink you mix in the blender made with rice, milk, and vanilla. My kids love it. Diego, my son, has two glasses every day. You can buy it on the street in Venezuela, and I used to get one every morning. The best *chicha* I ever had was the one sold by a man who would mix everything with his bare hands. It was delicious! My mother used to say she'd never go there, but I loved that man's *chicha!*

I like to make *asado negro* now. That means "black meat," and it's a very popular food in Venezuela. When I do it now, people always ask me exactly what I put in and how long they need to cook the meat. I don't know! I just feel it by putting my finger inside to see if it's done.

You can serve *asado negro* with rice and arepas. Arepas are made from corn flour, and some Venezuelans eat them every day, like my mother. She has an old, old iron pan, and every morning she makes an arepa on that pan. My mother can cook everything. When I was little, she was in the kitchen all the time, and if she wasn't cooking, she was shopping in the markets for the food. Everything had to be fresh. I never saw a can of food in the house. She cooked all day, every day, because we always had a lot of people at the table. When we were kids, we would all eat together at twelve o'clock. My father would leave work and pass by the bakery, the *panadería,* to buy bread for the meal. If you weren't at the table at twelve o'clock, like if you were there at 12:05, you could not eat with the family, and you went to the kitchen. This was my father's rule—twelve of us at the table together at noon.

We helped my mother cook sometimes, especially at Christmas. The traditional food was *hallacas.* They're kind of like tamales, because you use a leaf to wrap the ingredients together. When we were kids, everyone would help. Usually the little kids would put the olive or the raisin, what we call the *adorno,* on the *hallaca.* The big kids helped to wrap them, and we'd get the banana leaves from our own tree to do that. My mother would move extra tables into the kitchen so that we could all work together. It was fun because there were a lot of people there, even the neighbors. And drinking, I remember that. When we'd begin to cook, my parents would have some rum with Coca-Cola and lemon juice and put on the music. We'd be working and dancing around with all these people in the kitchen. We'd make three or four hundred *hallacas,* because we'd have a lot of people for dinner. Now, I make them with a friend every Christmas.

The last time my mother came here was five years ago. It's been a long time. I moved here because of my husband, Christian. His family had to leave his country, Chile, when Pinochet came into power. His father had been working in the presidential house with Allende. He wasn't a political man, but he had the last name, San Allende, and Pinochet's people would kill you if you were related to Allende in any way. So the whole family had to leave. Christian was eight, and his parents told him they were going on vacation. They went to Venezuela, where I later met him, and the aunts and uncles went to the U.S. The family was separated during the move, and they never saw some of the aunts and uncles again. It was very sad. When Christian's family finally came over to the U.S., I went with him.

I'm the only one here from my family. I really miss them, but I'm going to stay. I have to, because my kids are here. It's hard for me. When I do go back, I want to stay. I don't want to come back here. Last time I went, I stayed for six months. I'm very attached to my family; we're very, very close.

I like Boston now, though. I feel like it's my town, but it took a while. At first I didn't speak any English, and I was terrified to go out without Christian, because I knew people would speak to me in English. I felt like I didn't connect with anybody, not even the Central Americans I met who lived near us. They used to say to me, "You're white. You're not Latino." So it wasn't easy at first, but after two or three years, when I learned to speak English, I helped a lot of people who couldn't, and people began to accept me.

Then, when I was living in Roxbury, I had trouble with black Americans. My brother had a business there, and I never felt unsafe, but people would tell me it's a very dangerous place. I didn't know then that things were so different here. I remember one day on Blue Hill Avenue, there was a little bodega, and there was a black man working there, and he didn't want to sell me anything. I asked him for a lemon, and he told me, "No, I don't have a lemon for *you!*" I think the only white person on all of Blue Hill Avenue was me! I was shocked, but when you are young, you have your ideas, and I guess I thought I wanted to stay. When I was living there [in Roxbury], I worked in a bar, and the people began to get used to me, but only the ones that lived between there and my apartment. Finally, I did move, because I began to see the reality: it was no place for me to live and to try to understand the black people here. It was hard. I like black people. My brother-in-law is a Dominican. He's black.

In Venezuela, I never saw this. I think people here are very delicate about skin color. I never felt racism back home, though. My father was dark; he was Mexican. My mother is white. In my country, when you see a black person you say, "Hey, *negrito!*" People don't feel offended. It's normal. Actually, my nieces are very dark, because my brother is married to a black woman. My mother calls their kids "my little black peppers" because of their hair. You don't feel bad. Here, it's different. The communities are very divided, and I don't know why. You might have a community of Dominican people, another of people from Haiti, or Colombians, like in East Boston. The Portuguese people don't like the Brazilians here. You can't be like a family with your neighbors, be-cause, I don't know, the people here aren't friendly, like in Venezuela. There, I know all of my neighbors. If I need something, I knock on the door. You can knock on your neighbor's door if you feel like drinking coffee with somebody. There, it's normal. Here, no. Here, I know my neighbors, but they are not my friends. I say, "Hi," but that's it. I try to be friendly, though: when I collect my tomatoes and vegetables from my little farm, the garden out in my backyard, I have one of the kids bring something over to them.

Inside my home, we are Venezuelan: you respect everyone; you re-spect your family. We are very close, and we like to spend time together. Even though he's a teenager, my son Diego likes to be with us. To me, American teenagers are different. It doesn't seem like they want to be with adults, like they don't know how to talk with them. In Venezuela, the kids like to talk a lot. They discuss politics, everything. They're not shy with adults, and they are very close to the family, very respectful of the family. My kids like to go with us everywhere, even to the supermarket to buy stuff for arepas or *chicha.* Elsa pushes the cart, and Diego organizes everything, because he's very neat. Sebastian goes with Christian to buy the *queso blanco*.

So I don't have to worry about teaching my kids about my culture, because in our house, we live the culture every day. When you cook arepas, maybe you don't think you are teaching them something, but you are.

Xotchil's Venezuelan *Asado Negro, Insalata Repoyo, Plátanos,* and Arepas

Black Roast Beef with Vegetables, Cabbage Salad, Baked Plantains, and Corn Cakes

Serves 6

Asado negro, *or blackened roast, refers to the dark color the meat acquires when it's been caramelized in the sugar. The roast could be served simply with white rice or, as Xotchil did, with the salad, plantains, and arepas. Arepas are a staple of Venezuelan cuisine, sold throughout the country in* areperías *and eaten for breakfast, lunch, or dinner.*

2½ pounds boneless beef chuck or bottom round roast, trimmed

½ white onion, chopped

1 green bell pepper, cored, seeded, and cut in 1-inch pieces

1 red bell pepper, cored, seeded, and cut in 1-inch pieces

1 bunch scallions, chopped

3 cloves garlic, minced

3 carrots, chopped

2 bay leaves

½ cup soy sauce

½ cup dry white wine

Salt and freshly ground pepper

2 tablespoons vegetable oil

2 tablespoons sugar

Pat the meat dry with paper towels. In a large bowl, combine the onion, peppers, scallions, garlic, carrots, bay leaves, soy sauce, and wine. Add the meat and coat it with the marinade on all sides. Marinate for 6 to 8 hours.

Transfer the meat to a plate and season on all sides with salt and freshly ground pepper. In a large, heavy-bottomed pot, heat the oil and sugar over medium heat. Cook, stirring frequently, for about 2 to 3 minutes, until the sugar caramelizes and becomes a deep golden brown color. Add the meat and cook, turning occasionally, until brown on all sides, about 5 to 7 minutes. Transfer the meat to a plate. Add the vegetables from the marinade to the pot and cook, stirring frequently, until they begin to brown, about 7 minutes. Return the meat to the pot and add any remaining liquid from the marinade.

Bring to a slow simmer and cook, covered, for 1½ hours. Gently turn the meat over and continue to cook until it is tender when pierced with the tip of a sharp knife, about 1½ additional hours.

Transfer the meat to a cutting board. In a blender or food processor, puree the vegetables with the liquid from the pot until smooth. Season with salt and pepper. To serve, slice the meat into ¼-inch slices and arrange them on a platter. Spoon the sauce from the vegetables over this.

INSALATA REPOYO

1	small head green cabbage
1	cup mayonnaise
1	tablespoon sugar
¼	cup fresh lime juice
3 or 4	carrots, peeled and grated
	Salt and freshly ground pepper

Wash the cabbage under cold running water, remove the tough outer leaves, and cut into quarters. To shred, cut out the core and slice the quarters crosswise into ⅛-inch-wide strips.

In a large bowl, combine the mayonnaise, sugar, and lime juice. Add the cabbage and carrots and toss them until combined. Season with salt and pepper. Cover and refrigerate for 2 to 3 hours before serving. Can be prepared a day ahead.

PLÁTANOS

4 yellow plantains

1 tablespoon vegetable oil

Several tablespoons soft butter for serving

Preheat oven to 400°F.

Remove the tips of the plantains with a sharp knife. Using the tip of the knife, slit the peel along the length of each plantain and remove. Coat the bottom and sides of a medium-sized baking dish with the oil. Place the peeled plantains in the dish and bake in the middle of the oven until golden brown on the outside and soft inside when pierced with a knife, about 20 minutes.

To serve, slice each plantain lengthwise about halfway into its diameter and insert 1 to 2 teaspoons butter.

AREPAS

2 cups precooked white cornmeal*

½ teaspoon salt

2½ to 3 cups boiling water

Vegetable oil for frying

In a large bowl, combine the cornmeal and salt. Gradually add boiling water, pouring it slowly in a thin stream and mixing with a wooden spoon to form a ball. Cover and let rest for 10 minutes.

Divide the dough into 10 to 12 equal pieces. Moisten your hands with water and form pieces of the dough into balls. Press to form a cake about 2 to 3 inches in diameter and ½ inch thick.

In a large skillet, heat several tablespoons of oil over medium-high heat until shimmering. Working in batches, fry the arepas until a golden brown crust forms, about 4 to 5 minutes. Turn them over and brown them on the other side for an additional 4 to 5 minutes. You may need to add more oil between batches.

Arrange them on a plate and serve immediately.

* Found in markets specializing in Latino and Caribbean products. The cornmeal used to make arepas is a special, precooked type, *masa precocida,* different from the more common *masa harina,* or corn flour, used to make tortillas. For her arepas, Xotchil uses P.A.N. brand, which is popular in Venezuela and Colombia and easily found here.

Eating Alone

Saida Tridou, twenty-two, came to the United States from Morocco
in the fall of 2004, eight months before we met. She lives with her
husband, also from Morocco, in East Boston.

⬛⟫⟨⬛

TO WATCH SAIDA SORT THROUGH a platter of steaming couscous, methodically separating the tiny pieces that have stuck together in the cooking
process, is mesmerizing. She goes at the task quietly, her fingers working
their way through the granules as she moves from the left side of the tray
slowly over to the right, never stopping until all of the clumps have disappeared. This is something she will repeat several times during the cooking
process. Her face, wrapped in a beige head scarf today, reveals delicate fea-
tures that often appear thoughtful and serious. Now, however, they register
surprise, her brown eyes wide and her mouth open slightly when she gasps.
I have just told her how I prepare couscous, by throwing it into a pot of
boiling water and serving it immediately. "You never use the *couscousière*?"
she demands in amazement, referring to the pot used for steaming the
granules over the meat and vegetables. "You cook it in the water?" she asks,
making sure she's heard me correctly. When she says she can't wait to call
her mother back in Casablanca and tell her how Americans prepare couscous, I promise her that the next time I'll do it the way she's shown me.

Saida tells me that in Morocco, couscous that is served clumped together (the way mine always turns out) is not good couscous and that it's

Opposite: Saida serves the couscous.

81

important to take the time to break up the granules several times during the preparation. When she turns away from the stove now and walks across the room to get something from the refrigerator, her black ballet slippers make a soft pattering sound on the tile floor. Saida reminds me of a dancer: her movements are delicate and precise as she goes about her kitchen slicing, stirring, measuring, and, finally, working through golden mounds of couscous every fifteen minutes.

While the chicken and vegetables steam, she shows me some of the items that she brought from home to adorn her kitchen: the beautiful wooden *kesria,* a hand-carved platter she will serve the meal on today, and her prized *tajin,* a covered dish made of ceramic and painted in bold colors, which she uses to prepare her favorite Moroccan dish of the same name. When the phone rings, Saida excuses herself and goes into the next room, where she turns down the Egyptian news program that's been left on. She speaks into the receiver quietly in Arabic, nodding and playing with the ends of her head scarf. "No problem," she says after several minutes, and hangs up the phone.

Saida spoons the couscous onto the *kesria,* this time to serve it, carefully spreading the granules to the edges of the platter and mounding it slightly in the middle. Next, she arranges the pieces of chicken on top, followed by turnips, squash, carrots, and cabbage, which she alternates artfully on top of the meat. The vegetables are a warm golden hue from the turmeric that was added to the pot early on, and the ginger-scented steam is tantalizing. "You can't enjoy Moroccan food alone," Saida has told me before, and suddenly I understand clearly what she means when we sit just inches away from one another on the floor around a low table, using our fingers to scoop pieces of chicken, vegetables, and couscous off the same beautiful plate, marveling together at the delicate flavors of the dish. This is a meal that's meant to be shared.

If I could go back to Morocco today, I would eat *tajin*—*tajin* with chicken, or, if it was Friday, I'd have couscous. Friday is couscous day in Morocco, and after we go to pray, we always eat that. I can't do it here, because I'm usually working, but sometimes I do it on the weekend.

I remember the smells of the couscous cooking on Fridays in our apartment building in Casablanca. Everybody prepares it on Friday. My mother, even though she works, would always get up really early to

At home in East Boston.

cook so that we could have it after praying. I miss those mealtimes. It was always special. Everything is served on big plates, and you share it together.

Before I got married, I lived with my parents. My mother taught me to cook when I was older, maybe thirteen or fourteen years old. She showed me how to do the couscous and *tajin*. *Tajin* is delicious! It's meat or vegetables in a special sauce that you cook in a ceramic pot. When my mother was working, I liked to prepare something to surprise her when she came home. She encouraged me. My father also, I would prepare things for him. They didn't always agree with this because it was dangerous for me to use the stove when nobody was home, but I did it. I loved it! I love to cook, to try to do something new and to see if it's going to be good or not. So I taught myself a lot of things, but in my memory I had information from my mother. I remember a lot, because I memorized what she did.

It was fun to cook with her and to try to help with some parts of the preparation. I would do the easy things; maybe I would prepare the vegetables while she did the meats. She was a good teacher because she had patience. A lot of times I did the wrong things, but she'd always explain again.

I think about her when I cook now. Every day when I prepare Moroccan food, my husband says that it's good, but I say, "No, it's not like my mother's cooking." Sometimes I call her to get recipes and talk about what to do. For example, I know in general how to prepare the foods, but I ask about little things, like if I have to add *gingembre,* the ginger, or if I don't have to do that. It's the small things that I have to ask her. I usually cook Moroccan food here, but sometimes I cook other things like fries or fish. If it's not a Moroccan specialty, I still use a lot of our spices, like pepper, paprika, cinnamon, ginger, and especially the turmeric to make the food yellow.

My grandmother was a good cook, too, and I have lots of memories of her house in Kenitra, the city where she lived. It was always full of grandchildren—my cousins, my brothers, and me. I loved her food. She made traditional dishes like the couscous and the *tajin.* I didn't help because I was too little, but I liked being there with her. Because my mother worked—she was a teacher—we didn't always have time for all of the traditional dishes like my grandmother served.

I can't enjoy the food here. Even when I cook Moroccan food, I can't enjoy it. I don't know why. Maybe I need the ambience of all the family. We're just two now, my husband and I, but in Morocco we were together with everyone. Sometimes, if I have time, I prepare couscous, and I am happy because it's different from the other days when we are at work or school, but it's still not the same.

It's difficult to be alone here. Even if you have friends, it's difficult because the family is so far away. Maybe my husband is more habituated to it because he's been here for seven years. But I am learning a lot about things in this country, and there are many good things. I like that you have the ability to do anything. Nothing is impossible here. You can study and work and find the skills you need to do anything. It's different in Morocco, because there aren't as many opportunities. Everything is different, even the daily schedule. Here, we don't have time to sit at the table at twelve or one o'clock for the meal, but there, everyone must be home to take lunch together, so the schools and businesses close. In the United States, there's no time. I'm at school and my husband is at work. The only time is late at night when he gets home from the parking garage where he works.

So when things are difficult here, I stay busy. It helps me. For example, if I was home alone when my husband was working all day, it would be very hard for me to adapt, but when I am busy with my homework and my school, it's better. Sometimes I cook so that there's no time to feel bored. The cooking makes me think about my mother, my brothers, and my father, because I was always with them. We talk on the phone and e-mail every day now. One brother is in France, and another is in Morocco. I don't know if everyone will go back, but if I stay here and have a family, I am thinking I will send my children to Morocco for two or three years so they will have attachments with the family there. I don't want them to be detached and have no relation with our heritage. I want my children to know that in Morocco, at lunch, there is always a place for them at the table.

Cooking the food all the time helps me to remember that I'm Moroccan. So I always cook, and when we have a holiday, we try to celebrate like we do in Morocco. The last one was Eid el Adha, when each Muslim must buy a sheep. It's like a gift to God, a sacrifice. I did that here, but it was not so good. It was my first holiday, and we were alone. It was very different. In Morocco, the sheep is brought home, and my father would kill it. Sometimes my brothers would help him. But here we brought it home ready from the butcher. And then at home, we'd always barbecue it on the fire, and we'd have tea and bread, but here, even the barbecue is different. It's electric! It's not so delicious with the electric one.

I'll keep cooking my foods, though, even if I must do it differently here, because I think if I changed my cooking style, it just wouldn't be right.

SAIDA'S MOROCCAN COUSCOUS

Serves 4 to 6

Saida uses the couscousière *she brought back with her from Morocco to prepare this meal. A* couscousière *is a colander and pot that can be tightly fitted together and covered. The grains of couscous are placed in the colander to steam, absorbing the flavors of the meat and vegetables cooking in the pot below.* Couscousières *can be found in cooking supply stores or those specializing in Moroccan and North African goods. A large steamer or colander (with small holes) that fits over a pot can also be used.*

In Morocco, everyone shares a common plate by sitting on the floor around a low table. Couscous is often eaten with one's fingers, although spoons may be used. Saida's family always ate the vegetables and couscous from the platter first. When only the chicken remained, her mother would portion it for everyone.

1	small savoy cabbage, quartered
	Salt and freshly ground black pepper
⅓	cup vegetable oil plus 2 tablespoons, divided
1	chicken (about 2½ pounds), cut into 8 serving pieces
1	white onion, cut in half lengthwise and then cut into thin strips
6	plum tomatoes: 3 cored, seeds removed, and sliced; 3 cored, seeds removed, and grated
12 to 15	sprigs parsley
1	tablespoon ground ginger
1	tablespoon turmeric
4	small purple turnips, peeled and quartered
6	carrots, peeled and left whole
2½	cups couscous
1	cup plus 1 cup water, divided
1	acorn squash, quartered and seeded (or 2 small zucchini, left whole)
One	15-ounce can chickpeas, drained and rinsed

Prepare the cabbage first by steaming it in a small pot with 1 to 2 inches of water that has been seasoned with salt and pepper. Cook for 15 to 20 minutes or until the cabbage is soft. Drain and set aside.

Meanwhile, heat the ⅓ cup of oil in the bottom of a *couscousière* or a large pot over medium-high heat until shimmering. Add the chicken, onion strips, sliced tomatoes, parsley, ginger, turmeric, salt, and pepper. Cook until the meat begins to brown, about 10 minutes, stirring the ingredients frequently so that they do not stick to the bottom of the pan. Add the turnips, carrots, and enough water to just cover the chicken and vegetables. Bring to a boil and immediately reduce the heat to medium.

While the chicken and vegetables simmer, spread the couscous onto a very large plate or tray. Moisten this with 1 cup of water, working the water into the grains of couscous with your fingers until all are moistened. Pour the moistened couscous into the top of the *couscousière* or steamer and place over the steaming pot of chicken and vegetables. Cover. Allow the couscous to steam for 15 minutes.

Remove the top of the *couscousière* from the pot of chicken and vegetables. Add the squash, chickpeas, and grated tomato to the pot of chicken. While the chicken and vegetables continue to cook, pour the hot couscous from the *couscousière* onto a tray or large plate, spreading it with a spoon. Sprinkle several pinches of salt and the two remaining tablespoons of vegetable oil over the couscous. Gently work the salt and oil into the couscous with your fingers. Sprinkle 1 cup of water over this, again working it into the couscous so that all of the granules are moistened, breaking up any clumps that have formed. Pour the couscous back into the *couscousière* and return it to the top of the steaming pot of chicken and vegetables. Cover and cook for another 15 minutes.

Again, remove the couscous from the *couscousière* and pour it onto the tray, repeating the process of breaking up any lumps that have formed in the couscous but not adding water, oil, or salt this time. Pour the couscous back into the *couscousière* and steam it for 10 more minutes. Remove the chicken from the pot and set it aside on a plate. Add the cooked cabbage to the pot of vegetables and cook for 2 to 3 minutes to heat.

To serve, remove the couscous from the *couscousière* and arrange it in a circle on a serving platter. With a spoon, form a depression in the center of the pile. Place the chicken in the depression. Arrange the different vegetables alternately on top of the ridge of couscous and in a ring around the chicken. Season with salt and pepper.

Quiet in America

Xiu Fen Xiang, originally from China, is fifty-nine and lives in
Brighton, Massachusetts. She came to the United States in 1997 and
works as a cashier's assistant at Whole Foods Market in Brighton.
In China, she worked as an engineer.

XIU FEN IS IN HER element today, wheeling her carriage purposefully
down the aisles of C Market, a large grocery store in Chinatown. The sounds
of Mandarin, Cantonese, and Vietnamese surround us as we make our way
toward the produce section, maneuvering around the many families shopping on this Sunday afternoon. Xiu Fen calls my attention to the things she
likes to buy here: piles of leafy green pea tendrils, eggplant, water chives,
Chinese celery, and baby bok choy. There's a certainty to her movements
I don't recognize. When I usually see her, bagging groceries at the large
American natural foods market on the other side of town, she always looks
a little tired. The lines in her pretty face are more pronounced as she fills
my bags and we chat about one of our favorite things—food. Sometimes
I'll come upon her outside the store, where she collects the grocery car-
riages that are scattered about the parking lot. She'll tell me about a trip
she's planning back to Shanghai or a dish she cooked the night before, or,
if there's a special on something in the store she thinks I'd like, she'll let
me know about it. This is always spoken in English that has a sing-song
quality to it: her vowel sounds rise and fall with the words she struggles to
pronounce. Frequently she'll stop midsentence, furrow her brow, and close

Opposite: Xiu Fen Xiang.

her eyes as she searches for a particular word. Over the years, I've gotten better at guessing what she's trying to say and sometimes help her finish a sentence, which she seems to appreciate, nodding eagerly when I've gotten it right.

I've always wished I could say more to Xiu Fen, that she could tell me about her life before she came to the United States, the people whose faces peer out from the framed pictures in her apartment, the successful career she left behind in Shanghai. The connections we've made have always been through food—she asking what I've been cooking recently or I wondering how to prepare one of the Asian vegetables the store just got in. I love her suggestions for homeopathic remedies when she finds out one of my kids has been home with an upset stomach or if I come into the store with a cold. "Licorice is good for that," she'll advise, pointing toward the aisle where I can find the herbal teas and then turning to her next customer with another bag to fill.

But across town in her favorite Chinese market today, Xiu Fen is the customer. She roams the produce section with a light step, calling me over excitedly when she sees they've just restocked the lily bulbs. "Good for soup," she explains. Or she shows me the taro root she'll use for dessert.

"Ah, winter bamboo!" she cries out suddenly, parking her carriage in front of a large cooler. This is what she's really come for. It's one of her favorite things to eat, and she tells me it's hard to find in Boston. I look down at a pile of oddly shaped vegetable pieces that are a nondescript brown color. "Winter bamboo!" she says again. "You slice it, then cook. Very, very good! Much better than canned bamboo." She moves several aside before she chooses one, explaining that summer bamboo is delicious, too, but impossible to find in this country.

When we move into the seafood section, the distinct smell of salt and fish permeates the air. Here there are tanks filled with live sea bass and flounder, baskets heaped with menacing-looking crabs crawling over one another, and, behind the counter, an assortment of filleted fish. Xiu Fen points to a tray of tiny silvery-white fish, aptly translated as "silver fish" on the sign, and asks if I like them. When I tell her it's something I've never tried, she orders a pound. I marvel at the assortment here: sea ginger, conch, even seaweed. "Eat with sugar, vinegar, maybe some soy sauce and spices," Xiu Fen says when she sees me looking at the translucent green vegetable.

Several days later, when we are in Xiu Fen's apartment on the other side of Boston, she prepares no fewer than fifteen different dishes for dinner. Several of them, which she refers to as the cold foods, were already arranged artfully around the living room table when we came in. The others I watch her cook in her wok. Wearing a white lace apron that she probably sewed on the machine she keeps in the other room, Xiu Fen measures, mixes, stir-fries, and serves everything with a pair of wooden chopsticks she rarely puts down. Some of the dishes are straightforward: for example, the shrimp simply stir-fried with peas, and the sea bass cooked with green pepper. Others, like the eggplant served at room temperature, which I did not see her make, are more complicated, a blend of exotic flavors complementing the dish. My favorite is no surprise to Xiu Fen: the winter bamboo she cooked with soybeans, black mushrooms, tofu, and nuts. She was right: the fresh bamboo is so much better than the stuff in a can.

<hr />

I go to Chinatown when I need vegetables. Lemongrass, tofu, baby bok choy, everything is very, very fresh. But Chinatown is a little far away. I go maybe every three weeks only. I like to get special vegetables, the fresh bamboo. You can serve it with meat. Chinese people love this. And pea tendrils, I cook in oil with a little garlic and salt. You cook it very quickly. Then you must eat right away, because if you wait, it's no good. I can get the dried tofu there. It has a very nice taste. I cook it with some oil and mushrooms. It's very delicious with a little soy.

Every day I cook Chinese food. I like to eat shrimp and fish, and I prepare it like we do in Shanghai. I cook with garlic, sometimes aspara-gus. I do everything in the wok. I use a little oil and add garlic. When you can smell the garlic, then you add the vegetables. And ginger, I use ginger with fish and maybe chicken, but not with vegetables. Sesame oil, that's only for special vegetables, maybe to sprinkle on mushrooms be-fore you eat, but never for cooking. And soy sauce, I like to put that on chicken with a little sugar and some spice. That's for dinner. For break-fast I make Chinese cake, like moon cake. I make a lot and freeze them so I can have one every morning.

I'm a little tired because I always work hard. I work full-time. I go home and cook for myself—breakfast, lunch, and dinner. I make the things we have in Shanghai, like the rice, the noodles, and the dumplings. In the North, they eat noodles and steamed dumplings, and in the South, rice. Shanghai is between North and South, so I cook both. My neighbor in Shanghai was from the North, and sometimes I watched her make steamed dumplings and vegetables. Now I can do this!

Xiu Fen selects taro root for dessert.

My mom was a very good cook. She always did a lot for New Year's. A few days before, we'd go shopping to get everything. For the meal, you always start with a lot of cold foods. Later we'd have the hot food and then the soup at the end. It would take us a few days to prepare everything. And the spring rolls, we'd always make them. We would make a lot and bring them to friends—spring rolls because spring is coming. This year I didn't do anything special because I worked. In America, it's different, but in Shanghai, it's very, very exciting! The first night we usually eat the big dinner; it's like American Thanksgiving. The family, everybody, they come together and eat—brothers, sisters, my mother, always everybody together. Then, at midnight, there are so many fireworks in the street, and people everywhere. It's very beautiful!

I don't always cook everything for New Year's now. Before, when my friends were here, I'd have a party. They all went back to China. Their husbands didn't like it. It was the language. English is difficult, and people get frustrated, maybe a little bored. Our language is so different! I'm sorry, I want to learn more English, but I work a lot, and I'm very tired. I don't have time to practice. Sometimes I watch TV, or sometimes I read. I used to listen to English tapes that I bought in Shanghai, but I don't have time now. But I can speak Russian! Sometimes I speak with the Russians who come to the store. We had to learn it in school, because, when I was a youngster, China and Russia were very close.

That was [during] the Cultural Revolution. In China, everything changed. Oh, it was very bad then. Very bad! There was no school. I had to stay home. The teachers, they were considered bad, treated very bad. And the red color, it was everywhere. The clothes, we had to wear dark gray and green, nothing beautiful. Our hair, we had to keep it very short. It was a terrible time! And there was no good food, no fancy food, because everything was rationed. Like sugar, you could only have a little sugar every month. It was the same with oil, rice, with many things. So, for six years I stayed home with my mother. She didn't want me to go out, because she was very scared. So, I learned to cook. She cooked every day, and I watched her. She could cook anything! And sewing, I learned that. I used to sew all the clothes: my mom's clothes, my brother's clothes. And now, it's good for me; it keeps me busy.

It's nice here. I like America, because the air is fresh and it's quiet. I like quiet. In China, oh, a lot of people! Before, when I lived in Shanghai, I didn't have this feeling, but now when I go home I think there are too many people—on the street, everywhere. Here, after six at night, there's no one around. In China, there are always so many people. I like quiet. And the air, I like the fresh air in America.

My father left China, too. I never knew him, because he left when I was a baby. That was because we had the Cultural Revolution. He was in Taiwan, working in a famous hotel. Before he died, he was a chef, and he cooked American food, Chinese food, French food. He was the first chef in a big restaurant in Shanghai! A few years ago, I went to Taiwan to find my father's friends. They said, "Oh, your father, he was a very good chef." I was happy.

When I cook now, I think about my mother teaching me how to make all the foods. She taught me to eat slowly, to have patience, and also how to treat people. And now, I like to cook Chinese for my American friends, sometimes for people at work. They like it. They like my spring rolls! And when I go back to Shanghai, it's nice because everybody cooks for me—my sister, my sister-in-law. And the taste, it's so good, not like the restaurants here. I don't go to Chinese restaurants [here], because they're all the same.

I like Chinese food! I try American food sometimes, but, to me, it has no taste. When I eat salad, I feel like an ox eating grass! Sometimes, at the store where I work, I watch them cook. Some of the foods have no flavor. Some are too salty. Some of the desserts, oh, they're very sweet. I cannot eat them. But pizza, sometimes I like that. Cheese pizza is good!

Xiu Fen's Shanghai Fish and Vegetable Dinner

Stir-Fried Sea Bass with Green Pepper, Curried Scrod with Scallion,
Shrimp with Peas, Winter Bamboo, Pea Tendrils with Garlic,
Scallion Pancakes, and Sweet Taro Tapioca Pudding

Serves 6 as a multicourse meal

When Xiu Fen prepared this meal, she cooked one dish at a time and brought each to the table immediately, rather than trying to serve everything together. Although the winter bamboo stir-fry is more labor-intensive than the others, I highly recommend it if you are able to locate all the ingredients. Fresh winter bamboo, unlike the canned version, is tender and subtly flavored, which is why it's so prized in Asian cooking. The dish itself is beautiful, a contrast in color and texture.

STIR-FRIED SEA BASS WITH GREEN PEPPER

    1 pound fresh sea bass fillet, cut into 1-inch pieces
    3 tablespoons olive oil plus 1 tablespoon, divided
    1 medium green bell pepper, cored, seeded, and cut
      into 1-inch pieces
      Salt and freshly ground pepper

In a medium bowl, gently toss the fish with the 3 tablespoons olive oil. Let stand for 5 to 10 minutes.

In a wok or large skillet, heat the remaining tablespoon of oil over high heat until shimmering. Add the peppers, making sure not to crowd the pan (which will lower the heat). You may need to work in batches. Stir-fry the peppers until they just begin to curl at the edges, about 1 to 2 minutes. Add the fish and continue to stir-fry until just slightly browned on the edges and cooked through, about 30 to 60 seconds. Season with salt and pepper. Serve immediately.

CURRIED SCROD WITH SCALLION

¼ cup olive oil

1½ teaspoons curry powder

1 pound fresh scrod fillet, cut into 1-inch pieces

½ cup scallions, chopped

Salt and freshly ground pepper

In a wok or large skillet, heat the oil over high heat until shimmering. Add the curry powder and cook for 5 to 10 seconds. Working in batches, add the fish by carefully placing the pieces in the oil and allowing them to fry until partly cooked, about 1 to 2 minutes. With a spatula or tongs, gently turn the fish to cook its other side, and add the scallions. Fry for another minute or two, until the fish is just cooked through and the scallions are soft. With tongs or a slotted spoon, carefully lift the fish and scallions from the oil. Season with salt and pepper. Serve immediately.

SHRIMP WITH PEAS

1 tablespoon olive oil

½ pound medium shrimp, peeled and deveined, tails left on

½ pound fresh green peas

Salt and freshly ground pepper

In a wok or large skillet, heat the oil over high heat until shimmering. Add the shrimp and peas, making sure not to crowd the pan (which will lower the heat). You may need to work in batches. Stir-fry until just cooked, about 1 minute. Season with salt and pepper. Serve immediately.

WINTER BAMBOO WITH SOYBEANS, GINKGO NUTS, MUSHROOMS, AND TOFU

2 pieces winter bamboo* (about 1½ to 2 pounds)

2 tablespoons plus 2 tablespoons vegetable oil, divided

¼ cup soy sauce

2 tablespoons sugar

4 to 6 Chinese dried black mushrooms,** soaked until soft, drained, stemmed, and cut into ½-inch strips

½ cup canned soybeans, drained and rinsed

½ cup canned ginkgo nuts,*** drained and rinsed

8 ounces drained firm tofu, cut into 1-inch pieces

Salt and freshly ground pepper

1 tablespoon sesame oil

Using a sharp knife, cut off the woody bottom end of the bamboo and discard. Make a lengthwise incision in the shoot and remove outer husk, along with the leaves and sharp hairs that grow on it. Cut off the tip of the bamboo and shave off any remaining hairs and any remaining inner leaves until you have a smooth piece. (You will have reduced the diameter of the bamboo by more than half.) Discard the leaves and shavings. Cut the remaining piece of bamboo in half lengthwise and slice crosswise into pieces ¼ inch thick.

In a large skillet or wok, heat 2 tablespoons of the oil over medium-high heat until shimmering. Add the bamboo and stir-fry until golden, about 5 minutes. Add the soy sauce, sugar, and enough water to just cover the bamboo. Bring to a boil. Immediately reduce the heat to a simmer and cook, covered, until the bamboo is soft to the bite, about 40 minutes.

In a 10-inch skillet or wok, heat the remaining 2 tablespoons of oil over high heat until shimmering. Add the mushrooms, soybeans, ginkgo nuts, and tofu and gently stir-fry, being careful not to break up the tofu, until

---

* Found in markets specializing in Asian and health foods.

** Fresh mushrooms with a strong flavor, such as shiitake and portobello, can be substituted. Cooking time will vary.

*** Fresh ginkgo nuts can be substituted. Remove the shells by gently tapping the nut with the side of a large knife or a small pan. Boil the nuts for 1 minute to make removing the skins easier.

everything is cooked through, about 3 to 4 minutes. (Note: If using fresh mushrooms, you will need to sauté them ahead of time. Also, when adding the remaining ingredients, you may need to work in batches to stir-fry properly so that the ingredients are not crowded in the pan.) Add the bamboo and its liquid and continue to cook for another minute. Season with salt and pepper. Transfer everything to a serving plate and drizzle with the sesame oil.

PEA TENDRILS WITH GARLIC

2 tablespoons olive oil

1 clove garlic, minced

½ pound washed pea tendrils, coarse lower portion of
   shoot removed

   Salt and freshly ground pepper

In a large skillet or wok, heat the oil over medium-high heat until shimmering. Add the garlic and cook, stirring constantly, until it begins to turn golden, about 15 seconds. Add the pea tendrils (you may need to work in batches if the pan becomes too crowded) and stir-fry until the tendrils just begin to wilt, about 1 minute. Season with salt and pepper. Serve immediately.

SCALLION PANCAKES

Makes 6

- 2 cups flour
- ½ teaspoon salt
- 1 cup water
- 3 tablespoons vegetable oil, plus more for frying
- 1 cup scallions, chopped, white and first half of green part

  Salt and freshly ground pepper

In a medium bowl, combine the flour and salt. Slowly add the cup of water and, using a wooden spoon, mix the dough until it can be gathered into a ball. If the dough crumbles, add more water. If it is too wet, add flour. Turn the dough onto a lightly floured surface and knead it by folding it end to end, then pressing it down with the heel of your hand and folding it forward. Repeat for 2 to 3 minutes. Form the dough into a ball, place it in a bowl, cover with a cloth, and let rest for 10 minutes.

On a lightly floured surface, roll the dough into a large oval, about 9 by 18 inches and ¼ inch thick. Using a pastry brush, spread the 3 tablespoons of oil over the dough and sprinkle with the chopped scallions, salt, and pepper. Working from the long end, roll the dough jelly roll–style, and cut crosswise into 6 equal pieces. On a lightly floured surface, roll each piece to about 8 inches in diameter and ¼ inch thick.

In a 10-inch skillet, heat 1 to 2 tablespoons of oil over medium heat until shimmering. Add one of the scallion pancakes and fry until the edges are golden brown, about 2 to 3 minutes. Turn the pancake over and cook the other side until golden, about 2 to 3 minutes more. Sprinkle with salt and pepper, cut into quarters, and serve immediately.

SWEET TARO TAPIOCA PUDDING

6 cups water

1 cup tapioca pearls*

1 small taro root* (about 1½ pounds), washed well, peeled, and cut into 1-inch pieces

One 14-ounce can coconut milk

½ cup sugar

In a medium pot, bring 6 cups of water to a boil. Add the tapioca pearls and reduce the heat to low. Cook until the pearls become translucent, about 15 minutes, stirring frequently so that the tapioca does not stick to the bottom of the pan and burn. Add the taro and continue to cook, stirring frequently, until soft, about 20 minutes. Add the coconut milk and sugar and continue to cook until the thickness of porridge, about 20 minutes. Serve warm in individual bowls.

* Found in markets specializing in Asian products.

Remembering Where You Started

Roula Kappas, fifty-one, left her country, Greece, in 1968 when she was a teenager. She lives in Boston and owns the New Paris Bakery in Brookline with her husband, Jimmy, also from Greece.

ROULA CAREFULLY ARTICULATES HER THOUGHTS in a low, measured tone one moment, then raises her voice slightly the next to underscore a particular point. She spreads her hands over the table, marking off invisible boundaries as she moves from one subject to the next, explaining why her family first immigrated here more than thirty years ago and how Greece has changed since she's been gone, then listing the reasons why its food is still so much a part of her life after all these years. "I'm totally addicted to this," she says of spanakopita, the classic spinach and feta pie she's making today. Her mother, Ann, who's visiting from Greece for several months, helps her daughter clear the table, which has been covered in thick plastic to make rolling the phyllo dough easier.

The women use a *plastis,* a thin wooden instrument much like a rolling pin but longer, to create thin, translucent sheets that feel like silk when they're held up for me to inspect. They take turns rolling the twenty or so balls of dough that will be needed to layer the pie. This is a time-consuming process, but neither rushes through it; instead they carefully manipulate the pale, elastic dough with long, sweeping movements of the *plastis,* all the while making small talk or sometimes reprimanding one another good-naturedly.

Opposite: Roula (right) and her mother assemble dolmades.

At one point, when Ann starts to season the spinach and feta mixture for the filling, Roula takes the box of salt from her and says something in Greek. "My father is on a low-salt diet," she explains to us, "and my mother, sometimes she forgets."

The popularity of spanakopita in this country has overshadowed some of the other versions of *"pita,"* the pies available throughout Greece. "You have the *tiropita* with feta, ricotta, and milk," Roula explains. "And then there is the *kotopita* with chicken; we have another with eggplant." It's a shame Americans haven't caught on, I think, as I look around the kitchen at all the beautiful ingredients Roula uses in her cooking—piles of fresh mint and lemons, olive oil and kalamata olives, a stack of freshly washed collard greens—and I begin to wonder what else we've been missing all these years. Some of the items about the kitchen today will be used for Roula's version of dolmades, leaves stuffed with rice, vegetables, and ground beef and pork. These will be wrapped with collard greens rather than the more typical grape leaves, a variation perfected by her ancestors, the Pontians who immigrated to Greece from northern Turkey.

As Roula pours the spinach and feta mixture onto the sheets of phyllo dough, which have been carefully layered in a large baking pan, she tells me that many people in Greece no longer make this at home. Because of the number of *pita* bakeries selling them fresh every day, it's just easier to buy them. Roula, however, who has become adept at making spanakopita because she can't get it easily here, sometimes teaches friends back home how to prepare it when she returns every summer.

When she finishes layering the remaining sheets of dough over the spinach mixture, Roula scores the top with a knife, explaining that this will make it easier to cut after it's been baked. As she begins to mark the next slice, her mother gently nudges Roula's hand with the knife, moving it slightly to indicate the pieces should be larger. Roula sighs deeply, but in an instant gives in, scoring the next as her mother has instructed.

And when the much-awaited spanakopita is pulled from the oven and finally served, I am glad for the large portion on my plate. The crust, which is light and airy and tastes of fresh butter and olive oil, melts in my mouth, along with the creamy feta and thin leaves of perfectly cooked spinach.

<hr />

When we first came here, I was sixteen, and my mother continued to cook the Greek dishes. She cooked everything. I remember her bean soup; it's probably the national soup of Greece. You make it with white navy beans. Then there is lentil soup, and there's spinach and rice and green beans. And she'd make something like the French ratatouille. We have our own Greek version. We call it *tourlou.* Sometimes, we make *imam baldi.* Several months ago, I saw a recipe for it in the paper, and I was happy. This is a great food! You make it with eggplant and fresh onion, garlic, and parsley. We also have moussaka. My mother has made it, but it's a little complicated and not something we make all the time. We also make pastitcio with macaroni, and that's delicious. And then there are the appetizers that everyone likes. We have those when we have people over, like the *tzatziki,* made with cucumbers and yogurt, or *tara-mousalata* with the fish roe, and the *skordalia* with the potato and garlic. Actually you can make that with bread or potato and serve it with fried zucchini on the side. It's great!

I don't consider myself to be a really good cook, but I always cook. I don't depend on tins or frozen foods or TV dinners. I make spanakopita a lot. I make it at home, and I've also sold it in the bakery. If I start making it on a regular basis, I know it's going to sell. People love it.

It's always for better opportunities that people come to the U.S. That's why my parents came. My father was Russian born. There was a law in the early sixties that if you were born in Russia, you could come easily to the United States, so we came. In 1968, I was fifteen, and I really wanted to come. I wanted a change. Politically, things were hard. We had the coup d'etat and junta for seven years, beginning in 1967. I wasn't politically involved, so that was not my problem, but I just wanted a change. I loved it when I got here. I went to the Day School for Immigrants, in the South End of Boston, and loved it. There were a lot of Greek students, a lot of Italians, Puerto Ricans, too.

Then, when I went to Brighton High School, I was always hanging around with other immigrants there. I couldn't be Americanized. There was no way! I know other people do that, but I just couldn't do it myself. I'm not all the way Americanized now either; I'm like a Greek-American. I'm on the side of both cultures, a kind of cultural-marginal. Now, when I go to Greece, I speak the language and everything, but there are so many new words that have been added, and because I don't read the Greek papers, I'm not Greek all the way. I tend to have more in common with people who have been away from Greece and come back. There's a bit of a disconnection when I go home, but I try not to let it bother me. I have other things. I always try to make other connections myself.

Right now I don't miss the culture so much as I miss my people. People in Greece are warm people. They're Mediterranean people. They're loud! They're friendly! In Greece, we don't have so many psychiatrists like you do here, because there's no room for them. We're always talking. We don't need them! Sometimes it's too much, though. I think sometimes the people there overdo it, because they're all over you, always sitting around talking about everything in the cafés. In a small community, everyone knows your habits.

No, the thing I really miss is something I can't visit. It's Greece from the late fifties and early sixties, my childhood. It was a time you didn't have everything, and yet you could be happy because you had maybe one thing. Maybe all you had was a little transistor [radio] in the house. You didn't have a TV, but you went to the movies. There were a couple of movie theaters in Katerini, where I lived, and it was great to go out, maybe to spend a little pocket money on a movie or to buy *kokoretsi,* which is a specialty in Greece. You have little shops that sell it everywhere. It's skewered organ meat, like the intestines, the little hearts, everything. When we go back to Greece, my husband's plan the very first night is always to go immediately to get some.

We'd also spend our pocket money at the souvlaki places. Or on the tripe—when we were kids, I used to love tripe. This guy in Katerini would make it, and there were always a lot of people at his place. We'd wait in line and eat it right there. We thought it was wonderful. Would I like it now? I don't know.

Katerini was a real community then. But those days are gone. My older customers talk about those times here. They tell me they'd come to the bakery long before we owned it and buy an éclair with their pocket money. It's a different time now. Everyone has everything.

So I miss things that cannot come back again. But I do realize that things were hard for many people. At the time, I think I was too young to fully understand everything, that there were people in Greece who had nothing. In the forties and fifties, the country was highly agricultural, and where I was from, it was all tobacco. A lot of the people would kill themselves to grow it, and then maybe they were unable to make money because this went wrong or that went wrong. That's why they emigrated. My family never had tobacco fields. My father had a little business, and we made it, but other people didn't have any food. So if they were able to go to the States, it was the most wonderful thing that could happen. And right now, a lot of these people are rich here. Greeks have done extremely well, and a lot of them have been able to send money home.

I remember when I first came. That summer I worked in an insurance office. I loved it. I made decent money, and I was able to buy a piano for $720. I bought a bag. I bought shoes. At the time, I was hanging around with this Chinese lady who was telling me that all the money she makes she sends to China. I remember thinking to myself, is she crazy? She's not keeping her money to buy all these material things? Now, years later, I'm doing the same thing. I'm helping out, because you just never know. As much as I can, I try to do humanitarian work. I belong to a church, and I help out with the food pantry. Every time I have leftovers from the bakery, I bring them there. This is the way we were taught. Maybe so many years of church, so many years of hearing this, so many years of seeing situations made us want to do it. I mean, when I was a kid in Greece, I didn't necessarily see people losing things, because like I said, my immediate family, although we came to America, we were okay: I was taking piano lessons, I was taking English lessons, my father built a house, my mother dressed us well, we always had something to eat. But again, you never had the extra money. You had to be careful. There's a big difference between how Greece was then and now. Now everybody has something—*everything*—now.

So I really can never go back, back to that place I knew in my youth. You don't know what it is to live in a country other than your own for so many years and what it does to you. You're not American. You're no longer Greek. I don't know what to call you. You're in a situation with a different perspective that other people don't have. When you're some-where in between the two cultures, like me, you lose what's happening in your country right now. Because I'm not there, Greece is a place I don't really understand completely anymore. I've missed the direction of the country and the people for so long. But, you get a better under-standing of human nature by living somewhere else, because you see that everything is relevant and you are the product of a particular soci-ety. I'm not a philosopher—although Greeks are philosophers, believe me; we philosophize all the time!—but it doesn't matter how cultured and well traveled you are, human nature is the same everywhere. You just come with another face, and you try to recognize the things that come out from these different places.

I think people can be brainwashed by the beliefs of a particular re-gion where they live, and that really characterizes their temperament.

What comes to shape these beliefs is what happened before, the history and all these things. Kazantzakis, one of the big Greek existentialists from Crete, once said something like "I don't believe in anything, and I'm not afraid of anybody or anything. I'm free." I think people should consider this and be a little bit more sensitive to different cultures. You know, we have an Austrian woman who comes to the bakery every Tuesday to have lunch with us. We've learned a lot of things from her.

And the food? You cook because you like the taste. You eat it. There are certain foods that you, because you're Greek, eat. Americans may love it. Other cultures may love it. They may have it once or twice, but for you, that's part of your everyday substance, like the Greek cheeses—feta all the time or *kassri*—and Greek coffee every afternoon. It sort of gives you a continuity of what you are. I think it reminds you of where you started from. Food is a cultural thing, definitely. My mother is visiting now, and it's wonderful because she cooks every day, mostly Greek food. Yesterday she made stuffed green cabbage with rice. She makes her own yogurt. It's like we're eating in Greece again.

Roula's Greek Spanakopita and Dolmades

Spinach Pie and Stuffed Collard Greens

Although Roula makes her own phyllo dough, the spanakopita is more easily prepared with premade, frozen dough. I have not included Roula's phyllo recipe here, because I have found it difficult to prepare without a plastis, *which is a very long, thin (3 feet by 1 inch) rolling pin used by Greek cooks to make these pies.*

Roula's version of dolmades is delicious, made with collard greens rather than preserved grape leaves, which gives them a distinctly fresh flavor.

SPANAKOPITA

Serves 4 to 6

3 pounds fresh spinach, stems removed (to yield approximately 2 pounds), washed thoroughly and chopped

1 cup water

¼ cup plus ¼ cup olive oil, divided

½ cup white onions, finely chopped

¼ cup scallions, including some of the green part, finely chopped

¼ cup flat-leaf parsley leaves, finely chopped

¼ cup fresh dill leaves, finely chopped

½ pound feta cheese, crumbled (about 1 cup)

4 eggs, beaten

¼ teaspoon salt

¼ teaspoon freshly ground pepper

4 tablespoons butter, melted

16 large sheets of premade phyllo dough

In a large pot, steam the spinach in 1 cup of water with a pinch of salt added, turning occasionally, just until the leaves wilt, about 1 to 2 minutes. Spread on a large plate to cool enough to squeeze the excess liquid from the spinach, using your hands. Set aside.

In a large skillet, heat ¼ cup of the olive oil over moderate heat until shimmering. Add the onions and scallions and cook, stirring frequently, until translucent, about 5 minutes. Set aside to cool.

In a large bowl, combine the spinach, onion mixture, parsley, dill, feta, eggs, salt, and pepper.

Preheat the oven to 375°F. In a small bowl, combine the melted butter and the remaining ¼ cup of olive oil. With a pastry brush, coat the bottom and sides of a large (13-by-9-by-2-inch) baking dish with the butter mixture. Line the dish with a sheet of phyllo, pressing the edges of the pastry firmly into the corners and up the sides of the dish, allowing any excess dough to hang over the side. Brush the entire surface with the butter mixture. Spread with another sheet of phyllo and again brush the surface with butter. Repeat 6 times to make a total of 8 layers.

Spread the spinach mixture evenly over the layers of phyllo, smoothing it carefully into the corners. Place another sheet of phyllo on top and brush with butter. Repeat to make 6 top layers. If excess layers of pastry are left hanging over the rim of the baking dish, trim them with a sharp knife. Brush the top of the pie with butter. (At this point, you may, like Roula, want to score the top of the pie so that portioning will be easier after the pie has cooked.)

Bake in the middle of the oven until the pastry is golden-brown and crisp, approximately 30 minutes.

Cut into portions and serve hot or at room temperature.

DOLMADES

Makes 18 to 20

2 pounds collard greens, rinsed, stems removed and set aside

1 cup medium-grain white rice, rinsed

1 pound ground beef

1 pound ground pork

2 bunches scallions, including some green parts, finely chopped (about 1 cup)

1 medium white onion, finely chopped (about 1 cup)

½ cup fresh flat-leaf parsley leaves, chopped

½ cup fresh dill, chopped

¼ cup plus ½ cup olive oil, divided

½ teaspoon ground cumin

2 teaspoons salt, plus more for seasoning

½ teaspoon freshly ground pepper, plus more for seasoning

⅓ cup water

5 to 6 tablespoons fresh lemon juice

In a large pot, steam the collard greens in 1 inch of water, with a pinch of salt added, until tender, about 8 to 10 minutes. Drain in a colander and spread on a plate to cool.

In a large bowl, mix the rice, ground beef and pork, scallions, onion, parsley, dill, ¼ cup of the olive oil, cumin, salt, pepper, and ⅓ cup of water.

To roll the dolmades, spread a collard leaf, shiny side down, flat on a clean work surface. Place 2 to 3 heaping tablespoons of the rice mixture on the center of the leaf. Turn up the stem end of the leaf and then, one at a time, turn up each of the sides to enclose the stuffing. Beginning at the stem end, gently roll the collard leaf into a cylinder. If the collard leaves are very large, they may be split lengthwise.

Layer the bottom of a heavy 2- to 3-quart casserole with the reserved collard green stems. (This will help to prevent the stuffed leaves from sticking.) Stack the stuffed leaves, side by side with seams down, in layers in the casserole. Add enough water to just cover the dolmades. Season with additional salt and pepper.

Place the casserole on a burner over high heat and bring to a boil. Immediately reduce the heat to low and simmer gently, tightly covered, until the rice and meat in the collard leaves are fully cooked and the rolls are firm to the touch, about 30 minutes. Remove the dolmades carefully from the pot and arrange them on a serving dish. Before serving, drizzle with the remaining ½ cup olive oil and fresh lemon juice.

Can be served hot or at room temperature. (Dolmades can be made 1 to 2 days ahead and stored in a sealed container in the refrigerator.)

Eating the Flag

Magdani Valera, twenty-one, and her sister, Riqueldys, eighteen, live
with their parents and younger brother in the Roslindale section of
Boston. Originally from the Dominican Republic, they came here in
2003 with their family and are both studying at Bunker Hill
Community College and working as cashiers at CVS.

⚜

THE VALERA SISTERS WEAR THEIR dark hair pulled tightly off their faces,
giving prominence to their large brown eyes, which are at times inquisi-
tive, at others, playful. Dressed in identical jeans belted tightly at the hips,
hoop earrings, and gold chains, it's easy to confuse these two young
women. Magdani and Riqueldys spend a lot of their time together; they
easily answer for one another or pick up where the other has left off in
conversation, often espousing the same opinions and drawing on similar
experiences. They answer my questions in the hip lingo of American
teenagers and possess an irreverent sense of humor, teasing their mother
good-naturedly as they all work in the kitchen or laughing about particular Americans they've encountered at work or at the community college they
both attend. "Americans are so serious," Magdani tells me, and Riqueldys
nods, adding, "Yeah, I see it at work all the time. They look stressed out
when they come in the store."

Today they are cooking *sancocho,* a Dominican favorite, a stew of pork,
plantain, yucca, and calabaza, a squash similar to pumpkin. They work
together with their mother, Yudys, who, as her daughters explain, is quiet

Opposite: Magdani (left) and Riqueldys peel potatoes for *sancocho.*

today because the conversation is mostly in English. Otherwise, Magdani tells us, "She's like a radio. She never stops." This becomes apparent when the phone rings and Yudys wedges it between her ear and shoulder, speaking into the receiver in rapid Spanish while she walks about the kitchen measuring rice, stirring the soup, or washing dishes. Soon the calls become more frequent as news of the *sancocho* spreads to the aunts, uncles, and cousins living in the area, who are now making plans to stop by for a bowl.

Magdani and Riqueldys peel vegetables with small kitchen knives while their mother browns pork in a huge aluminum casserole she brought from the Dominican Republic. This is the kind of pan any good cook would covet, dented and black on the outside, with a smooth interior and a bottom thick enough to create an even heat for cooking. While Yudys works at the stove, Riqueldys prepares the yucca, a vegetable that I've found almost impossible to peel because of its tough skin. Riqueldys, however, does this easily, making a shallow incision along the length of it, inserting her paring knife under this, and easily snapping the thick skin off with a flick of her hand, which makes a satisfying popping sound.

As we wait for the *sancocho* to cook, Magdani shows me the family's rice stash, stored off the kitchen in a closet all its own. A huge container filled with white rice and weighing at least fifty pounds sits on the floor with a large four-cup scoop resting on top of it. "Dominicans really like rice," Magdani laughs when she notices my surprise at the amount they have on hand. Today it will be served with the *sancocho,* which is boiling rapidly on the stove and is a beautiful ochre color from the pureed calabaza squash. The smell is heavenly with the sweet aroma of caramelized pork and plantain, countered by the scent of fresh lime juice.

<hr />

Magdani: It's not that different here; even the food's the same. It's like we live in a small Dominican Republic, because there's so many Dominican people, and all the bodegas, the markets, are Dominican too. Just the weather's different. The way we eat, it's the same here as it was there. We eat the flag. That means we eat rice, beans, and meat. That's the flag, and Dominicans eat that almost every day. We always cook the same things— not always the flag, because, you know, you get sick of it every day—but we cook Dominican food, because that's what we're used to.

Sometimes we make *sancocho.* It's like a thick soup with meat and vegetables. On the Fourth of July we had some Dominican friends over, and we did *arepitas a mano*. They're like little cakes made out of corn flour and milk and cinnamon that you wrap in plantain leaves. We did it on the barbecue, but they didn't taste the same as the ones we make in the Dominican Republic because the flour's not the same, and over there we cook them on rocks on a fire in the ground. It tastes better that way.

Some of the recipes we can't do. A lot of the food back home is just better. There's this place in Salinas beach, near where we lived. This woman, Tanita, cooks there. Oh my God, she cooks so good! She has a *comedor,* a restaurant, in her house. You bring your own bowl and you buy her food. You can take it back to your house or you can eat there. She lives fifteen feet from the beach, so you sit there and look at the water and smell the air. It's really beautiful. She makes rice, beans, and fish. You don't even know it's fish because it's so rich. And her salad, it's so good! She gave us the recipe, but we can never do it like she does.

We shop at Latin markets, so we can get some of the same stuff that we get over there. You feel like you're in the D.R., the Dominican Republic, when you shop at these places. It's the same atmosphere as the markets in our country, because almost everybody's Dominican and we all know each other. The people are really friendly. They're always yelling, "Hey, what you doin' today? I'm coming to pick up some food and stuff for a party. You want to come too?" When you go to an American place you see the difference. It's all tranquil, and nobody's talking too loud.

Riqueldys: That's the thing. Dominican people—oh, my God!— sometimes I get tired because they talk too loud! Well, American people, they talk to you, too, but it's different. Like when I'm working in CVS, they come to me with stories. It doesn't matter if they don't know me. They say, "Oh, this is just the worst day! I was walking here, and you'll never believe what happened to me." I don't say nothing. If they feel comfortable talking to me, all right, but in the Latin grocery, it's just different. Everybody's friendly and happy. They're always talking to you. They'll tell you, "Hey, don't buy this one! Take that one! That one is really good." Or, "Hey, you should go to that place. It's cheaper! It's better!"

I like it here, though. It's not too hard. You have to follow some rules here—it doesn't matter if it's in the street or at work—but you get used to it. I think the difference is that in the U.S., people respect things. It's different in the D.R. If you drive over there, you need to have twenty-five eyes all around you, because you're always gonna see something.

They drive like crazy over there. I know when somebody does something wrong on the road here, they must be Dominican. Dominicans drive crazy! Over there, you can see kids that are ten years old driving, and that's a huge problem, but in the U.S. people respect rules. I like that.

Magdani: One thing that's kind of hard here is our schedules. It's sometimes hard for us all to eat together. In the D.R. we had lunch together every day. When we finished, we'd stay there talking. Over there, everybody's chillin'. They talk, they eat, and they sleep. Here, our hours at work are different, so we never get together. When I'm in school, I come home at two o'clock and sometimes I have to work at three, so I have to eat, change, and hurry to go back to work. My sister has to do the same thing. Now my brother's working in construction with my father, so they come home after three or four, and my mother works at night.

On Sundays, though, we try to cook together, even if it's late. I'll do the beef, Riqueldys does the rice, and my mother will make the beans. But in the D.R., every Sunday was a special day. We'd go to my grandmother's, and she'd make something good like arroz con pollo, our chicken and rice, or she'd make the *sancocho.* When you eat *sancocho,* it's a huge event, because everybody loves it so much. In the D.R. we do a funny thing when we eat it. Well, not us, but the men. They take off their shirts. That's just a funny tradition we have. They take off their shirts before they sit down, because they know the *sancocho* is gonna be hot and they know they're gonna sweat. They just can't wait for it to cool to eat, so they all remove their shirts! My uncle does that. Not the women though, they can wait for it to cool.

Riqueldys: In the D.R., we always had people visit. That's why we'd have to cook a lot. Sometimes people would go to your house, even if you weren't expecting them, so you'd have to have something special to serve them. We don't plan it before, the way you do here. You just go. But I like it better if they call, like Americans do, because over there, if you want to go out, sometimes you're stuck. Like you might be going out and—*ding dong!*—somebody shows up. So you have to stay. After an hour or something, you can say, "You want to come with me? I have an appointment." But you have to invite them in for a while first.

There are lots of things about America I like better, like the way Americans are with their kids. It's different. Dominicans want to have their children like laptops. They want them close by all the time. It doesn't matter if their kid is thirty years old, it's like he'll always be a baby. And Dominican kids, even if they're thirty or more, still stick with their parents. They can't be alone. I think we need to change this and let them learn by themselves.

American kids are more responsible. Their parents treat them differently. You see it when you shop. They might be helping their mother buy something, like maybe stuff for the house. Then you see the Dominicans, and they're going straight to the toys. They're always with a toy or with gum. And the kids, they open it! The parents say, "Oh, my God, what you doin'? I'm telling you, don't open the candy! Now I have to pay for it!" Then the kids cry. The Americans, they explain things. They say nicely, "You know, you can't be opening those candies, because you don't have the money to buy them. You know that." It's really different.

Americans have more rules for their kids too. They say, "You can play from three to five. That's your time to play, and then you need to clean up. You have to help in the house, and you can't always have fun." In the Dominican Republic, you just play, play, play. That's it. Dominican kids need to learn that they can play, but they also need to clean up and study. They cannot do everything they want. They have to follow the rules that somebody gives them.

Magdani: Yeah, I see it when they come to the store. If they're Latin, you see them yelling at their kids, but when they're American, you see they treat their kids like older people. They talk with them. They'll ask their kid, "Oh, do you remember what I was going to buy?" And I'm like, that kid don't remember that! He's too little for that! They talk like they're with a friend. I like that, though, because they teach the kid to be responsible, and also to be friends with the parents. They make the kid think that he's a young person with responsibilities. Latin people treat you like a kid. You can be fifty-five, and they never let you grow up.

Riqueldys: If I have kids here—and I'll probably be here, because things aren't so good over there—I want to teach them to respect rules and to be more independent, like American kids. But some things I'll do the same as Dominicans, like the food. When I have my kids, I want to eat at the table together. I want to make it part of our lives every day, that we have to eat together and that we have to help in the kitchen, like we do in D.R.

Riqueldys and Magdani's Dominican *Sancocho* and *Bollito*

Stew with Squash, Yucca, Plantains, Pork, and Dumplings

Serves 6 to 8

There are countless versions of sancocho *in Latin America, but it is especially popular in the Dominican Republic. Riqueldys and Magdani use pork, but beef or chicken could be used instead. I have seen recipes that call for fish. When made without meat, it makes a hearty vegetarian stew. Like most stews, it's best made one day ahead of serving to allow the flavors to fully develop.*

SANCOCHO

1½ pounds boneless pork shoulder, trimmed and cut into 1-inch pieces

1 pound pork ribs, halved

Juice of 2 or 3 limes (about ⅓ cup)

3 cloves garlic, minced

2 tablespoons dried oregano

1 tablespoon adobo seasoning*

Salt and freshly ground pepper

3 tablespoons vegetable oil

1 onion, chopped

1 stalk celery, chopped

½ green bell pepper, cored, seeded, and chopped

½ red bell pepper, cored, seeded, and chopped

2 green plantains,* peeled and cut on bias into ¼-inch slices

2 yucca,* peeled and cut into 1-inch pieces

2 small yams, peeled and cut into 1-inch pieces

2 potatoes, peeled and cut into 1-inch pieces

1 small calabaza squash* (about 1 pound), peeled, seeded, fibers removed, and cut into 1-inch pieces (butternut squash can be substituted)

8 to 10 sprigs fresh cilantro

15 sprigs fresh *recao** (additional fresh cilantro can be substituted)

Marinate the meat in the lime juice, garlic, oregano, and adobo seasoning overnight.

Remove the meat from marinade, reserving the liquid. Season with salt and pepper. In a large pot, heat the oil over medium-high heat until shimmering. Working in batches, add a few pieces of meat (shoulder pieces and ribs) at a time to the pot and cook until lightly browned on all sides, about

* Found in markets specializing in Latino and Caribbean products. For the adobo seasoning, 2 teaspoons of ground cumin, ½ teaspoon of black pepper, and ¼ teaspoon of cayenne can be substituted.

5 minutes. Add more oil between batches if necessary. Transfer the cooked meat to a platter and set aside. Add the onion, celery, and bell peppers to the empty pot and cook, stirring occasionally, until soft, about 5 minutes.

Return all of the meat to the pot and add the reserved marinade and enough water to cover by 2 inches. Bring to a slow simmer.

Cover and cook until the meat is tender, about 1½ hours. Add the plantains, yucca, yams, potatoes, calabaza, cilantro, and *recao*. The liquid should cover everything. Add more water if necessary. Continue to simmer, uncovered, until the vegetables are soft, about 30 minutes. Remove approximately a quarter of the mix of vegetable pieces from the pot and puree in batches, along with a small amount of broth from the soup, until smooth.

Pour the batches of vegetable puree back into the pot of soup and stir gently. Add the *bollito* (recipe follows), gently dropping them into the stew. Simmer, uncovered, for 30 minutes. Just before serving, remove the sprigs of cilantro and *recao* and season with salt and pepper.

BOLLITO

2 green plantains

Peel plantains: Using a sharp paring knife, cut off the tips of the plantain and discard. Using the tip of the knife, slit the peel along the length of the plantain and remove.

Using the edge of the knife, gently scrape the meat of the plantain into thin shavings. Work these with your fingers to form a soft dough.

To form the *bollito,* pinch off 1-inch-sized balls of the dough and, using your fingertips, roll them gently in the palm of your other hand to form small cylinders.

A Happy Straddler

Soni Gupta is forty years old and originally from India. She came to
the United States in 1990 for graduate school. She works part-time as
a consultant in the field of affordable housing development and lives
with her husband, Dave, and two daughters, Urvi and Tara, in the
Jamaica Plain section of Boston.

LITTLE URVI, AGE THREE AND A HALF, smiles shyly at me from her perch
on the counter. She looks like a centerpiece in the middle of Soni's work
space, sitting surprisingly still for a small child as she watches her mother
prepare a fillet of tilapia. Her outfit, a gold, black, and red printed dress
from India, complements the colors of the polished granite countertop, as if
the space were made specifically for her. A row of mirrorlike beads hangs
from the neck of her dress, and she pulls at them while she watches her
mother move about the room. Soni slides a stainless steel container toward
her, and Urvi reaches for it eagerly. It's her job to sprinkle spices onto the
dishes her mother is preparing. Soni lifts the lid to reveal compartments
filled with cayenne pepper, turmeric, the cumin and coriander she grinds
herself, and garam masala, a mixture of spices she's brought back from
Delhi. Urvi slowly puts the spoon into the cumin, scoops some of the finely
ground powder, and allows her mother to guide her hand over to the fish,
which will be rubbed with the spices before it's cooked. She repeats this with
the coriander and turmeric, her movements concentrated and precise. "Now

Opposite: Dave and Urvi inspect the garam masala that Soni brought back from
India.

we need the *namak,* Urvi, but I'll do that," Soni says, looking at me. "*Namak* is salt. It's hard for her to sprinkle the big granules with her fingers."

Soni turns around to check something on the stove and the ends of her silk magenta dress, also bought in India, reflect the afternoon light streaming in from the window. Like her daughter, Soni moves in a focused, methodical manner, gathering the ingredients for *roti,* the bread she will make with Urvi, watching as her husband, Dave, pours milk into a pot to make *paneer,* an Indian cheese, and sprinkling salt over the fish she is about to cook. Dave works on the other side of the large counter, and Urvi sometimes turns around to watch him. He, too, is wearing traditional clothing: a beige *kurta,* or loose shirt, and pants to match. "Here's a guy who, even though he grew up in Spokane, Washington, loves everything Indian," Soni says of her husband. "I really think he must have been an Indian in a previous life."

When I ask Dave if he's considered living there, he doesn't hesitate. "Definitely. We hope to go back." He says he appreciates the closeness of family life, the way that Soni's family is always around, something Urvi and her little sister, Tara, enjoyed. "I also love the way that India is so vibrant," he says. When I ask him what exactly he's referring to, he says, "Everything. The colors. The smells. It's so different from here."

Soon the kitchen takes on this quality, with the scent of cumin and coriander wafting through the air as the fish cooks. When Soni uses a spatula to flip the fish, the deep golden color of the turmeric is indeed vibrant in the pan. Many of the items on the counter, in the cupboards, and hanging on the walls have been brought back from India, so that, in addition to the intoxicating scents, there is something exotic about Soni's kitchen. While the fish cooks, Soni shows me the dried bay leaves from her mother's garden; they're much larger than the variety found in most stores here. Other items also come from home: her mortar and pestle, used to grind the numerous spices she uses in her cooking, and the *masala dani,* where they're stored after they've been ground.

When the cries of Tara, who is one and a half and has just awoken from a nap, can be heard coming from the other room, Dave slips out of the kitchen to get her. She, too, is placed on the counter next to her older sister, who is busy rolling *roti* with Soni. Urvi pushes the rolling pin across the light brown dough—made with whole wheat flour—while her mother helps guide her hands. "*Rotis* are made when the family is sitting at the table," Soni explains. "There is always someone in the kitchen—in the old days it would have been the cook or the household help—making them and bringing them out one by one."

In Soni's kitchen here in Boston, it seems that Urvi will be the one to take on that task.

⊱✕⊰

I cook a lot of rice because it feels like I'm going back to my roots. We also do dals; that's the lentils cooked with onions and ginger. For convenience I go to the Indian store every other week. I bring things back from India, too. I feel that certain spices, like cinnamon stick, mustard seeds, and bay leaves, are just better there. You can smell the difference. And then there's the garam masala. I buy it in this place in Delhi where they grind it. I mean, really, if you were a good Indian housewife, you should do it at home. And for the longest time I was doing that. I still roast and grind my own spices, but the garam masala, it's a lot of work to mix all those spices, so I just buy it when I'm there. In the old days, we used to grind everything with a mortar and pestle, but now I see a lot of electric grinders in people's kitchens in India. Actually, things are changing there now: lots of modern conveniences, even Western-style restaurants that have started to come in. Frankly, I fail to see the benefits of this, of globalization in general, for the Indians.

When I was young, everything was done by hand. I was always in the kitchen observing my mother and my grandmother, and sometimes I got to cook. Like the *rotis*—it's a passion with kids to be able to roll them, and I see it now with Urvi, my oldest. Sometimes I get impatient because she makes such a mess, but then I remember how I just loved making *rotis*. In India, they're made twice a day, so there was always ample opportunity for me to roll them. And now, I have the reputation of being one of the best *roti* makers in my family, something my dad still proudly proclaims. I think it's just practice. You need a light hand when you roll the dough so that it will puff up into a ball when it's cooked.

I began to really cook with my mother when I was about eight or nine. She's very serious about food, so sometimes it was a little scary, because things had to be done in a certain way. I think in general, Indians are fussy about the way things get cooked. Nothing ever tastes bad there. In every house I've ever been in, the food was always delicious. So when I was allowed to help my mother, it was always on her terms because it had to be good. As I got older, she would let me have a little more leeway, like maybe let me fry the onions—there's a lot of frying of onions—and I remember sautéing them to a crisp a few times, and we had to toss them out. She was still tolerant, though. Later, when she thought I was ready to cook, she let me do a few things on my own, like okra the Indian way or the dals.

We don't have cookbooks—absolutely nothing is written down—so I learned by watching. My mother and I were close. She spent a lot of time in the kitchen, so naturally, I would spend a lot of time there, too. She was a good teacher. I still call her for certain recipes. The other night I called at midnight her time because I was cooking for friends and I was stuck. We were making this sweet called *gulab jamun,* and I just couldn't do it.

My husband started copying her recipes into this little book for us. He brings it to India every time we go. He makes her give him quantities and tells her to describe exactly what she's doing. He'll say, "No, don't just say, 'This much curry powder.' Tell me exactly what you're putting in." Sometimes the men in my family try to tell him how to make things, and it's funny because men don't cook in India. But they all think they know so much about it and will sit around and tell Dave how things are prepared. It's hilarious because they've never even stepped into a kitchen! They all think they have the last word, though.

My mother cooks with my kids, too. She's coming this summer, and when she's here, there's always a lot of activity in the kitchen. It feels really nice. There are a lot of things she'll cook that I just can't always do, like suddenly we'll be having the breads like the *roti* and *paratha* all the time when she's here. The kids love it.

When I cook now, my kids are always around. They'll come in for a taste of something, like the *paneer.* It's a cheese that we make a lot, and they love it. Before, in India, it would have been unheard of not to make *paneer* at home, but now a lot of people get it in the market. I wouldn't dream of buying it, though. I really love making it! My younger one loves it. She just wanders over for a piece, heads back to what she was doing, and then comes back for more.

They like Indian food. There are some things they absolutely love, and then, with others, I'm still working on them. Like my older one, she can't eat a lot of hot chili, whereas, in India, that's what all the kids are eating. It's just what they're used to.

When I think about keeping the culture with them, the food part of it is big, and not just in terms of what we cook, but other things, too. We're always inviting people over. In India, we use food to bring people into our homes, to be a part of our lives. So, now, we're always getting people to come over because we don't want the girls to grow up isolated. We don't have family in Boston, and growing up with aunts, cousins, and my grandparents was a big part of my life and such a very sad thing to be without, I think. Over there, everyone is in each other's lives; there's just more of a connection. I could go a couple of days here without seeing anyone but Dave and the girls, and that feels strange to me. It's not how I grew up. I was surrounded by people constantly. Actually, it can drive people crazy, but that's what I crave. Although, I can imagine if I were living there now, it would be hard, because once you live in a country that's so different—as different as the U.S. is from India—you can never belong anywhere. That's the reality of my life. I'm straddling. I used to fight it, wondering, where do I belong? But I'm a happy straddler now. I can see the ills and the good of both places. And if I can get my kids to grow up to be global creatures, I think they'll understand that there's a world beyond America, that they can be comfortable in different worlds.

In some ways, I am raising them like American kids, though. I want them to be independent, the way Americans are raised. Indian kids are just coddled too much. I didn't have many responsibilities until I was about twenty-four, and I want my kids to be different. I want them to embrace responsibility. I think it's a fabulous way to grow, something I never had. Even little things in India are different, like children being fed by their parents until they're eight or nine. It's ridiculous! Here, they can use a fork and, if not, their fingers. It doesn't mean they're neglected!

But in terms of Indian culture, I try to give them a piece of it, to teach them to be outgoing and invite people into their lives. Also, I want them to have respect for the environment, for animals, and to not take things that money can buy for granted. Like the food: in India, you just don't throw things away, not even the tiniest bit of leftovers. It's been very hard for me to see so much being thrown away here. In the U.S., there's a lot of environmental awareness and understanding about social justice amongst a small group of people, but if you think of it in terms of American society as a whole, [respect for things is] really more prevalent in India, because, in general, people don't have the kind of resources that we have here, so they are more respectful of every little thing. In India, you don't throw money away; you don't throw things away. Plastic is making an appearance there, unfortunately, but it used to be all stainless steel, and everything would be reused; like newspapers would be folded to make little bags for groceries. There's a whole recycling industry there because it's been necessary. Here, there's too much of an abundance of things, like water. I go to people's houses and they'll have the water running while they're doing something in the kitchen. It makes me cringe! We don't have a lot of water in India.

Yes, I guess the food is one of the biggest things. I want it to really be a part of my girls' lives. When we're in India, it's wonderful because there's so much for them to experience, like the markets; they're incredible! The fruit and vegetables are just beautifully arranged: they start at ground level and get stacked in tiers. It's so much fun to have that array of fresh food that's grown nearby. People still eat seasonally. In winter, there are certain vegetables you eat, and in summer there's an abundance of other things. And I miss that. I miss the seasonality. I try to do that here by going to the farmer's markets. In India, that's where we'd always shop. I love how the people at the market know you: they know my mother, and they know what vegetable she'll want. I miss the constancy of that.

And the sweet shops; Urvi just loved them when we were there! After we got back, she'd say, "Mama, let's talk about all the sweets we ate in India again!" She loved them, loved looking at all the incredible displays that are so tempting. They're all so pretty: pink and green and sprinkled with pistachios. I used to make some of them with my mother when I was little. That used to be my favorite thing to do with her, to just sit on the kitchen floor with newspaper spread everywhere and spend a half a day making sweets!

Soni's Indian Lamb *Biriyani, Tali Machhi, Matur Paneer, Bhartha, Roti,* and *Halwa*

Spiced Saffron Rice with Lamb, Fried Fish with Spices, Peas with Homemade Cheese, Spicy Eggplant, Flatbread, and Sweet Semolina

Serves 6 for dinner

Soni loves to cook and made several dishes on the day I visited her kitchen. The biriyani *is something her mother first taught her, and she prepares it now when she has guests for dinner. The* tali machhi, *Soni's aunt's recipe, could be served as an appetizer or main course to accompany the* matur paneer, bhartha, *and* roti. *It could also be served more simply with rice. Soni says most Indian cooks make their own garam masala, the spice mixture that is called for in these dishes. Although it's readily available in supermarkets, you could easily make your own using the recipe included here. Finally, be sure to try the* halwa; *it's a light, soothing dessert after this spicy Indian meal.*

LAMB *BIRIYANI*

- 1 cup plain yogurt
- Juice from 1 lemon
- 1 small red onion, finely chopped (about ½ cup)
- 3 cloves garlic, minced
- 2 tablespoons fresh ginger, peeled and finely chopped
- 1 teaspoon ground cumin
- 1 teaspoon garam masala (recipe follows)
- ¼ teaspoon cayenne pepper
- 1 teaspoon plus 1 teaspoon salt, divided
- 1 pound lamb (from leg), trimmed and cut into ½-inch pieces
- ¼ cup plus 3 cups water, divided
- 2 cups basmati or long-grain white rice, washed and drained
- 1 cup milk
- ½ teaspoon saffron threads
- 2 tablespoons plus 1 tablespoon ghee, divided (recipe follows)
- 3 or 4 bay leaves
- 8 to 10 cardamom pods
- 2 or 3 cinnamon sticks, broken into pieces
- ½ cup sliced almonds, lightly toasted

In a large bowl, combine the yogurt, lemon juice, onion, garlic, ginger, cumin, garam masala, and cayenne pepper. Add the lamb and toss so that all of the pieces are coated. Marinate for at least 1 hour. (Meat can marinate overnight.)

Add the teaspoon of salt to the lamb mixture and toss so that it's evenly distributed. In a large pot, bring the lamb and its marinade and ¼ cup of water to a boil. Reduce heat to medium and simmer, covered, until the meat is cooked through, about 20 minutes.

Meanwhile, preheat the oven to 325°F. Bring 3 cups of water and 1 teaspoon of salt to a boil in a 3- to 4-quart saucepan. Stirring constantly, pour in the rice in a slow, thin stream and cook over medium heat, uncovered, for 10 minutes. Drain any water that remains.

Heat milk (in a microwave or on the stove) until very hot but not boiling. Add the saffron threads and soak for 10 minutes.

Brush the bottom and sides of a medium (2-quart) oven-proof casserole with the 2 tablespoons of ghee. Pour in half the rice, spreading it evenly with a rubber spatula into the corners of the casserole. Sprinkle half of the saffron milk over this. Distribute half of the bay leaves, cardamom pods, pieces of cinnamon stick, and almonds over this. Spoon the lamb mixture over this, carefully spreading it evenly over the rice. Pour the remaining half of the rice over the layer of lamb. Sprinkle with the remaining saffron milk and distribute the remaining bay leaves, cardamom pods, pieces of cinnamon stick, and almonds over this. Drizzle the remaining 1 tablespoon of ghee over everything.

Cover the casserole tightly with aluminum foil. Bake in the middle of the oven until the lamb and rice are tender and most of the liquid has been absorbed, about 20 minutes.

GARAM MASALA

  2 teaspoons cardamom seed

One 2-inch stick cinnamon

  1 teaspoon whole cloves

  1 teaspoon black peppercorns

  1 teaspoon fresh grated nutmeg

  1 teaspoon cumin seed

In a heavy saucepan over medium heat, toast the spices, stirring constantly, until lightly browned, about 2 minutes. Cool.

In a spice grinder (a coffee grinder that has been thoroughly cleaned of coffee grounds will do), finely grind the toasted spices. Can be stored, tightly covered, for up to 6 months.

GHEE

Makes about ¾ cup

2 sticks (½ pound) unsalted butter, cut into pieces

In a heavy saucepan over very low heat, melt the butter. Remove from the heat and let stand for 5 minutes.

Skim the foam from the top and discard. Pour the melted butter slowly into a container, discarding the milk solids in the bottom of the pan. Ghee can be stored, tightly covered, for 1 month at room temperature and up to 6 months in the refrigerator.

2 tablespoons turmeric

2 tablespoons cumin

2 tablespoons coriander

Six 4-ounce fillets of tilapia or other firm white fish

1 teaspoon salt

4 tablespoons ghee (recipe above)

In a small bowl, combine the turmeric, cumin, and coriander. Spread onto a plate. Drag the top side of each fillet through the spice mixture to coat it generously. Sprinkle the fillets with salt.

In a heavy-bottomed skillet, heat the ghee over medium heat until shimmering. Place the fish, spiced side down, onto the skillet and cook until the fish is halfway done, about 3 to 4 minutes. Carefully turn the fillets over and cook them on the other side until just done, about 3 to 4 more minutes.

Transfer the fillets to a tray lined with paper towels to absorb any excess oil. Serve immediately.

MATUR PANEER

2 tablespoons ghee (recipe above)

⅓ cup red onion, finely chopped

2 cloves garlic, minced

2 tablespoons fresh ginger, peeled and finely chopped

½ teaspoon ground cumin

½ teaspoon garam masala (recipe above)

2 tomatoes, pureed in a blender or food processor to yield about 1 cup

4 cups shelled peas

  Paneer, cut into ½-inch cubes to yield 1 cup (recipe follows)

  Salt and freshly ground pepper

2 tablespoons fresh cilantro leaves, chopped

In a heavy-bottomed skillet, heat the ghee over medium heat until shimmering. Add the onions and cook, stirring frequently, until almost soft, about 5 minutes. Add the garlic and ginger and continue to cook, stirring, until the vegetables are translucent, about 2 minutes. Add the cumin and garam masala and continue to cook, stirring, for 1 minute. Add the pureed tomatoes and continue to cook until the juice has reduced by half, about 10 minutes. Add the peas and cook just until done, about 3 minutes. Add the *paneer* cubes, stirring gently. Season with salt and pepper.

Transfer to a serving dish and sprinkle with the chopped cilantro.

PANEER

½ gallon (8 cups) whole milk

¼ cup water

6 tablespoons fresh lemon juice

In a large, heavy-bottomed saucepan, slowly heat the milk and water nearly to a boil, stirring frequently to prevent scorching. Remove the mixture from heat and gently stir in the lemon juice. The milk should begin to separate. If not, return to heat and continue to stir gently until it separates. Remove from heat.

Drape several thicknesses of cheesecloth over a colander in the sink. Using a slotted spoon, carefully transfer the curds of cheese to the colander. Gather the ends of the cloth and twist to hold the cheese together while it drains in the colander. Place a heavy object, such as a ceramic bowl, on top of the wrapped cheese until the excess liquid has drained, about 20 minutes.

Paneer can be stored, tightly sealed, in the refrigerator for several days.

BHARTHA

- 5 to 6 small eggplants (preferably Asian), approximately 3 pounds
- 2 tablespoons ghee (recipe above)
- 1 medium red onion, minced
- 1½ teaspoons whole cumin seed
- 3 medium-sized fresh tomatoes, coarsely chopped
- 1 to 3 teaspoons finely minced Indian *jwala** peppers (more or less depending upon the heat intensity you desire)
- Salt and pepper
- 2 tablespoons fresh cilantro leaves, finely chopped

Preheat the oven to 450°F. Wash the eggplant and pat dry with paper towels. With a small, sharp knife, cut several ½-inch-deep and 1-inch-long gashes into the skin. Place the eggplant in a shallow baking dish and bake in the middle of the oven until tender and almost falling apart, about 30 minutes. (The eggplant also can be roasted over a medium flame until soft. Turn frequently so that the skins do not get overly charred.)

Transfer the eggplant to a large plate or bowl. Cut it in half lengthwise and carefully scrape the pulp away from the skin. Discard the skins. Coarsely chop the pulp.

Meanwhile, in a large heavy skillet, heat the ghee over medium heat until shimmering. Add the onion and cumin seed and cook, stirring constantly, until the onions are soft, about 5 minutes. Add the tomatoes and hot peppers and continue to cook, stirring occasionally, until the tomatoes begin to soften, about 5 minutes. Add the eggplant and continue to cook until the eggplant is very soft, about 10 minutes. If the eggplant begins to stick to the pan, a small amount of water can be added. Season with salt and pepper. Transfer to a serving dish and sprinkle with the chopped cilantro.

* Also known as Indian finger hot peppers. Found in markets specializing in Indian products. Jalapeños can be substituted.

ROTI

Makes 12 rounds

Note: You will need a gas stove with a direct flame to make this properly.

2 cups whole wheat flour

1 to 1⅓ cups lukewarm water

3 tablespoons melted ghee (recipe above)

Pour the flour into a large bowl and form a cuplike well. Add 1 cup of water and work the mixture with a fork until the dough begins to come together. (You may need to add the remaining ⅓ cup water if the dough is too crumbly and hard to work.)

Gather the dough and turn it onto a floured surface to knead. Knead the dough by folding it end to end, then pressing it down and pushing it forward several times with the heel of your hand. Repeat for 4 to 5 minutes, or until the dough becomes smooth and elastic.

Gather the dough into a ball, place it in a lightly greased bowl, cover with a cloth, and let rest for 30 minutes. Divide the dough into 12 equal pieces. Using your hands, shape each piece into a ball. On a very lightly floured surface, roll each ball into a 5-inch round with a rolling pin.

Without adding oil or ghee, heat a heavy-bottomed skillet or cast-iron pan over medium-high heat. When the pan is very hot, add one of the *roti*. Shake the pan back and forth to prevent the *roti* from sticking. Cook until bubbles begin to appear and the bread is lightly browned, about 1 minute. Using tongs, turn the *roti* over and cook for another minute. Transfer the *roti* to cook over an open flame by placing it directly on the burner of a gas stove set at medium heat. When the *roti* begins to puff up like a ball, about 15 to 30 seconds, flip it using the tongs. Cook the *roti* on the other side for another 15 to 30 seconds. Remove the *roti* from the flame and brush the top half with ghee. Stack the *roti* on a plate and serve immediately.

HALWA

4½ cups warm water

½ cup sugar

¾ cup soft wheat semolina (farina)*

2 cardamom pods

3 tablespoons ghee (recipe above)

In a bowl, mix the water and sugar. Set aside.

In a medium-sized, heavy-bottomed pot over medium-high heat, dry-roast the semolina, stirring constantly, until golden brown, about 4 to 5 minutes. Add the cardamom and continue to roast for 1 minute. Add the ghee and mix. Add the water mixture by pouring it slowly into the semolina in a thin stream while rapidly whisking. Continue to cook, whisking frequently, until the semolina has absorbed some of the water, about 5 to 6 minutes. The mixture should be the consistency of thin pea soup. Remove from heat and serve.

* Found in large supermarkets and markets specializing in ethnic products. Cream of Wheat can be substituted.

This Is America?

Genevieve Dei, thirty-five, is originally from Ghana. She came to
Boston with her husband and two young daughters in 1999. She works
as a nurse's aide and is also attending classes at Quincy College to
obtain a bachelor's degree.

GENEVIEVE WALKS TOWARD THE KITCHEN, tying an apron loosely
around her waist and reminding her girls, Abigail, eight, and Barbara, six,
to put their coats and backpacks away. Everyone, including Genevieve,
has just returned from school. She begins to pull yams, peanut butter, and
plantains down from the shelves above the stove as she chats with a friend
who has just stopped in. When the phone rings, Genevieve picks up the
receiver and hands it to her cousin, Cynthia, in the other room watching
TV with the girls, and then turns around to tell me what's on the menu
tonight. It's *nkatekwan,* a groundnut stew popular in Ghana, something
Genevieve cooks frequently. Sixty-four-year-old Margaret, Genevieve's
mother, who is staying with the family for several months, sits quietly in
the corner. She wears a traditional Ghanaian cotton dress and head scarf
in matching shades of blue and purple, the scarf similar to the orange and
red one Genevieve is wearing. She looks regal with her high cheekbones,
jet black skin, and deeply set eyes, which scan the room authoritatively.

When the cooking begins, a clear division of labor in this tiny kitchen
becomes apparent. Genevieve, Margaret, Cynthia, Abigail, and Barbara all
take turns performing particular tasks. Abigail begins by cooking the peanut

Opposite: Genevieve Dei.

butter slowly on the stove, all of her concentration focused on keeping the mixture from burning as she stirs it gently with a large wooden spoon. Genevieve stands close by, occasionally directing her daughter in their native language, Tre. "This is Abigail's responsibility," Genevieve tells me. "She needs to know how to do it right, so it won't burn."

When it's time to prepare the chicken, Margaret rises from her chair in the corner and approaches the counter with a large knife, her printed dress trailing behind her. She calls out in Tre to Abigail, who moves next to her to hold the chicken carcass steady while her grandmother cuts it into pieces. Genevieve explains that it's important for older children to work closely with an adult female in the family to learn cooking techniques so that they will be prepared to take care of their own families someday. When Margaret has cut a piece of breast from the carcass, she spreads it flat in her hand and holds it out to me ceremoniously. "Always for the husband," she instructs in a voice that is low and rhythmic. "He bought the meat for you, so you must give this part to him."

While the soup simmers, Cynthia comes into the kitchen to make the *fufu*. She stands over the stove kneading the golden dough repeatedly with a flat wooden spatula over the heat until it is a thick, malleable consistency. "Cynthia does the *fufu* best," Genevieve says. While she works the dough, Barbara and Abigail scramble about with bags of groceries their father, Daniel, has just brought in. They unload packages of chicken thighs and legs into the freezer chest in the corner and stack bags of rice and green plantains on the shelves. They set the table when Genevieve begins to serve the meal, ladling a rich, golden stew over a pale yellow mound of *fufu*, making a striking contrast of earth tones.

Following the Ghanaian tradition, we eat with our hands, dragging the *fufu* across the bowl to gather the thick soup. Barbara and Abigail do this expertly, managing to get big handfuls into their mouths and then wiping their bowls clean with the *fufu*. The soup is delicious; the subtle peanut flavor is perfectly balanced with the acidity from the tomato and the spike of ginger and hot pepper. Lifting their bowls to their faces, the girls manage to get the last precious drops, and then, without being asked, carry everything to the sink, where it's washed and returned to the cupboard.

⬗✕⬖

When we were kids and they used to tell us to come and pound the *fufu*, sometimes we'd run and hide. It's hard! Nobody likes doing it. Like if we'd come home from school and find that they had the *fufu* on the fire, we'd run back the other way. Then we'd hope that by the time we came back, one of the other kids would have already pounded it. But sometimes, when we didn't help, my mother would just give us the cooked cassava and plantain and not the *fufu*. She'd say, "If you didn't pound it, you have to eat yours like that." So you wouldn't always want to hide, because you'd really want the *fufu*.

I learned to do it when I was a kid. It's like a dumpling that you can eat with stew. I would make it with my grandmother. We all used to cook with her—both the boys and girls helped. Our job was to pound the cassava and plantain. We'd do it in a big mortar and use a pestle, which was really heavy. The bigger kids did that, and there would usually be two of them pounding because it's a lot of work. So that's one job that we didn't like.

The groundnut soup is another thing we'd do. We would go to the mill to grind the nuts to make a paste. It's a fresh, local peanut butter that's so, so good, not like the peanut butter here. We'd also go to the market to get tomatoes, hot peppers, cassava, even snails. Whatever we needed for that day we could get at the market. We would never do a weekly grocery shopping like you do here, because everything has to be fresh. My grandmother used to go to the market with us, but there came a time when she couldn't walk very well, so she would tell us exactly what to buy. I started going with my mother when I was a little girl. I'd look at what she was doing so I could do it myself one day.

I was surprised when I came to America. I thought it would be perfect, like a new heaven. I imagined it would be so different from Africa, and I wouldn't see anything bad, like people sleeping in the street. You hear the things at home about America: people who have been here say it's such an incredible place, and you can tell by the way they look, with all their jewelry and new clothes, that it must be perfect. I saw American movies when I was there, and everything on the TV looked so beautiful. So when I came here, I was surprised and thought, oh, so this is America? I was shocked! Everything wasn't perfect. I even saw rats here. Just like we have rats back home, you have them here, too. Now I'm starting to think, whatever happens here, happens there.

Some things are different. Here, you walk around and you don't know [anyone]. In Africa, you talk to everybody, even if you don't know them.

Genevieve (center) prepares a Ghanaian meal with (from left) her daughter Abigail, cousin Cynthia, and mother, Margaret.

And what I really love is that everybody watches out for everyone else, especially for the children. Here, it's totally different. None of my neighbors are around. We might say hello, but we don't know each other very well, and we don't look after one another. It's like everybody's busy. I have a couple of people in the neighborhood that my girls used to play with, but I still need to keep an eye on them to make sure they're okay. In Ghana, the kids can go off by themselves. When I was little, I used to go to the market or wherever I wanted. You didn't need to worry about things like shootings or somebody beating you up or kidnapping your kids. There are none of those problems in Ghana. I'm more worried here.

My kids were so happy when we went home last summer. They didn't want to come back, because they had such a good time playing around and going off by themselves. I remember when Abigail was a year and a half and she could just walk, she would go to the neighbor's. I wouldn't have to worry because I knew she'd be fine and that they'd come get me if I needed to pick her up. Here, everybody has to call before they go anywhere. When I first came, I thought, wow! But, hey, you're in America, so you have to do what Americans do. We just have to adapt. It's harder for the kids, though; they don't understand. They say, "Why can't we go there? Can't we go to this person's house?" And I tell them, "No, we have to call and find out when it is a good time."

I try to keep our culture with the girls. I speak our language, Tre, with them. I teach them respect. They know if I have a visitor, they cannot sit with us and just jump in and say something. We really respect our elders in Ghana. I work in a nursing home now, and I would never put my mother in one of those places. In Ghana, we take care of our family. If an elderly person needed to cross the road, someone would stop the cars and walk that person across the road. We respect them.

I teach the girls to help, too. They know the routine, and they help a lot. They clean the bathroom, wash the dishes, and fold their own laundry. They really like to cook, too! We make a lot of the things from home. Barbara likes to make the *fufu,* so we show her how to mash it up. Abigail is the one that really likes to cook, and I let her. But sometimes she takes forever, like peeling the plantains or cutting up the tomatoes. They both are a big help, though.

I want them to understand our traditions, to always remember that they are from Ghana. Abigail is becoming more Americanized, but Barbara is like a local, typical Ghanaian girl. She loves to eat the soups, the hot peppers, and the *fufu.* They both love to cook our foods, but sometimes Abigail prefers to drink Coca-Cola and eat McDonald's. Sometimes, if I have *kenke*—it's like a cornmeal cake—and I have McDonald's, Abigail will go for McDonald's. But Barbara will always ask for the *kenke.*

I plan to go back someday. I'll go after the girls finish high school here. Right now, they're little, so I think they don't really understand everything. All they want to do now is have fun and play. So right now, if I tell them I'm taking them back to Ghana, they'll say, "Yeah, we'll go." Once they grow up though, it will be different. They may want to stay here. So maybe I'll have to come visit them. It will be difficult to be separate, but maybe I'll visit every summer. I'll cook all the foods for them, just like my mother does when she visits me now.

Genevieve's Ghanaian *Nkatekwan* and *Fufu*

Groundnut Soup and Plantain Flour Dumplings

Serves 6

In West Africa, fufu *was traditionally made by boiling, peeling, and pounding tubers such as yam and cassava or sometimes plantain into a smooth paste with a pestle and a large wooden mortar. The dough was formed into balls and served with stews such as* nkatekwan. Fufu *can also be prepared more easily using flours derived from yam, cassava, or plantain, which is the way Genevieve prepares* fufu *in her Boston apartment today. The* fufu *is used to scoop the pieces of chicken and peanut sauce, making utensils unnecessary.*

       1 onion, chopped

   One 3-inch piece fresh ginger, peeled and chopped

       2 jalapeño peppers, cored, seeded, and chopped

       2 cubes adobo seasoning*

     ¼ cup plus 2 cups plus 2 cups water, divided

       1 whole chicken (about 2½ pounds), skin removed, and cut into 8 serving pieces

    1½ cups (12 ounces) unsalted, all-natural peanut butter

        Salt and freshly ground pepper

       2 tablespoons vegetable oil

 5 or 6 plum tomatoes, chopped

 1 to 2 tablespoons lemon juice

In a blender or food processor, puree the onion, ginger, jalapeño, adobo seasoning, and ¼ cup water. In a large bowl, combine the chicken and onion mixture and marinate overnight.

In a small saucepan, mix the peanut butter and 2 cups of water. Cook over low heat, stirring frequently, until the peanut butter is caramel in color, about 15 minutes. Cool.

In a blender, puree the peanut mixture with the remaining 2 cups of water until smooth. Set aside.

Remove the chicken from the marinade (reserving the liquid). Season the chicken with salt and pepper. Heat the oil in a large pot until shimmering. Working in batches, add a few pieces of the chicken at a time to the pot and cook them until lightly browned on all sides, about 5 minutes. Add more oil between batches if necessary.

Transfer the cooked chicken to a platter and set aside. Add the tomatoes to the empty pot and cook, stirring occasionally, until soft, about 5 minutes. Add the pureed peanut mixture, the reserved liquid from the marinade, the chicken, and the remaining 2 cups of water. Simmer, uncovered, until the oil begins to separate from the peanut mixture along the edges of the pot, about 1 hour. Skim the oil and season the mixture with salt, pepper, and the lemon juice. Serve with *fufu* (recipe follows) or rice.

---

* Found in most markets specializing in Latino and Afro-Caribbean products. For the adobo seasoning, 2 teaspoons of ground cumin, ½ teaspoon of black pepper, and ¼ teaspoon of cayenne can be substituted.

FUFU

1½ cups plantain, cassava, or yam flour*

1 teaspoon salt

3 cups water

In a medium saucepan, combine the flour, salt, and water. (The mixture should be the consistency of thick pea soup.) Over medium-low heat, cook the *fufu* dough slowly, working it constantly with a wooden spoon by pulling it away from the edges of the pan. Continue until the dough is thick enough to be rolled into balls that hold their shape, about 5 minutes.

Cooling the *fufu* enough to work it with your hands, shape it into 12 balls by rolling a small handful around on a flat surface that has been moistened to prevent sticking. Serve with the *nkatekwan*. This can also be served with Lili's *kedjenou* (page 203).

---

* Found in markets specializing in Afro-Caribbean products. Genevieve used Tropiway Plantain Fufu Flour.

More Relaxed but a Little Tired

José Carlos Ramírez, twenty-eight, left El Salvador in 2002 and lives
in East Boston with his family, which includes his wife, daughter,
mother, sister, and several nephews. A lawyer in his country, José
currently has two jobs cleaning and working maintenance. He attends
Bunker Hill Community College and hopes to obtain a law degree
in this country.

THE EAST BOSTON NEIGHBORHOOD WHERE the Ramírez family lives is
vibrant on this beautiful Saturday morning in May. The sounds of *cumbia,*
salsa, and merengue float through the windows of cars passing though this
busy intersection. We walk by a small market selling Latino products;
the doorway is bathed in sunlight and frames two teenage boys wearing
T-shirts and jeans, who watch the action on the street with feigned disin-
terest. As we make our way to the row of three family buildings where José
lives, a sleek jet glides surprisingly low, just skimming the rooftops. The
startling roar of the engine comes next, slicing through the sounds of the
neighborhood, a reminder that Logan Airport is nearby.

José, his wife, Ana, and their little girl, Gabriela, three years old, show us
into their third-floor apartment. Aminta, José's mother, wipes her hands
on a dish towel and smiles when José introduces us. Saturdays are Aminta's big cooking day; she makes quesadilla, a sweet cake in the Salvadoran case, for the Central American market around the corner, as well as

Opposite: José pours ingredients for quesadilla batter with his mother and daughter
while his sister and nephew make *pupusas.*

pupusas, a Salvadoran specialty made with corn flour and filled with beans, cheese, or shredded pork, which she cooks for her large family almost daily. I struggle in Spanish to ask about the food she'll be cooking today, when José's sister, Evelyn, comes into the room. "Another excellent cook," José says, introducing her to us.

In the kitchen, Aminta shows me the ingredients she's set out for the quesadilla and *pupusas.* Miguel, four, and Ángel, two, friends from the apartment downstairs, are playing on chairs in the corner and look up eagerly, as if they've been anticipating our arrival. Ángel runs over to Aminta, who scoops him into her arms for a quick kiss before turning toward the stove to check on a large pot simmering with beans.

Aminta pulls a chair over to the table for her granddaughter, and together they pour the rice flour and sugar into a mixing bowl she's set out to make the quesadilla. Ana, who speaks in a thick Central American accent and has a good command of English, talks about her mother-in-law's cooking, her husband's heavy work schedule, the challenges of raising Gabriela in a place far from home, and the English classes she takes at the same community college José attends. "It's another life for me here. In my country, I was somebody. I was a lawyer, like my husband. So, I'm starting again now," she says.

Ana talks freely, jumping from one subject to the next in sharing her experiences with me. She is not at all deterred by the cooking that is going on around her—Aminta and Evelyn reaching around for bags of rice flour and shredded pork—or by little Ángel, who runs through her legs to chase his brother about the kitchen. Soon, a teenage girl appears at the table, stepping in front of Ana for the bowl of corn dough and shredded pork. She quickly shapes a *pupusa,* clapping the dough between her hands, and then places it onto the hot griddle in the middle of the table. Before I am able to find out who she is, she disappears down the hallway.

While I'm listening to Ana, I realize that Aminta has already begun to pour ingredients into the bowl for the quesadilla. *"¿Cuánto?"* (How much?) I ask, pointing to the bag of rice flour Aminta has in her hand. She shrugs and indicates with a finger approximately how full it had been before she started cooking. I copy the ingredients into my notebook as Aminta tosses pinches of salt, baking powder, and small handfuls of grated parmesan into the bowl faster than I can write, and all the while Ana is still talking to me. Meanwhile, little Gabriela works the batter, using her tiny fingers to break up the clumps of sour cream her grandmother has just added. When Aminta tells her she's finished, she smiles and puts them to her lips.

José, who stands next to his daughter, occasionally hands ingredients to his mother as he listens to his wife talk, nodding about something she has just said. When Aminta passes a spoon to José, he explains, "My mother always asks me if it should be more sweet." After trying a generous scoop he tells her, *"Un poco más"* (a little more), and passes the bag of sugar across the table.

As Aminta makes room to pour the batter into pans, Ana describes the differences she finds between Salvadoran and American culture: "In my country, mothers are home with the kids. Mothers are like your best friend, because you're always together. I want Gabriela to know our culture. I think one of the best places to be with your family is when you're eating. For me, the kitchen is special. It's three times each day to be with your family."

José waits for his wife to finish. His eyes look tired behind the wire-rimmed glasses he wears, and he gestures toward several chairs in the corner of the kitchen. "In this country, it seems like parents don't have enough time for the kids, because they need to work a lot. This is our situation right now," he tells me. "My mother came here so I could become a lawyer in our country. Now I am here because I had to leave my country. I just want Gabriela to have a good life. I want her to be happy." A concerned look remains on his face when he watches his little girl run through the apartment with Miguel and Ángel, and he reaches out to pat the top of her head when she passes.

I look around the kitchen, soaking up its warmth and the earthy smells of rice flour and sesame seeds coming from the oven, where the remaining pans of Aminta's quesadilla bake, and I can hear the playful shrieks of Gabriela, Miguel, and Ángel in the next room. I consider the many family members who have come through here today to make a *pupusa,* laugh over a hot chocolate, or sit with a warm piece of quesadilla, and I can't help but think that José needn't be worried.

<hr/>

We eat here like we would at home. We have lots of beans and soups. My daughter, Gabriela, loves *sopa de frijoles,* bean soup. Sometimes we put an egg in it for her, or *queso seco,* the cheese, or you can add *chicharrón,* the pork. I want her to learn our customs, and for me, the food is really important. Oh, sometimes she eats hamburgers, like at Burger King, and she loves the french fries they have, and that's okay, but I want her to know things about my country, too. Like when I take her to

El Salvador, I want her to try our specialties, like *ticucus.* I don't think she's ever had that. It's made with corn and has beans inside, and we usually eat it for Semana Santa, holy week.

When I was young, maybe ten years old, I'd cook with my mother, like Gabriela does now. All of my sisters and brothers would help. We'd make the tamales with her every weekend, maybe seventy or eighty of them. It was a lot! I would get up early and go to the place where you grind the corn. I'd bring the *masa,* the ground corn, back home, and she'd have all the other ingredients ready—the chicken, potatoes, the salsa, and sometimes the *loroco* [a flower that's added to some dishes, sometimes in its bud form]—and she'd fold everything into a banana leaf. My job was to tie them. We'd put them in a big pot to cook, and when they were done people would come to our home to buy them. We sold *pupusas,* too. They're like tortillas filled with pork or beans and cheese. Only my mother and my sister, Evelyn, made the *pupusas.* So, I'd help with the salsa and the *cortido;* that's the cabbage salad that you eat with them.

We lived humbly, and my parents worked hard. My brother and sisters and I helped when we weren't in school. It was fun, because we told jokes and funny stories. Sometimes, though, we were angry, because we didn't want to always cook. Sometimes my brother and I wanted to go play soccer. But my mother was working, so we all helped.

I miss those times with all of the family around, especially the holidays. We lived in the city, and during the holidays people who live in the country come into the city. Everyone would be together. We'd roast a turkey, and my mother would make a salsa with tomatoes, peppers, onions, and garlic. Delicious! Things are different here. For the last two Christmases I was working, and I wasn't able to be with the family. In El Salvador everyone has a day off at Christmas. I miss that.

I had to come here. I was working as a criminal prosecuting attorney in Metapán, the city where we lived. I loved this job, but it was very dangerous: I was shot at twice. The scariest time, though, was the day they followed my family. I knew I had to leave. When I talk to my friends back home, they tell me I made the right decision, because things are really bad right now. So here I am in the U.S., more relaxed, but a little bit tired.

I'm working two jobs as a cleaner. It's not cleaning like taking the trash out; I think it's more like maintenance work. I work in a condominium building. When someone needs to change a lightbulb, they call me and I go to change the lightbulb. If the carpet is dirty, I shampoo it. This is in the day. At night, it's cleaning in a gym in Quincy. I like it there, because I'm alone and nobody bothers me. I'm also going to school. I want to study law and to become a lawyer in this country someday.

Things are better here for us. We have a better life. You have to work really hard, but if you want to buy a pair of shoes, you can. In my country, if you want shoes, maybe you have some money to buy them, but you won't be able to go out to eat with your family for two weeks. So we have more opportunities here, but we've lost something, too. For Gabriela, I think she's lost some of the freedom she had in El Salvador. There, she could go anywhere. We knew everyone, and we had lots of family around to watch her. Since she has come here, she has to stay in the apartment all the time. She wants to go out on her own, but she can't. I think she is really frustrated.

In East Boston, we don't have many friends. It's hard to become friendly with people here. We haven't even met many Hispanic families. Sometimes I think Americans are right when they think something is wrong with Hispanics. Some of them seem so angry to me. I don't know why, but sometimes when one Hispanic person sees another, he's not friendly, and it's like they don't trust each other. I don't know what happens to people. Maybe they've forgotten their origins.

I want Gabriela to know the good things about our culture and to be proud of it. I'm going to try to bring her back home next September. Here, she spends a lot of time with my mother, especially when I'm working, and that is good. My mother likes to cook with her, and when they do that, I think she learns about Salvador. My mother will tell her about different ways to prepare things, like the quesadilla, the way she sometimes did in Salvador when she would make the cheese herself with the *requesón,* the curd. I think it's important that they spend this time together.

I really want Gabriela to understand that the family is the most important of all things. Even if I can't spend a lot of time with her now, I want to be a good example for her. I am a professional in my country. I want to become a professional in this country, too. I want her to look at her parents and think, oh, they are studying and they work hard. I need to do that, too. Now I don't have the time to be with her a lot, so I'm glad she has my mother and my wife. Some things are hard, like mealtime. Now I don't eat meals with my family, not breakfast, lunch, not dinner. I never have a day off, because I'm going to school and then I have to work. Someday, though, my dream is to have only one job, not two or three. What I really want is to have one job where I only work forty hours a week, not eighty. And someday, I'd really like to be able to leave Gabriela at her school in the morning and pick her up when she finishes in the afternoon. That would be nice.

JOSÉ'S MOTHER'S SALVADORAN QUESADILLA

Sweet Cake

Serves 8

Not to be confused with the Mexican dish of the same name, Salvadoran quesadilla is a sweet, rich cake made with cheese. It's easy to prepare and is a great dessert to make with children. José's family serves this with hot cocoa for breakfast or sometimes as an afternoon snack. It's also delicious with coffee or tea.

 1 cup heavy cream

 ½ cup ricotta cheese

 1 large egg

 ¼ cup cream cheese, softened

 1 tablespoon freshly grated parmesan cheese

 ¾ cup sugar

 1½ cups *harina de arroz* (rice flour)*

 ¼ teaspoon salt

 ½ teaspoon baking soda

 1 tablespoon sesame seeds

Adjust the oven rack to center and preheat the oven to 350°F.

Mix the heavy cream, ricotta, egg, cream cheese, and parmesan in a large bowl until smooth. Add the sugar and mix well. In a separate bowl, mix the rice flour, salt, and baking soda. Add this to the cream mixture and mix just until the ingredients are incorporated. Spread it into a lightly greased 9-inch cake pan and sprinkle with the sesame seeds. Bake until the cake springs back when touched in the center, about 30 minutes. Let stand for 10 minutes.

Can be served slightly warm or at room temperature.

* Found in the ethnic cooking sections of large supermarkets and in markets specializing in Caribbean and Latino products.

Bringing Good Things with Food

Liz Kugell, fifty, moved to the United States from Brazil in the
mid-1980s. She lives in Brookline, Massachusetts, with her fifteen-
year-old son, Alex, who was born here. Liz works as the director
of activities at the Coolidge House, a home for the elderly
in Brookline.

LIZ IS PREPARING SUNDAY LUNCH in her boyfriend's apartment today,
located on a quiet street behind Boston College, on the outskirts of the
city. Her son, Alex, fifteen, and nephew, Guilherme, in his twenties, come
in and out of the kitchen, checking on the status of the *peixada,* a traditional Brazilian fish dish that Liz learned to make from her grandmother.
The boys laugh about Liz's sometimes unconventional cooking pursuits,
explaining how they'll hear her moving around the kitchen at odd hours.
Liz cuts them off: "It's true! I cook all the time, any time! Like the other
night, I had blueberry cake ready by midnight. It was fresh for breakfast!"
Alex looks over at his cousin with a knowing smile, and they both nod. He
opens the cupboard and rummages around until he finds a container of
cereal, which he pours into a bowl, and follows Guilherme out into the living room. "Alex, what about your test on World War II tomorrow? Did
you study everything?" Liz calls after him.

"Don't worry," he says.

Liz watches the receding back of her son and looks as though she might
say something, but turns and walks over to the refrigerator instead. The

Opposite: Liz gets ready for Sunday dinner.

heels of her boots click across the linoleum floor as she moves from fridge to sink to oven, unloading fresh cilantro, tomatoes, and onions onto the counter, bending down to pull several pans and covers from a low cabinet, and reaching for a large knife on the kitchen table. Having just returned from work, she's dressed in a long wool skirt and coffee-colored knit top, which accentuates the beige tones of her hair, skin, and eyes. Liz has an expressive face: one moment her brow furrows and her lips are pursed as she looks around for a sharpening steel for her knife, and the next, her dark eyes sparkle with mischief as she moves the knife quickly against the steel, its blade flying through the air. "You want to frighten men? Sharpen knives in front of them!" she laughs. When Liz speaks, she stretches her vowels in the Portuguese' manner, and her stories about a childhood in which the kitchen was one of her favorite places take on a rhythmic quality.

A large Himalayan cat with luscious white fur sits regally atop one of the cushioned stools in the middle of the kitchen, following Liz's every movement with her pale blue eyes. When Liz slams the side of her knife against a garlic clove to peel it, the cat jumps at the sound, tail twitching and clearly annoyed as it walks out of the room. Liz says the cat and Alex come with her when she moves between this apartment and her own, where they all split their time during the week. With plastic dish gloves— vegetable juice bothers her skin—Liz chops some red onion, tomato, scallion, and cilantro and begins to layer these in the large pot on the stove, where she'll cook the fish.

"I'm a fast cooker," she tells us, slipping her gloves off and reaching for the sugar and eggs she'll need for the crème caramel she's making for dessert. "Cooking is one of the few times when my mind is totally connected," she adds, motioning to Alex that she needs his help. He walks back into the kitchen and stands awkwardly next to her by the stove, his hands fidgeting with the seams of his jeans. She passes a container of sugar to him and says he should pour it slowly into the pan while she whisks. Alex is several inches taller than his mother, and Liz has to look up at him when she warns, "Be careful, Alex, it's crumpy!"

"You're not speaking English," he jokes, laughing. "It's *clumpy,* not *crumpy!*" Liz laughs, too, and then tells him he can go away after he's added the sugar. Although Liz learned most of her Brazilian recipes, like this dessert, from her grandmother, the family's maid was the first to introduce her to the stove. When Liz was eight or nine, the maid couldn't come to cook for the family one day, and Liz remembers running several neighborhoods away to ask her how to prepare rice for the midday meal. She stops halfway through the story and looks around the kitchen. "Oh, I guess I should make rice," she says to herself, moving toward the cupboard to grab another pan.

When the smells of cilantro, tomatoes, and fish fill the kitchen, Liz calls for Alex to set the table. He begins to complain from the other room, asking why it needs to be set. Liz puts the large wooden spoon she's holding onto the table and sighs. "Alex, it's Sunday. Remember? We're having lunch."

⚯

Cooking is like therapy for me. When I'm cooking, I'm quiet, and that's when I think. If I see myself getting upset or angry, I go cook. You can bring good things to people with your food. You can make them smile, and when they pass that smile to you, you have the world back in your hands. It takes one smile for everything to get fixed. I try to explain that to my friends and to my son. I tell Alex that it doesn't take too much, that if you are angry and the person apologizes, you give your smile back and accept their apology. I tell him if he cannot accept that apology right away, that he needs to go play some music for a while, because he's got to find something that [distracts] him from any disconnection and resentment. It doesn't have to be cooking, but you have to find something. So I'll tell him, "Mama cooks. You go play the piano."

I learned the tricks of Brazilian cooking from my father and grandmother. My father taught me to marinate the meat. He used lime to give it that zesty taste. He would go to the central market, get the meat, and then take it home and prepare it. You could get anything there, and all the food came fresh every day! It was a huge market; you could even get a kitten there if that's what you wanted. My godfather had a spice store, and they'd bring me there in the morning, and he'd give me a cinnamon stick. I would chew that thing all day; it was better than a lollipop!

The market was fun. We had family who owned several stores, selling vegetables and things. And then my uncle had a farm, and we could go and eat everything fresh there, too. Like fruit, we would have fruit only when it was in season. The papayas, wow! You should see the papayas over there! I remember watching them ripen up in the tree. You'd see the little fruits—because everybody has a papaya tree in the back yard— and you'd be watching those papayas, waiting until you could eat them, salivating because they were almost ready. And the mangoes, it was the same thing. We only ate them at a certain time, never in the summer.

Liz and her son, Alex, add yucca flour to the *peixada*.

With the guavas, it was the end of the year only, and apples, only at Christmas, because they came from Argentina. So I'd have to wait until December to have an apple! But Brazil is different now; you can eat anything whenever you want it, like here. In my time, it wasn't like that, and I think you appreciate it more when you have to wait. I used to love apples, and because I'd have to wait for them to come from Argentina at Christmas, when I would eat that apple, it would be in my heart for the rest of the year. Over here, I go to the market and get whatever I want. Do you think I buy apples now? No.

I first started cooking with my father when I was nine. My mother worked a lot, so my father was home more, and he did the cooking. I was really close to him. He was behind me for many things. He taught me how to read, how to write, how to appreciate history and life. So I learned a lot from him, but also from my grandmother, too. She cooked Brazilian, and I loved to eat her food. She made the *tutu,* that's our traditional bean dish, and before she died, she taught me the right way to prepare it. She said the trick was that when you cooked the garlic, it had to be golden, not burned. Because she was from the north of Brazil, she cooked with lots of spice, like cilantro seed, the coriander. She'd make this fish, *peixada.* She'd put it in a stone pot with tomatoes and onions and oil and cover it with cilantro. I like to do that now.

The food was the nicest part of my life when I was a child. And I appreciate that I can give that to my son. I don't really miss anything about Brazil, just my father. Sometimes I think he was a dream in my life. I have pictures of him all over the house, and I tell Alex about him. I think about him when I cook his food. The thing I loved was his smile—a big, happy smile. I remember him laughing in the market. He had a loud, joyful sound, such happiness inside him. But then he became sick, and I saw him suffering a lot. But before that, he was hilarious. I always tried to please him. The only time we fought was when I wanted to go out and he wouldn't let me. I would tell him I was responsible, that I wouldn't smoke and drink, that I wanted to go dancing. I loved dancing! He was the one that taught me how to dance. He danced so well! I have a hard time dancing with other men now, because he was so good. We used to dance around the house. And now, I do that with my son sometimes. He's a very nice dancer, too.

But when my father and I would fight, the way we'd handle communication between those fights was with music. He'd be shaving in the bathroom and behind the door he'd sing a love song, something about how he knew he would love me for all his life, that every time I left him, he would love me, and when I came back he would still love me. He'd be singing this song, and I would be screaming at him! Oh, I miss him, but he's in my heart. I tell Alex that there's no such thing as death as long as you keep someone in your heart, that I'll never leave him as long as he always remembers me. My father taught me that.

I'm both Brazilian and American now. I didn't need to forget my Brazilian side when I came here—that's the charming side, the side I get from my father. My dad would walk into places, and he would flirt with everyone. My friends tell me I'm the same. People may think I'm flirting, but really, I'm just friendly. We express more in Brazil. From my father, I got the charm and the need to be friendly with people. And then the American side is the need to obey regulations, because I try to follow the rules, to obey the system here. And the freedom—you begin to understand that the legacy here is the freedom. I enjoy the freedom, and it's become a part of my life now. But I never felt like I needed to lose my identity to become part of this culture. I kept it. I use it when it's needed. I'm still partly Brazilian.

There are things about my culture I try to teach Alex, like the way generations interact. The teenagers here, they don't know how to talk to adults. They don't know what to say to you. In my country, they do. Like my cousin's kids—they kiss me, they hug me, they talk to me about everything. They tell me about their girlfriends, they ask me if I have a boyfriend. You see this in our culture, in European culture, too. You will see a ten-year-old child guiding his grandmother or grandfather. They take care of them. You do not see that here. I tell Alex, "Call your grandmother. Check your grandfather. Let's go visit them now." This is my culture, my values.

There are some days I feel like I'm my father, oh, my God! Maybe because I'm raising Alex like a Brazilian, the way I was raised. Although, one thing that's different is I do teach him how to treat women, because I was not raised in a society that does that well. You see, I really didn't belong there. I hated it! Women are second-class citizens in Brazil; we're raised to serve. Men think it's okay to go out and do anything they want, like betray us, and then come back and everything will be fine. So when I first came to the U.S., this was normal to me. If a guy cheated on a woman, I thought this was acceptable. It was like I was brainwashed! And when you live like that, you don't have control of your life.

When I go back, I still see those things. Women have some power now, but not like here. In America, we have power in one way, but really, I think society is run by men. There's still a double standard, but it's much worse there. For example, there, if I open my mouth, someone might say, "I don't think this is for you to discuss, because you're a woman." But a man could say anything, and no one would care. You know, I'm the first woman in my family to get a university degree, but some people don't look at that in such a positive way. And for some women, I'm like a threat: I don't belong. They accept things that I don't, that I never did.

When I go back now, I have fun, but then I always want to come back here. I find Brazilians are behind thirty years. I always wanted to leave, maybe since I was young, eight or nine years old. I always knew I wanted to go somewhere else, like France or England, to study. I came when I was twenty-seven. I didn't have problems assimilating. I knew English. I wasn't fluent, but I could speak, and I made friends. I had my mother-in-law. And I learned so much about food! After I got married, my husband would take me to all kinds of restaurants, and I'd have things I never had before. That's when I started to do everything: Japanese, Chinese, Indian. For him, I'd try to do the best. He'd come home, and there would always be something different. So I got to learn more about food from all over the world. But now, it's really the Brazilian dishes I like to cook.

LIZ'S BRAZILIAN *PEIXADA*

Fish Cooked with Tomatoes, Onions, and Cilantro

Serves 4

In Brazil, Liz and her grandmother always prepared this dish with suru-
bin, *a firm white fish popular in that country. When she makes* peixada
*now, she uses swordfish and serves it with white rice seasoned with several
pinches of anise seed, which she adds to the water before cooking.*

1½ pounds swordfish or other firm white fish, such as
    halibut or monkfish, cut into 1-inch-thick steaks or
    fillets

¼ cup fresh lemon juice

¼ cup plus 2 tablespoons extra virgin olive oil, divided

1 small red onion, cut into very thin rings

4 plum tomatoes, cut into thin wedges

½ bunch cilantro, leaves chopped (about ½ cup)

3 whole scallions, finely chopped

1 clove garlic, minced

   Salt and freshly ground black pepper

   Optional: ¼ cup *farina de mandioca torrada*
   (toasted yucca flour)*

Place the fish in a bowl and sprinkle with the lemon juice. Let it sit for
20 minutes.

In a medium-sized Dutch oven or heavy-bottomed pot fitted with a cover,
add the ¼ cup of olive oil. Arrange the vegetables in layers by first placing
half of the sliced onions in the bottom of the pot, followed by half of the
tomatoes and finally half of the chopped cilantro. Spread the fish and the
lemon juice over this. Sprinkle with salt and freshly ground pepper.

Cover the fish with layers of the remaining onions, tomatoes, and cilantro.
Sprinkle the scallions and garlic over the vegetables and drizzle with the
remaining 2 tablespoons of olive oil. Sprinkle with salt and freshly ground
pepper.

Cook, covered, on medium-high heat until the liquid from the fish and
vegetables begins to boil. Reduce the heat to medium and cook until the fish

---

*Found in markets specializing in Brazilian and Afro-Caribbean products.

is done, about 10 minutes. (The cooking time will depend on the thickness of the fish. Allow for approximately 10 minutes per 1-inch thickness of fish.)

Optional: Liz thickens the juices from the fish and vegetables with toasted yucca flour to make a gravy. To do this, carefully remove the fish and vegetables from the pot and place them on a serving platter. Pour the remaining liquid from the pan into a small saucepan. Season with salt and pepper. Bring this to a boil and whisk the toasted yucca flour into this, stirring for 30 to 45 seconds, or until the mixture becomes thickened, similar to the consistency of Cream of Wheat. More yucca powder can be added if necessary. To serve, place a large dollop of the mixture on each plate. Serve the fish and vegetables on top of this.

Keeping the Connection Flowing

Aurora Bautista, forty-three, moved to the United States from the Philippines in 2003. She lives in Jamaica Plain with her American husband and two teenage children, who are from a previous marriage and were born in the Philippines. Aurora is a professor of behavioral sciences at Bunker Hill Community College in Charlestown, Massachusetts.

⤙⤚

HI LO, THE LARGE LATINO supermarket in the Hyde Square section of Boston, is uncharacteristically quiet on this weekday afternoon. On Saturdays, when I sometimes come here, I've had to work my way past groups of shoppers—usually women—chatting in Spanish as they pick through piles of limes that sell ten for a dollar or running after children who have disappeared down the soda and juice aisle. Today, however, the store seems like a different place: no half-unloaded crates of corn flour or fifty-pound bags of rice make passage difficult through the narrow aisles; no salsa music streams through the loudspeakers, and only two cashiers work the registers that line the front of the store. Later in the day, when the subway station down the street lets out the commuters heading home for dinner, business most certainly will pick up.

Aurora practically has the place to herself while she peruses the aisles for the ingredients she uses in her Filipino foods, some of the same products that cooks from other former Spanish colonies, like the Dominican Republic, Puerto Rico, Venezuela, and Colombia, use in their traditional dishes. As

Opposite: Supermercado in Hyde Square, Boston.

we step into the produce section amid piles of green and yellow plantains, yucca, calabaza squash, jalapeño peppers, and yams, Aurora stops to inspect some avocados. They are stored in boxes on the floor, and she bends down to sort through them, choosing two that are large and unblemished. "I make a dessert with these," she says, explaining that she'll serve them the way her mother always did, mashed with milk and sugar. "I love it for dessert, but my kids, they don't really like this one," she smiles.

The scent of cilantro and *recao* is pungent in this part of the store; piles of the deep green herbs are heaped on tables next to packages of peeled garlic and assorted peppers. Aurora scans the area and then shrugs, telling us she was hoping to find some fresh tamarind today. "Maybe in Chinatown," she says, picking up her basket.

Aurora makes a trip here every few months to get ingredients for dishes like *arroz a la cubana,* a Filipino rice dish made with beef, tomatoes, and raisins, or the chorizo and mild cheese, *queso de bola,* she likes to keep on hand to make the Spanish-influenced Filipino dishes her kids love. We move toward the rear of the store, where the concrete wall behind the cooler is painted a cheerful pink with the large letters "MEATS" in red, giving the place a festive, warm Caribbean feel. We walk past portions of pork shoulder, loin, and pig's feet, next through the chicken section— wings, thighs, legs, and feet—until we get to the beef. Aurora looks through plastic-wrapped packages of bones until she finds one that has generous portions of meat still attached. "My son will say, 'Where's the meat, Mom?'" she tells us while she checks again to make sure there isn't another package with even more beef. She'll use this to make the sauce for the *arroz a la cubana;* the beef will be stewed with tomatoes, onions, and raisins and poured over rice. In the Philippines, it's traditional to serve this with a fried quail egg placed on top, something she forgoes here, because quail eggs aren't easy to find.

As we meander through the aisles, Aurora points to the ingredients she sometimes buys, explaining it's not every day that she can cook the dishes she learned to make from her mother and grandmother. When she stops in front of the freezer section and grabs a box of *plátanos maduros,* prefried frozen plantains, she laughs: "This is my short-cut version. Anything short-cut I like to do. Besides, it's midterms now." She says she doesn't feel guilty about not making everything from scratch, that her mother often did the same thing, because she, too, worked full-time. "Here's another lazy thing," she says, tossing a box of prepared empanadas from the freezer into her basket.

In a few weeks, she explains, she might have to go to Chinatown to get the ingredients she can find only there: the special soy sauce and cane vinegar made in the Philippines, which she needs for her adobo, a stewed meat dish served with rice, which she makes several times a month, or the shrimp and wrappers she uses for *lumpia,* the Filipino spring rolls.

Today, though, with several shopping bags full of Spanish cheese, chorizo, beef bones, and the two boxes of ready-made, frozen empanadas and fried plantains, her "lazy" staples, Aurora will be set for a month or so.

✄

I end up cooking the Filipino food, like really trying to make a traditional recipe, maybe once a week now. That's something everyone looks forward to, even my husband, who's American.

Food and family are the things we try to hold on to. We celebrate Easter with my cousin, and we go to my aunt's maybe once or twice a year. Then it's all about food. At my cousin's house, we'll plan for a celebration and say, "Okay, let's do some cooking!" and we'll start talking about our favorite Filipino foods, and everyone will get assigned a particular dish. What's interesting is the food is mixed, because some of us are married to non-Filipinos, so it's never all Filipino food. Like my husband, he doesn't eat pork, so I have to substitute for some of the dishes.

The thing my kids really talk about is *lechón.* You cook a whole pig outside in a pit. They haven't had it in five years. If we lived in New York or California, we could get it, because they have the Filipino festivals there. I remember when I was in California and I first saw it. I thought, oh, my God, it's here! This is my chance! I don't know anyone who's actually done it here, because you need a big yard to cook it. The closest thing we have is the *chicharrón,* the fried pork, which I can get in the Spanish places down the street. It's a little different, because they deep-fry the meat instead of cooking it on the open flame, so it's more crunchy. It's close enough, though.

Sometimes we grill at my cousin's. A couple of years ago I told her I'd do the barbecue Filipino style. You have to skewer the pork and marinate it in soy sauce, ketchup, sugar, and garlic. This is our typical food, almost like street food. You'll always find this at parties over there. So that's what we grilled at my cousin's that time, and everyone said, "Oh, my God, you did the barbecue! How'd you do it? You should make more!" And I was like, oh, yeah? It's a lot of work skewering all of those pieces!

And then we'd have the rice: it's like Spanish-style fried rice with tomato sauce. When I go to my cousin's, I bring things, because I can get the chorizo and the white cheese at the Spanish markets. The chorizo is what they really love; once I got some for my aunt for Christmas. We use it for our pork and chicken stew. That's a typical dish from my island, and my grandmother always cooked it a lot. And then there are certain things they send to me from back home. When my mom comes, she'll bring these handmade candies that are a regional specialty there. It's more than just the food; it's the connection, and sending it to us keeps the connection flowing. I know if I really wanted a certain food, I could probably find something close to it here, but it's a good feeling when my parents send things to me. Sometimes I'll think, oh, I remember this one, or my cousin will call and say, "Hey, come on over. Your mom just sent all this stuff!" So we'll sit there all afternoon and start picking at something like the dried spicy anchovies and drink a lot of Coke together.

I didn't really start cooking until maybe after college. I was home then and looking for a job. So in between going on interviews, my mother would say, "Okay, now you have to learn how to cook." It was her belief that if you were going to get married, you needed to learn. And I felt it, too. I knew I'd have to run the house someday. All my mom's generation—all the aunts—they were all career women, but they also ran the house. So they set such a high standard, and I knew I'd have to be able to do everything well. And I think that even without my saying it, my daughter is doing the same thing. She'll ask, "What if I don't like the food when I go to college? What if I crave for something?" I think that's why she watches what I'm doing in the kitchen now. One thing she really wants to learn is the adobo. It's similar to the Spanish one, but ours has garlic, soy sauce, and vinegar. Adobo is what you want to eat when people talk about Filipino food. It's a cooking style, a national style, really. It's one of those things you learn. I really wanted to make it the way my grandmother did, but she was one of those cooks who'd say, "Oh, you just do this." And I'd wonder, what is *this*? A third of a cup of vinegar? How much soy sauce? And she didn't know. Everything to her was feel. There were never any measuring cups. So I'd watch her carefully, because for me, my grandmother's food was the best food. Even my mom couldn't do it the way she did. And now, as long as I can get the Filipino vinegar and soy in Chinatown, I can do the adobo sauce, too.

Back home, we'd always spend Sundays at my grandmother's. Sundays are still special here, and when I can, I'll make a big Filipino breakfast with fried rice, eggs, and corned beef. That's what we'd have on Sunday mornings growing up. We'd always eat with the extended family, and I do miss that. But we look forward to the gatherings that we have now, and it's nice, because my kids get together with other Filipinos and see what they're doing. So, we've created our own holidays here, like Thanksgiving, which is a new one for us. The harder ones are Christmas and New Year's, because they are such big family affairs back home.

I'm happy to be here, though. I think there are benefits for my kids. They know if they were in the Philippines, they wouldn't be able to travel around. It's a class issue. The grandparents would drive them everywhere, because there's this feeling that it's not safe to take public transportation. It's a divided society. I was sort of sheltered when I was growing up and was never really allowed to go out on my own either.

And now, I think I'm in between two cultures. Even when I was in the Philippines, I struggled, because I had spent a lot of time in the States, and I started to incorporate what I'd picked up. Eventually, I chose to go away [to the States]. I love the freedom; I think that's American. But in terms of being Filipino, I have a strong belief in roles, for example, the expectation of what it means to be a mother. I know I'm supposed to guide my kids, to help them and have big hopes for them. Really, I'm supposed to do everything for them, and sometimes I have to consciously get out of that way of thinking, to be aware that I'm doing that. It's a balancing act, but I multitask; for example, I'll make them breakfast, but they can do their own laundry. And church, I've consciously decided that they're big enough that we don't have to go to church every week.

My kids would probably say they're more American now. They've asked me, "Are we now Fil-Americans or are we still Filipinos living in America?" I think they've been asked this kind of thing at school. So I threw it back to them and said, "How do you feel?" It's like, when does that line happen when you become Filipino-American? It's a question I've grappled with, and I know they have, too. When do you change? I'm not sure myself. It hasn't happened to me yet. So they continue to struggle with that. They know they're not going back. They want to stay. And if ever they go back, it's to visit, not to live there. And for me, it's nice to visit, but I'll stay here, too.

I know the Filipino thinking is still with me. Like at the college where I'm teaching, I'm always comparing things to what we had when I was in school: just a blackboard and chalk. If we wanted to watch a video in class, it was a big deal. You'd have to move to a special audiovisual room. Over there, the classrooms don't have a lot of things. We had limited books. Here I'm inundated with materials to enrich my teaching, so I'm one of those people who is always trying new things, because if the college is giving us all of these resources, why not use them? I guess I'm coming from a place where there was very little.

And I try to tell my students that I was once in a similar situation as they are now. I think it's a good starting point to get them to open up. I tell them that I had to go through the same thing, like learning how to be a student in the U.S. and how hard it was at first, how I came from a background where you sat there and just memorized so you could throw everything back to the teacher. I tell them how, when I came here, I was asked to share, to talk, to give my opinion to the group. It was so hard. Now in my own classes I ask students to write their responses in a little notebook, where they can put their opinions down. That way everyone gets a chance to share something. And because I make them write it first, they are more comfortable, because they've thought about it already. I think it makes things a little easier.

AURORA'S FILIPINO ADOBO

Braised Chicken with Soy Sauce and Garlic

Serves 4

Aurora sometimes makes this with beef or pork, cut into strips. She said the recipe can also be adapted for tofu. In Manila, Aurora's family often brought adobo on picnics, where it was eaten at room temperature. When dining at home, however, it was always heated and served hot with rice and the staples that appear on most Filipino tables: fish sauce, cane vinegar, and fresh hot peppers.

- 1 cup cane vinegar* (cider or rice vinegar can be substituted)
- ⅓ cup dark soy sauce*
- 3 tablespoons whole black peppercorns
- ¼ cup garlic, finely chopped
- 2½ pounds assorted chicken legs, thighs, wings, and split breasts
- 3 tablespoons vegetable oil

In a large bowl, mix the vinegar, soy sauce, peppercorns, and garlic. Add the chicken and toss gently so that all of the meat is coated with the marinade. Cover and refrigerate overnight.

Remove the chicken from marinade (reserving the liquid). In a large pot, heat the oil over medium-high heat until shimmering. Working in batches, add a few pieces of chicken at a time to the pot and cook until lightly browned on all sides, about 5 minutes. Add more oil between batches if necessary.

Return all of the chicken to the pot and cover with the reserved liquid from the marinade. Bring to a gentle simmer. Cover and cook until the meat is done, about 30 minutes.

Can be served immediately, or, as is typical in the Philippines, the dish can be refrigerated overnight, reheated, and served the next day.

---

*Found in markets specializing in Asian products.

Food, the Great Icebreaker

Yasie Saadat, thirty-one, is originally from Iran and lives with her
parents and sister in Newton, Massachusetts. The family came to the
United States in 1989, when Yasie was in the seventh grade. She
recently completed her MBA and occasionally teaches cooking classes
at the nearby Brookline Adult Education Center.

IT'S YASIE'S VOICE THAT SOMEONE might be drawn to first. Clear and
melodic, it rises and falls with the twists and turns of her story. When she
tells me about the Persian foods in her native Tehran, she speaks quickly,
gliding over the Farsi words *taftoon, barbari,* and *sangak* as she describes
the wonderful brick-oven breads she longs for here. But then her conversation may slow, and she'll articulate her thoughts more carefully, especially
when she tries to explain the difficulties an Iranian might face coming to
this country. It's as if she herself is still attempting to understand the complicated nature of the situation even as she speaks.

Now, however, she's offering me slivers of lemon-, coconut-, and saffron-
flavored candy, beautifully arranged in their package. They were purchased
in Isfahan, a city that both Yasie and her mother, Touba, insist is a place not
to be missed. "It's an art city," Touba says, pouring cups of tea from the
large brass samovar they brought back from Iran. "There's a saying," Yasie
explains, "something like, 'There's Isfahan and then there's the rest of the
world.'" The candy lives up to the praise: the pale orange piece I slip into
my mouth is a perfect balance between saffron and sugar.

Opposite: Yasie and Touba sip tea.

181

The women pick up their tea cups, for a moment turning away from the piles of herbs on the counter and the sliced eggplant that has been salted and sits sweating in a colander by the sink. Yasie tells me they have tea together every day, just like they would in Tehran, and I watch as they lift the delicate cups to their lips simultaneously. There is an understated elegance about this house: the kitchen with its sleek contemporary cupboards, the arrangements of sunflowers, asters, and zinnias on the counter, the silver bowl of dried rose petals on the coffee table in the living room, the framed watercolors with verses from the Koran hanging on the walls, and the handmade Persian rugs scattered about. Yasie and her mother, dressed fashionably in earth tones that accent their dark hair and eyes, seem worldly yet gracious and humble at the same time.

The two women work together efficiently in the kitchen, mostly quiet as they slice eggplant and chop herbs. Yasie might stop to point out a particular step in the cooking process, or Touba will recall something, like the first time Yasie made a cake for the family. "She was so young to make a cake," Touba tells us, explaining that her daughter had found the recipe on her own in a magazine. "And it was so good!" Yasie smiles, acknowledging, however, that what she's cooking today—*kashk-o bedemjan,* fried eggplant with yogurt, and *kou kou sabzi,* an herb casserole—are dishes that she didn't learn from a recipe. These are foods her mother first taught her to make years ago. Today, though, it is Yasie who is in control in the kitchen, and only once or twice does Touba question her daughter about something she's just done. "It's not time to turn it?" she asks at one point, indicating the green herb mixture cooking on the stove. "No, I already did." Yasie shakes her head quickly, and the black curls she's pulled back in a barrette tumble about her face. When I ask whether her sister, Saba, or her father—both back in Iran for several months—like to cook as much as she and her mother do, Yasie smiles. "I think my father considers himself a very good cook," she says, and the women both laugh.

The salted almonds Touba put out earlier with the tea are addictive, and I eat them, growing hungry as the beguiling scent of sautéed parsley, dill, chive, and fenugreek fills the kitchen. I admire the intricately designed silver bowl that holds the almonds and ask Yasie if it, like the rugs, paintings, and tea set, is from Iran. "You know, I guess I never realized how much stuff we've brought back with us," she smiles. That doesn't even include the cooking ingredients. Throughout the morning, the women pull jars of dried herbs from the cupboard, their contents indicated in Farsi on pieces of masking tape. They take containers of aged cheese and plastic bags of dried fruit from the freezer. One bag is filled with tiny red berries, which

Yasie tells me are called *zereshk,* something they can't get here. They are tart, like cranberries, and often used to flavor rice dishes. Another berry, *tout,* her mother's favorite, grows on trees and has a sweet, slightly fermented flavor. Touba tells me she planted one of the trees in their yard in Tehran so she'd always have plenty of the berries.

When the *kou kou sabzi* is done, Touba takes the pan from Yasie and carefully cuts what resembles a pale green omelet—the cooked herbs that have been bound with egg and breadcrumbs. She arranges the pieces artfully on a serving dish. Next, Yasie drizzles *kashk,* a fermented whey product that tastes similar to yogurt, and saffron liquid over the fried eggplant, cleaning the edges of the plate with a towel. She points to the recipes she's printed for me, explaining that she's noted how to replace the *kashk* if I'm unable to find it in my supermarket. I take them from her gratefully, the first time I've ever been handed recipes in the course of writing this book. Yasie's are typewritten and detailed, something she developed for her cooking classes.

Like so much about this kitchen, with its display of beautiful Persian artwork and the quiet competence of these women, who have spent the morning chopping, stirring, and sautéing, the food they've prepared is sublime, a unique combination of subtle flavors. There's the musty sweetness of the saffron oil, the acidity of the *kashk,* the bouquet of herbs cooked gently to perfection. It's quite unlike anything I ordinarily eat. We could almost be in Tehran.

My mother is definitely the guide for my cooking. She's a very good cook, and she's always been artistic with the way she presents things. So I've never gone out and bought a recipe book; it was always my mother who was the source. I think in our culture, recipes are passed down. There might even be a stigma about cookbooks, like, oh, she didn't know how to cook, so she *had* to go buy a cookbook. It's not something you'd want to admit to—not being a good cook—definitely with my mother's generation anyway, although now I think things might be changing.

To me, Persian food is comfortable. I think it's very tasty. It's rich and colorful and diverse, and it caters to the tastes of many different people. There's meat, but there are lots of things for vegetarians, because meat isn't always the main ingredient. Actually, I wish more people knew about it. If they did, I think they'd really like it. When I introduce it to my friends, they absolutely love it.

I've wondered why it's not so popular here, and I still haven't really found the answer. I think that people who have Iranian friends definitely know about it. But if they don't, they might never have tried it, because it's not really advertised. I think the Iranian community keeps to themselves; they tend to gather in, especially if there's something negative in the news about Iran. They might try to avoid talking about it, thinking maybe it would just go away. It's something I've wondered about. I don't handle it that way, maybe because I've grown up here. I think that gives you a different confidence about yourself, that it's okay to be whoever you are. The older generation might not feel that way, though. They tend to be a little more careful, because they consider the way they're perceived here. They try to go with the flow as much as they possibly can.

It's different for me. I'm just exactly on that borderline: I came early enough that I feel pretty comfortable here, but also I was over there long enough—twelve years—that I didn't forget the language or the culture. In certain respects, I feel I am very American, and in some situations, I feel a lot more comfortable in this country. But when I go back, I still feel like I belong. We have our old house—although it's changed a lot because it hasn't been kept up—but it's still my house, the place where I grew up, where I lived in first and second grade. So, when I'm there, it's like I never left. It's like I just woke up from this really long dream, and I've always been there. Certain things are so familiar, but at the same time, the culture has changed so much, and the people I remember have changed. Then, all of a sudden there's that thing that hits you in the face and you think, what am I doing? I really *don't* belong. It's such a contradiction, and it can be pretty difficult. I think it takes some time to get used to.

When I first came here, I knew that everything had completely changed for me. Starting from twelve on, everything was different. I was in a new world, and I had to adjust to the differences. Had I stayed in Iran, it would have meant I would have been in the same situation, the same culture, all my life. It would have been more comfortable, but I wouldn't have learned as much. I've gained a lot of perspective coming to the U.S. at such a young age and being in a totally different environment. It forced me to step out of that naive innocent world that I was in.

I think when I first got here, I had this expectation that things would be exactly as they were in Iran, that people would look the same, and that maybe only the streets would be a little different and the language wouldn't be the same. I really thought it would be a smooth transition. I had read books about the U.S., and I kind of knew a little of the history. In Iran, there are many other countries and cultures that are talked about. Even at a young age, you get a lot of exposure to the world. So I just assumed that I knew U.S. history, and I just expected people to know about me. But people had no idea where I was from. We lived in a tiny town in Wisconsin, and we only had one high school, one junior high, one of everything. In school, I was the only person other than someone from India that was from a different country. Even then, the Indian kid grew up here. I was the only one that didn't speak the language. When people asked me where I was from and I told them Iran, they were like, where's that? I was shocked! I thought, how can you not know? And they were like, is it in Asia? Is that India? Are you Arab? There were so many misconceptions; people would ask me things like "Do you guys live in houses over there? Do you have cars? Do you have snow?" I started to wonder if they thought I was from Mars! I don't know what they thought. So that was just very surprising to me. It was a little laughable, but it was also upsetting, and I remember thinking, okay, what do I do now?

I did make friends that first year, though. They were curious, but they were friendly, and they did accept me. I felt welcome there. But then we moved to Tennessee, and I didn't feel welcome at all. It was just the way people dealt with you that was sort of like, we don't want to have anything to do with you; we don't want to learn about you. We were there for five years, and that's where I went to high school. It wasn't the best time. But now we're here, and I love Boston.

I guess now I feel like I just want to be able to say I'm from Iran and feel totally comfortable and not have to explain myself to people. I don't want to speak on behalf of Iranians here, but I think that sometimes some of them maybe feel like they have to apologize for all the bad things that are said about us. With every bad piece of news, maybe they feel a little ashamed or embarrassed about it, because in some way, we're associated with it. Some people here understand me, but, you know, sometimes when I outright say I'm from Iran, I can see the judgment that's going on in some people's heads, and I start thinking, oh, they probably think of me as this, they probably think of me as that. So, I wish that would go away.

I think the biggest thing that would change people's attitudes and clear this misperception is to understand that everyone is kind of the same at the end of the day. We're all human beings, we all have the same aspirations in life, and we're not really that different. Yeah, people have different beliefs, and yeah, you have people over there that are a little bit fanatic. But you also have people here that are fanatic. Unfortunately, in our case, it just so happened that a certain group ended up representing everybody. So you can't really judge a whole group of people based on one thing or one particular group within that larger group. I guess I just want people to have an understanding of that.

Actually, I think food is a great icebreaker. Once you kind of see that, oh, these people have this food that tastes really nice, that looks good, and that has this wonderful smell, it kind of speaks for itself. You see that maybe there's more to them than you had thought. They enjoy eating, they enjoy music. What else do they enjoy? Oh, they enjoy living and being with people. So, I think food is a way to accomplish that.

It was really interesting for me to see people's reactions when I taught a cooking class last year. We did *kou kou,* a green herb soufflé, and everybody loved it. It was just amazing to me, because they had never seen such huge amounts of herbs used in cooking. They think of herbs as one piece of parsley for garnish, but this dish is all herbs. They couldn't believe herbs could be used that way. I also did some rice dishes with them. I try to teach things that aren't too exotic, because then maybe only one or two people would like them. Rice is a major part of our food, and it's cooked in many different ways. Most of the ingredients can be found in stores here, so an American cook could do it. I also like to introduce soups. In Iran, we have a variety of what you call soup; they're based on the Western recipes. But we also have *awsh,* which are the traditional Persian dishes, more like a stew. Again, herbs are a major part of these foods; every *awsh* has its own combination. So you put a lot of herbs and dried beans and noodles into them. When we did that, everyone really loved it. And what I really liked was that people thought, oh, this is something I can make for myself.

I learned almost everything from my mother. When I was younger, we could be in the kitchen together, and she would instruct me. I think now we get in each other's way a little bit. It works out when I'm learning something new from her; otherwise, we just have different ideas: she thinks it should be done this way, and I think it should be done that way. One time we tried to make the bread called *sangak,* a sourdough that they bake on little pebbles in a brick oven. When they cook it, they just throw the dough right on the hot pebbles, and of course when you take it out, the pebbles are attached to it. The baker gets rid of them, but sometimes when you take it home, you have to be careful that there isn't a little one still there. So once we collected pebbles and washed them and everything, but it just didn't work. I miss the good breads. We can't get them here.

I really love to cook. In some ways, it's a good escape. I also like to paint, and when I get started, it's like I become disconnected from everything. You just go into that world of paint, and all that exists for you is the paint and the colors. And then once you're done, you're back to reality, and you're like, I can't believe two hours just passed. It's sort of the same thing with cooking. You get into that zone. And you're so involved with whatever you're doing, it makes you forget about everything else.

Yasie's Persian *Kashk-o-Bedemjan* and *Kou Kou Sabzi*

Grilled Eggplant with Yogurt Sauce and Green Herb Omelet

Serves 3 or 4 for dinner or 6 to 8 as appetizers

These are wonderful summer dishes when eggplant and herbs are in season. Yasie sometimes serves the kou kou sabzi *for a light lunch or dinner. Both recipes could be served hot as main dishes, although Yasie most often serves them as appetizers at room temperature with flatbread. Dmitra's pita bread (page 20) would be a nice accompaniment to this meal.*

KASHK-O-BEDEMJAN

5 Chinese eggplants (about 2 pounds)*

Salt

¼ cup plus ¼ cup vegetable oil, divided

1 tablespoon *kashk***

¼ cup onion, finely chopped

1 teaspoon dried mint

1 teaspoon saffron liquid (recipe follows)

Cut the tips off the eggplants, peel, and slice them in half lengthwise. If using the larger globe eggplant, you may need to cut it into quarters lengthwise so that the pieces are no larger than an inch wide. "Sweat" the eggplant (to reduce some of its bitter taste): Place the eggplant pieces in a colander and generously sprinkle salt over them. Allow them to sweat some of their liquid for about 20 to 25 minutes. Rinse well and pat dry with paper towels.

In a large skillet, heat ¼ cup of the oil over medium heat until shimmering. Add the eggplant and cook, covered, turning occasionally, until lightly browned on all sides, about 10 minutes. (You may need to do this in two batches if your skillet isn't big enough to fit all of the eggplant. Add more oil between batches if necessary.)

In a large bowl, lightly mash the hot eggplant. Cool. Add the *kashk* and mix. Transfer to a serving dish.

Meanwhile, in a small skillet, heat the remaining ¼ cup of oil over medium-high heat until shimmering. Add the onions and cook, stirring occasionally, until golden brown, about 5 minutes. With a slotted spoon, remove the onions from the oil and sprinkle them over the eggplant. Add the mint to the hot oil and cook for 5 to 10 seconds only. Remove the mint from the oil and sprinkle it over the eggplant.

Drizzle the saffron liquid over the eggplant and serve with pita or lavash bread.

---

* Compared with the more popular globe eggplant, Chinese eggplant has thinner skin, a more delicate flavor, and fewer seeds, which tend to make the vegetable bitter. However, if you cannot find Chinese eggplant, choose globe eggplants that are small and thin, indicating they have fewer seeds.

** Found in markets specializing in Middle Eastern products. You can make something similar with ¼ cup of sour cream mixed with ½ teaspoon of lime juice and a pinch of salt. Use the same amount of this as is called for of the *kashk*.

SAFFRON LIQUID

1 teaspoon saffron

2½ tablespoons hot water

Break up the saffron threads with your fingers. Add the water and stir. (This will keep for several weeks in the refrigerator.)

KOU KOU SABZI

- 1 cup cilantro, finely chopped
- 1 cup flat-leaf parsley, finely chopped
- 1 cup dill, finely chopped
- 1 cup chives or scallions, including green tops, finely chopped
- ½ cup spinach leaves, washed and finely chopped
- 4 large eggs, beaten
- ⅓ cup fine breadcrumbs
- 1 teaspoon cinnamon
- ¼ teaspoon turmeric
- ¼ cup dried fenugreek leaves (optional)
- ½ teaspoon saffron liquid (recipe above)
- 1 teaspoon salt
- ½ teaspoon freshly ground pepper
- 3 tablespoons vegetable oil

In a bowl, combine the fresh herbs and spinach. In another bowl, mix the eggs, breadcrumbs, cinnamon, turmeric, fenugreek (optional), saffron liquid, salt, and pepper. Pour the egg mixture over the herbs and combine.

In a large nonstick skillet, heat the oil over medium heat until shimmering. Spread the oil around the pan to coat the bottom and sides. Pour the herb mixture into the pan, spreading it evenly with a spoon. Reduce the heat to medium-low and cook, covered, until the egg is cooked through, about 10 to 12 minutes.

To serve, carefully invert onto a serving platter. Cut into wedges. Can be served hot or at room temperature.

Man in the Kitchen

Dakpa Zady, who will not tell me his age, saying only that he is "a very old man," is originally from Côte d'Ivoire. Zady, as he likes to be called, is a contractor and house painter. He lives in the Hyde Park section of Boston.

⚒

THE TINY COUNTER IN ZADY'S kitchen is stacked with ingredients he picked up at the Afro-Caribbean market yesterday. There's a package of tilapia—two fish that have been gutted and sliced into thirds with heads and tails left intact—bags of frozen okra and fresh spinach, a small pile of chicken bones, and a bowl of shrimp, whose shells have been removed. Empty pots and pans are spread over the stove in preparation for the various dishes that Zady and his girlfriend, Lili, will cook today. He lights the burner under one pan and slices mushrooms into the oil that is now shimmering. Their sweet, musty scent fills the apartment, and Zady sings quietly as he stirs. He makes slow, graceful circles around the pan with a large wooden spoon, his lean, muscular arms seeming to move to an intricate dance rather than to stir mushrooms. "Oh, my girl is here," he says suddenly, glancing out the second-floor kitchen window, which looks down on the street. "Now I better help her out." He turns off the stove and slips downstairs with a jacket in his hand.

The bright morning sunlight streaming into the apartment reflects off a flat-screen TV that looks huge against the small wall behind it. Afro-pop drifts quietly from the other room, drowned out momentarily by the rustle

Opposite: Zady and Lili at the stove.

of paper and plastic in the hallway downstairs. Zady and Lili make their way up to the second floor, murmuring in French and depositing grocery bags and boxes on the sofa, chair, and end table. After several trips out to Lili's car, ingredients and kitchen equipment take over the small apartment. A wooden crucifix on the glass coffee table is moved aside to make room for containers of *foutu,* a type of dumpling made with plantain flour that Lili prepared at home earlier this morning, a pot filled with chicken pieces that have been partially cooked, ziplock bags of dried, ground okra and fish powder she brought back from her trips home to Côte d'Ivoire, and the *mandioca,* or yucca, she grated and strained several days ago, which she'll use to make *plakalay,* a type of dumpling popular in her village. On the side table next to the couch, Zady unloads a pair of scissors, a large wooden mortar and pestle, and Lili's prized calabash. The large bowl, made from the shell of a gourd, is smooth with wear, making it the perfect surface to roll her *plakalay* into balls. Zady peers into several bags until he finds what he wanted to show me. A frozen cylinder of *atieke,* or grated cassava, the classic staple in Côte d'Ivoire, is wrapped tightly in plastic. The tiny white granules resemble couscous, and, like couscous, they are steamed and served with stewed meat and vegetables. When I ask Lili if she also made this at home, she shakes her head, explaining it's a lot of work and something she can buy at her market.

When everything's been unloaded, Lili surveys the stove, moving aside the pots Zady has set out and replacing them with her own. She adds chopped onions and water to two separate pots of the parboiled chicken she's brought. The one on the left will be *kedjenou,* a popular stew from home. When I ask about the other, Lili shrugs and looks at Zady. "Call it sauce gumbo," he instructs, and Lili nods.

In Zady's pot on the front burner, onions, mushrooms, carrots, and chicken bones are cooking. He adds the tilapia pieces, explaining there's no name for this stew, because it's just something he cooks here. It does, however, reflect the kinds of meals his mother always made, even if she wouldn't have added quite so many ingredients. "I can just imagine what she would cook with all these things," he says, gesturing around to the piles of vegetables, pots filled with chicken, and bags of spices. "She doesn't have that many things."

Lili chops carrots on a small cutting board she balances on the edge of the sink. She adds them to her pots on the stove, stirring them slowly and watching quietly as more and more ingredients go into Zady's pot, which is nearly overflowing now with the fresh spinach and okra he's pureed in the tiny blender he calls his "toy" and poured over everything. "You will not have consistency from me!" Zady laughs, pointing to Lili's stews on the rear burners. "But hers are the traditional recipes. Mine, when you come back, will always be a little different." Lili looks over the rims of her glasses at Zady, who is humming and stirring. It's hard to guess what she might be thinking, because her face is fixed in a serious expression, and she doesn't talk as freely as Zady. She adjusts her glasses and focuses her attention on the hot pepper she's holding, cutting off a tiny piece which she adds to the stew. The *kedjenou* should be just slightly spicy, she explains when I ask. Zady, meanwhile, makes me pronounce the word several times to be certain I've gotten it right. Pointing to my notepad, he instructs, "Spell it *k-j-NU*," to help me with the pronunciation, adding that a lot of Americans mispronounce French words. He repeats it several times, slowly enunciating the syllables in his deep baritone. He watches as Lili pours a beige powder from a plastic bag into the pot of sauce gumbo and tells me it's the ground fish powder that goes into a lot of their home cooking. "You really have to brush your teeth with that one," he warns.

When the various stews have simmered for a while, it's time to make the rice. Zady pulls a fifty-pound sack from a low cupboard in the corner of the kitchen and holds it open for Lili to scoop. Before she can begin, he takes the pan from her and says something in French. "He wants me to make a lot of rice," she explains with a sigh. Zady reaches for a bigger pan and begins to scoop it himself. "I always cook the rice last," he says, lifting the cloth bag back into the cupboard. "It tastes great when it's hot, and there's nothing better than that!" He goes into extensive detail about its preparation—only an inch of water to cover the grains because an inch and a quarter will yield soft rice, and an inch and a half, overcooked mush not worth eating. He pours several tablespoons of olive oil into the pan, and when I ask about salt, he shakes his head emphatically, telling me it ruins the flavor.

He and Lili begin to debate whether she should do the *aloko* today, a popular appetizer in Côte d'Ivoire made by deep-frying slices of ripe plantain and tossing them with salt. He walks around the kitchen, looking through boxes and bending down to peek into cupboards in search of the plantains. Zady has a subdued, even energy when he moves, as if he were conserving some for later, an acquired trait, perhaps, when you grow up in a place that, as Zady's told me, is always very, very humid. When he locates the plantains—both nearly black, the best kind for *aloko*—he passes them to Lili. She heats the oil to deep-fry them, and Zady tells us he makes them differently, with just a little oil in the pan, "like a pancake," so that it's healthier. "That's not *aloko,*" Lili says quietly, shaking her head.

When it's time to eat, Lili takes a ball of her *plakalay* and several small spoonfuls of the *kedjenou* and the sauce gumbo she's made and sits in the armchair next to the TV. Zady makes a place for himself across from her on the couch. His plate is piled high with rice, cooked the way he likes it: dry and slightly brown on the edges. There's a large helping of his dish without a name, the green color from the pureed spinach and okra vibrant against the white rice. He eats slowly, savoring the flavors as he talks about his mother's cooking and life in Côte d'Ivoire and warning us to watch out for the fish bones. When Lili gives a ball of *plakalay* to each of us, Zady passes. "If I eat that, I won't have room for my rice," he tells her.

⸎⸎

When I tell them back home that I cook every day, they think I'm joking. My brothers can't even imagine me cooking. Men just don't do that there. My mother was the only one who cooked when I was growing up. No, for men, their responsibility is to provide whatever it takes to make a good meal, but you never see them in the kitchen. My family is certain I must have a woman here who cooks for me every day, because I'm educated and in America. They think it's impossible that I'd have to do it for myself. But, in fact, I don't have that basic thing. Even if they have nothing else, they still have someone that will cook for them every day. Where I'm from, that's the least a man can have.

So I can't tell them that I cook for my girlfriend; I haven't said anything. They would probably feel disgust or worry that she owns me, that I've lost my manhood. Actually, they might be scared for me! But I do cook. I cook for her when she comes. The traditional foods, she excels in those. But she's busy because she goes to school, she works, and then she has to take care of her kids. I feel bad for her because she works hard, so when she comes, I cook. I do vegetables with meat or fish. And always some rice. She really likes my cooking.

In my village, the food is rice. You always ate rice. If you have no rice, it's like you are starving. There never was much choice: whatever we had, that's what we would eat, and we grew our own rice, so that's what we ate. But there was a time when we didn't have much. That was when my mother left. She was fighting with my father for some reason, so she went to another village for a while. Oh, my God, what a disaster it was!

We had nothing, because my father, he cannot cook! He's not a food guy; he's more like a drink guy. But still, we needed to eat! You couldn't believe what a void—I mean, the family was just nonexistent. I can't even imagine now. She went for a long time. Oh, she was really mad! We were hungry. My brothers tried to cook but, oh, my God! For someone who never cooked to all of a sudden try to put food together, forget it. We were just eating to survive; there was no enjoyment in it.

You don't really have a choice about what to eat the way you do here. It's not like, oh, I feel like pasta or, oh, I'd like chicken or, maybe I'll eat a hamburger. Are you crazy? In America there are a lot of choices, but over there the problem is just finding something that day. So you eat to survive. Fortunately, my father was a hard worker, so, when we were young, we always had our rice, and he could hunt, so sometimes there was meat or fish, too.

When I went away to school, it was different. I lived with my aunt for a while, because there was a fourth grade in her village. All the relatives were sending their kids to her, so there were maybe ten of us in one house. It's not like the amount of food could just increase based on the amount of kids to feed. No, it stays the same no matter how many people there are. So we were fighting just to get a little bit. I can't believe we survived. There was very little to eat. But then, I passed a test in sixth grade and got to go to another school, where we were taken care of by the government. We lived on the campus, and there was a cafeteria, so I had food from that point on. It's a different lifestyle. And then I got a scholarship to come to this country when I was about twenty.

Oh, the food! There is no country like America that has so much food. Whatever you want, you can get! When I first got here, I was amazed by how much you could have. In one pot, there might be so many pieces of chicken, and you'd think, oh, my God! There was so much, and it was all the same thing! I mean, back home we might have two legs or two wings, but over here there might be seven pieces of wings—only wings!—or so many legs, and you'd think, Wow! How can this be? How can there be so many wings in one pot of soup? Back home there are certain parts of the chicken you don't even know about, because you've never had them. Someone else eats those—the good parts. So you come here and you see all of it; whatever part you want you can have.

I started to learn to cook when I came here. There were four of us in my program, and we were a bunch of guys who had been taken care of all our lives by our mothers and then our school, so we only ever had to show up and eat. All of a sudden we found ourselves in a place where none of us knew how to cook. I just started to put things together on the stove. Basically, we wanted to make our rice, because we have to have our rice, but sometimes we'd try to make a sauce, like maybe we'd boil vegetables with meat. In the beginning, the seasoning was the difficult thing, because sometimes we might put too much salt in. Or we might forget the salt. Another mistake we made is we would put the food on the stove and go watch TV. Then, all of a sudden the alarm would go off and the next thing we knew, firefighters were invading the building. Yeah, not once, several times!

So I just had to learn. It's not like I read it from cookbooks. In Africa, well, the place where I'm from, there are certain things that are natural. Like cooking. You have to know them; you don't learn them. It's like dancing, like the drums. They don't teach people how to do the drums; you just do it. You can't learn it. Singing, it's natural. You have to be able to sing, or you don't know how to sing. Cooking, usually it's the ladies who do that, so to read a cookbook or to go to school to learn cooking, no, never. School is for something else. It's another level, and only those that are educated go to school. But cooking? Even in the villages where the people are primitive, they know how to cook. So how can anyone go to school to learn cooking? Here, I know it's different, but in Africa, if you tell them you're going to school to become a chef, they will laugh. They cannot even imagine that. They would not believe that there are people in America going to school for cooking. And making a presentation with food? They don't think about that. If you're hungry, just find something to eat. And a cookbook? "Come on, what are you looking for in a book?" they'll ask. In Africa, even kids, young girls, twelve years old, know how to cook. So how can a grownup go to school for that? They cannot picture it. You go to school to be an engineer, a doctor, an economist. You do not go to school to be like your mother, who cooks.

A girl learns by watching her mother. She can start as early as ten, eleven. The only reason we had problems when my mother went away was my sister was not with us then. Otherwise, she would have taken over, because if a woman doesn't know how to cook, she's not going to find a good man. Yeah. The fact is, if you cook, your man will come home. If you're not going to make him a good meal, he's going to find one somewhere else. And it's not going to be with his mother! So you have to really be good, because your man will always stay where the good meal is.

I really haven't spoken with my mother for a long, long time. We talk on the phone, but there's very little that we can exchange. First of all, I really didn't master my native language, Beté, because I went away to school at a young age. So I cannot go into detail about a lot of things. I can speak a little, but I have to mix it with French, and she doesn't speak French. When I call, I ask her how she's doing and let her talk. I can understand her, but if I try to say something, I can't be abstract, and I can't articulate certain ideas. It's frustrating. I cannot really talk to my mother. It's very, very difficult. And I don't go back because it's so expensive. Sometimes it's just better to send them the money. I tell them I could spend two thousand dollars to visit, or I could just send it instead. They really need the money.

They don't have the opportunities you have here. The government is in control of everything. I couldn't do what I do here. People would laugh at me. They would say, Are you crazy? We send you to school and now you paint houses? They would expect me to be in a big office with a big Mercedes and always wearing a tie. It's not that I don't want that, but you have to do what will help you survive. And it doesn't matter what that is, because in this country, nobody will mock you for it. But over there, everybody wants to be in a big office. I think the mentality of the people has to change. They have to realize that success in life is not just getting a high degree and working in an office. You need to do whatever is necessary to take care of yourself and your children and to help the country, too. We all need to take part so that things will improve, so the roads will be clean, the houses will look nice, the neighborhoods will be in better condition. We have to stop waiting for the government to do all those things. We need someone like the little contractor, like you have here. People need to begin to do these things. That's the great thing about this country. You can be a doctor if you want, but you can also put your diploma in the drawer and put on your dirty clothes and go into the street and try to make it. There's no one telling you that what you're doing is beneath you.

When you look around, you find there's no such place like America. There's so much diversity, so many people doing different things. Life is not boring: the food, the people, even the weather changes. You can always find something to feel good about, the change of seasons, for example. Maybe you like skiing in the winter. If not, there's always something else. You might be enjoying the sun one minute, and the next, it's gone. In Africa, nothing really changes. It can be humid all your life.

But here, everything is so dynamic; things are always moving. And then, sometimes before you know it, you're too old. Time goes so fast.

I've moved around since I was very young, but this is the place I've lived the longest. I'm going to stay. Sometimes I miss people. I miss the ambience of the country; it's very fun! You don't see people worried like, oh, I have to pay my bills or, oh, my God, my rent is due. You have no such concerns, because there are always people who take care of you. When I go back, there's always someone who will feed me: my cousins, my friends' wives, my mother.

You know, when I was growing up, whatever my mother made, it was always the best thing of the day. I grew up eating her food, so it was always the ultimate; there was never anything better. And I think when you go home and you eat your mother's meal, that's when you can say, the day is over and I can go to bed, because now I've been fed. Sometimes I think, without that, it's like nothing.

Zady's Rice and Lili's *Kedjenou* and *Aloko* from Côte d'Ivoire

Crispy White Rice, Spicy Chicken and Okra Stew, and Fried Plantain

Serves 4 to 6

In Côte d'Ivoire, kedjenou *is sometimes made with eggplant instead of okra. Here, you could use one medium eggplant, peeled and chopped into ½-inch pieces, instead of the okra. Add the eggplant when you add the tomatoes. The* kedjenou *could be served with Genevieve's* fufu *(page 153), which is nearly identical to the* foutu *that Lili prepared.*

RICE

3 cups long-grain white rice

¼ cup olive oil

Measure the rice into a 4-quart saucepan. Add enough water to cover rice by 1 inch. Add the olive oil. Bring to a boil and immediately reduce the heat to a simmer. Cover and cook until all the water has been absorbed and the rice is just done, about 15 minutes. The rice should begin to form a golden crust along the edges of the pan.

KEDJENOU

2½ to 3 pounds chicken, cut into serving pieces
    Salt and freshly ground pepper
   3 tablespoons vegetable oil
   1 medium onion, chopped
   4 cloves garlic, minced
   1 bay leaf
4 to 5 sprigs fresh thyme
 One 8-ounce can tomato sauce
   4 plum tomatoes, chopped
 One ½-inch piece hot chili pepper, seeded and finely chopped
   1 Maggi bouillon cube (optional)
   2 cups okra, chopped

Season the chicken with salt and pepper. Heat the oil in a large pot over medium-high heat until shimmering. Working in batches, add a few pieces of chicken at a time to the pot and cook until lightly browned on all sides, about 5 minutes. Add more oil between batches if necessary.

Transfer the cooked chicken to a platter and set aside. Add the onions and garlic to the empty pot, reducing the heat to medium and stirring occasionally, and cook until soft, about 5 minutes. Return the chicken to the pot and add the bay leaf, thyme, tomato sauce, plum tomatoes, chili pepper, bouillon cube (optional), and enough water to cover. Simmer, uncovered, until the chicken is cooked through and begins to fall off the bone, about 45 minutes. Add the okra and continue to cook for 20 minutes. Season with additional salt and pepper. Serve with rice.

ALOKO

3 very ripe plantains

Salt

2 cups vegetable oil for frying

Peel and slice the plantains into ¼-inch rounds. Season with salt.

In a 2-quart saucepan, heat the oil until shimmering. Test the oil to see if it is hot enough for frying by dropping one slice of plantain into the pot. If the plantain turns golden brown in 45 to 60 seconds, the oil is ready. Remove the test slice of plantain and cook the remaining slices in small batches until golden brown.

Remove from the oil with a slotted spoon and drain on paper towels. Serve immediately.

Part of You Goes into the Cooking

Patricia Channer, fifty-two, is from Costa Rica. She lives in the West
Roxbury section of Boston and works as a house cleaner and private
chef. Patricia often cooks with her niece, Shirley Cruz, twenty-six,
who lives in an apartment nearby.

※✕※

"SHE REMINDS ME OF MY grandmother," Patricia says, nodding toward
her niece. "Same face, same body," she adds, tossing a handful of chopped
yucca into the pot boiling on the stove. We are in Shirley's kitchen today,
and she is rifling through her cupboards, pulling out some of the foods she
brought back on her last trip home to Costa Rica: coffee; *leche pinito,* her
favorite brand of powdered milk; and jars of *salsa lisano,* something Patricia's mother—Shirley's grandmother—makes with tamarind, a sour-
tasting fruit that grows in tropical climates. Her grandmother also puts
peppers, onions, and allspice in her special sauce.

"I gotta pack a whole suitcase of food I know I won't have for a year or
so," Shirley says as she passes the jar of *salsa lisano* over for me to have a
taste. She smiles when I tell her it's delicious, two dimples appearing on
her smooth face. Shirley and Patricia are preparing *sopa de pata de vaca,* a
soup made with beef; Patricia sometimes uses cow's feet sold at her local
market. Both women were raised by Patricia's mother and, at different
times, grew up eating this soup. When Shirley's mother, Patricia's sister,
left for the United States, Shirley and her brother stayed behind in Costa
Rica for several years, living in their grandmother's house, where there

Opposite: Making Abuelita's *sopa.*

were vast gardens, farm animals, and always plenty of delicious food. "Shirley's always calling my mom when she wants to cook something," Patricia explains, and even though they've both been here for a long time, they still miss her cooking.

"Yeah, when I wanna make *frijoles blancos y mondongo,* the beans I love, or the rice pudding, or the tamales—especially the tamales—I call my grandmother," Shirley says. "The last time I made them, I had to call her a few times to make sure I did it right."

Patricia nods, watching the niece who looks so much like her, with the same *café con leche* skin and big smile. She pulls a piece of folded paper from the small bag slung over her shoulder and tells us that she, too, called her mother just this morning to talk about the soup. Nobody uses recipes, she explains, and when she goes back home, her mother tells her to just come over and watch if she needs to know how to do something. "Oh, I forgot the carrots," she says, reading from her list and then turning around to open the refrigerator. "Look, they must get these big old mamas from Costa Rica," she cackles, waving a huge carrot in the air. She peels and grates the carrot while Shirley slips into the bedroom to get her laptop. The sounds of salsa stream out of the speakers when she comes back into the room. "We always danced when we cooked," Patricia smiles. "Like my cousin, he would come and spin me around in the kitchen. And my mom, when we're cooking, she'll always be dancing. And she's seventy-two!"

When I ask about the bag swinging from Patricia's shoulder as she moves her hips to the music and chops at the same time, Shirley laughs and tells us her aunt never takes it off, not even to cook: "Never! When she was little, she slept with her purse! Even at her wedding last year, she didn't take it off!"

"I need it!" Patricia cries. "It's part of me."

Patricia's presence takes over this kitchen: not only is she a large woman, at nearly six feet tall, but she chats constantly as she moves about, explaining when to add particular ingredients or how she's varied the soup slightly from the way her mother makes it, and occasionally stopping to sing along with the music. She stirs the huge pot, which now contains the cow's feet she picked up at her favorite Latino supermarket, the chopped yucca, onion, carrot, potatoes, and calabaza. Meanwhile, Shirley chops the chayote, another type of squash that is small and pale green in color. When she's done, she steps aside to let her aunt collect it for the soup. Next, Patricia adds a small handful of fresh cilantro into the steaming pot and soon a distinctly Latin scent of beef broth and the earthy, almost musty aroma of yucca begin to fill the apartment.

Shirley watches the cooking from across the kitchen, leaning into the table with her chin resting in the palm of her hand. "This is around the time everybody wants to know when the soup will be done, remember?" she smiles at her aunt. "¿*Ya,* Lita? ¿*Ya,* Lita?" (Now, Grandma? Now, Grandma?), she calls out in a high-pitched voice.

"That's what Shirley would say to my mother when she was little," Patricia explains. They called her 'Lita.' It's short for *'abuelita,'* or grandma," and then, looking around the kitchen quickly, she cries, "Oh, no, Shirley. The dumplings!"

The younger woman jumps from her chair and runs to the cupboard for a bowl, cornmeal, and some flour. "You make the dumplings," Patricia instructs. "You do it better." When Shirley pours cornmeal from the bag into the bowl, she looks at me with a guilty smile. "Sorry, I don't know about that calculating stuff," she says, adding some water from the sink without measuring. When the dough is mixed, the two women stand over the bowl and roll tiny handfuls into oblong balls. Patricia collects these on a plate and drops them into the soup. "When we were kids, we'd make them into different shapes," Shirley says, grabbing more dough from the bowl. They continue to reminisce, moving seamlessly between Spanish and English, as they laugh about Patricia's mother, describing her garden in Costa Rica where the cilantro, chayote, and the other vegetables needed for her much-loved specialties grow. When all of the dumplings have begun to float on the soup, Patricia gives it another stir and brings the large wooden spoon to her lips. "This baby is ready!" she cries.

"Oh, that smell," Shirley says as she moves next to her aunt, her eyes closed as she takes in the steam rising from the pot. "That smell brings memories, like I'm back home again."

⊰※⊱

I've always wanted to cook since I was small, because everyone else was doing it. I remember when I was maybe about four, my mum gave me this set of little pots and pans to play with. One day, she took some rice from her pot on the stove and put it in my little pot, and she said, "Go ahead, stir it. It's cooking!" But I remember being disappointed and thinking that mine was different from hers, because it didn't have any steam coming out of it.

When I got a little older I got to cook with her or with my mother's mom, Alberta. Wow, she used to cook! We'd do a lot around Christmas.

Patricia and Shirley prepare the *sopa.*

During the year we'd raise a pig and a rooster, so we'd have it for Christmas Eve dinner. We'd marinate the rooster in *salsa lisano*—it's like a sauce with tamarind and peppers—and then we'd cook it. And the pig, that was a lot of work. We made lots of different dishes with that. We'd use the feet to make jello, we'd marinate the leg and bake that, we'd make *chicharrón.* Well, my uncle Rodolfo would do the *chicharrón.* He'd start a fire in his oven outside and cook the fattiest part of the pork. First he'd marinate it—you know, we don't eat nothing without marinating it in Costa Rica!—and then, after it's cooked for a while, he'd put chunks of green plantain in it. So the *chicharrón* would cook outside, and my mother would do the leg inside. She'd rub it with garlic, papaya, and lots of spices. Then she'd baste it with Coca-Cola to caramelize it. She'd also make fruitcakes—twenty-two at Christmas!—and she'd share them with the neighbors.

Then we'd all make the tamales. We had five girls and one boy, and at Christmastime it was like we were in a production line when we made those tamales. My mum would be checking the pork and somebody else would go and baste it. Everybody was helping out, doing this and that. It was a lot of fun. You'd start a couple days before Christmas, and then, when you finally put the dinner out, it was a full table.

I do some of the things now for Christmas. I make the tamales, the fruitcake. I go to the Spanish supermarket and I get a pork leg and roast it. And I try to do the sauce for the pork. And the chicken, sometimes I make the chicken, too. Usually, if I'm going to make something, I call my mom. My niece, Shirley, does the same thing. She's always on the phone with my mom when she needs to cook. My sister, my cousins— we all call each other when we need to know how to do something. "How do we do this?" we'll say. "How did Granny used to do that one?" And if we can't call family, we'll call Costa Rican friends.

I still want my foods when I'm here. I know it's not the same, and I can't get everything. Like the cheese, the *queso turrialba,* that's what I really want. You can just eat it and eat it. That's the first thing I get when I go back. Then I'd go to a taverna and have some draft beer. We call it *cerveza cruda.* It's from a barrio, and they pour it in pitchers from the drums. It's delicious! Actually, you can find it in parts of New Jersey because of all the Costa Ricans. So definitely I would have the cheese and a beer, and then I'd go in the sea. That would be nice.

I've been here for almost twenty years now, and things are easier. The language was hardest at first: I felt like I was in a drum. Even though I had studied English at home, I was afraid to talk, because I was embarrassed about my accent. I thought I would make a fool of myself. I still wanted to be independent, though, like to go shopping alone and not have to bring a friend to translate for me, so I began to watch TV programs and read in English. That really helped me loosen up.

One of the things I still miss is the camaraderie there. Costa Ricans are really friendly, very giving. Once you live in a place, you become so much more a part of it than you do here. I think because there are so many people who come to America from different places around the world, maybe people put up a little wall here. You can say, "Hi," but people don't like to get that close. I have a neighbor here who's a Filipino lady. We say, "Hello," but that's all. In Costa Rica, we'd be having dinners together.

But it's been good for me to be here. I'm stronger now, and I think I've gotten a lot of positive things from American culture. I think about Costa Rica less. When I first came, my friends and I always ended up talking about home. Sometimes I'd have to put it in the back of my mind so I could get accustomed to being here instead. And it's been good. Now I'm more outspoken. In Costa Rica, because we're similar to the British, we don't want to hurt anybody's feelings. So you might not say something because you don't want to seem rude. Costa Ricans never want to be rude. Before, for example, if I thought a certain color didn't look good on you, I wouldn't tell you. I might say, "I wonder how blue would look." Being here, I'm more outspoken. I say things now. I'll tell you it isn't the right color. And with guys, I don't let them get away with things here.

My friends are always calling me now, because they know I'm the one that likes to cook. They'll say, "Are you cooking today? When are you going to make one of your inventions?" They like my soup. So I'll put all these things in a big old pot—cow's feet, yucca, potatoes, cilantro, maybe pork tail—and this neighbor will come and then that friend will come. Sometimes I cook at my friend's or at my niece's because my kitchen is small. They'll help me. They might peel the yucca or cut up an onion, but that's it.

We have a saying in Latin America: *"Se pelea."* It means that something is fighting against itself, and we say that when we cook sometimes. It's like Americans who say that too many hands spoil the soup. And, you know, it's amazing, because that really happens! If I'm cooking and somebody adds something, it tastes very different than if I made it alone. So usually, they cut the things up, but I'm the one who puts everything in the pot. When you cook, you put a part of yourself in the dish. If somebody adds something to my soup, it might clash.

Patricia's Costa Rican *Sopa* and Dumplings

Beef and Vegetable Soup and Corn Dumplings

Serves 6

Patricia says the cow's feet, something her mother always used, gives this soup its rich flavor. If you can't find cow's feet, however, stew beef can be substituted.

1½ pounds cow's feet or beef stewing meat, trimmed and cut into 1-inch pieces

2 stalks celery, chopped

3 cloves garlic, minced

1 tablespoon whole allspice

1 bay leaf

1 tablespoon dried thyme

One 15-ounce can small white beans or cannellini beans

1 small onion, chopped

2 carrots, peeled and grated

2 potatoes, peeled and cut into 1-inch pieces

2 small ears of corn, cut into 2-inch lengths

1 small yucca, peeled and cut into ½-inch pieces*

1 chayote, peeled and cut into ½-inch pieces* (summer squash or zucchini can be substituted)

1 small piece of calabaza squash (about 1 pound), peeled, seeded, fibers removed, and cut into 1-inch pieces* (butternut squash can be substituted)

½ small scotch bonnet pepper, cored, seeded, and chopped* (1 or 2 jalapeño peppers can be substituted; always wear gloves or wash hands immediately after handling hot peppers)

12 to 15 sprigs fresh thyme

⅓ cup chopped fresh cilantro leaves and stems

½ cup water

1 package Goya seasoning (Sazón Goya)* (a mix of 1 teaspoon ground cumin, 1 teaspoon *annatto* seed, and ½ teaspoon ground coriander can be substituted)

Salt and pepper

* Found in markets specializing in Latino and Caribbean products.

Place the cow's feet or beef stewing meat in a large pot. Cover with water and add the celery, garlic, allspice, bay leaf, and dried thyme and bring to a slow simmer. Cook, covered, until the meat is tender, about 3 hours for the cow's feet, 1½ to 2 hours for the stewing meat.

Drain the beans and place them, along with ½ cup of water, in a blender or food processor and puree until smooth.

Add the remaining vegetables, herbs, pureed beans, and Goya seasoning to the pot. The liquid should cover everything. Add more water if necessary. Continue to simmer, uncovered, until the vegetables are soft, about 30 minutes. Season with salt and pepper.

Add the dumplings (recipe follows), gently dropping them into the soup. Continue to cook for about 5 to 7 minutes or until they are cooked through. Remove the dumplings from the pot with a slotted spoon and set aside on a plate. Ladle the soup into bowls and place 1 or 2 dumplings in each.

CORN DUMPLINGS

½ cup cornmeal

½ cup flour plus additional for working the dough

¼ teaspoon salt

1 teaspoon sugar

1 teaspoon baking powder

⅓ to ½ cup water

Combine the cornmeal, flour, salt, sugar, and baking powder in a mixing bowl. Stir in enough water to just combine. On a lightly floured surface, with floured hands, shape the dough into 12 small cylinders, approximately 1 inch long.

Teaching Both Ways

Ha Hoang, forty-two, left Vietnam in 1983. She lives in the
Dorchester section of Boston with her family and works as a
paraprofessional at a nearby elementary school. Ha frequently
cooks with her sister-in-law, Chee, and Chee's children, who live
next door.

※＞〜＜※

EIGHT-YEAR-OLD MINH SITS ON THE floor under the counter where his
mother and aunt are cooking. In his lap is an open book; above him are
bowls filled with fresh mint leaves, lettuce, and rice stick noodles, the ingredients Ha will need to assemble her spring rolls, which Minh and his sister,
four-year-old An, love. When Ha asks her nephew if he'd like to help,
Minh says, "I can help by eating," and continues with his book. Ha smiles
and shakes her head, but when his mother, Chee, says something to him in
Vietnamese, he puts the book down. He climbs onto a stool next to his sister, who is watching her aunt deposit several clumps of cooked rice noodles
into a bowl. Little An leans forward to pull the translucent white noodles
toward herself, and the plastic crown on her head slips down over her eyes.

Chee's kitchen has ample counter space for everyone to work. Ha's children, who are older than Minh and An, attend Vietnamese school on Saturday mornings and missed out on the day's cooking. Minh, who will go
to his school later in the afternoon, tells me about the dances he will per-
form with his friends for the New Year celebration, which is now just two
days away. When he hears me asking his mother about the plate of food

Opposite: Ha makes spring rolls with her nephew, Minh.

219

that adorns the center of the dining room table, he joins the conversation. "It's *bánh tét,*" he says pointing to what his mother has told me is sweet rice that's been rolled in banana leaves and is always served for the New Year. "It's round for the face of the sun," he explains. His mother encourages him to tell me about the other version they serve, called *bánh chung.* "That one is square, because before they didn't know if the world was round or square," his high-pitched voice says with authority. "So that's why they made it that way."

Chee hands Minh a peeler and points to the cucumber by the sink, telling me that the holiday is something the kids love, because they receive red envelopes filled with lucky money from friends and family. Minh peels his cucumber quickly, making a game of flicking the peels into the wastebasket that Ha has moved next to him. "Sometimes we use pickles, not cucumbers," Ha says when she sees me jotting notes into my pad. When Ha speaks, it's always in a soft, almost restrained voice, and I have to listen closely if, like today, there's a lot going on around us. Her demeanor is somewhat restrained, too, and she walks about the kitchen softly, taking up as little space as possible, stepping lightly behind Minh to get to the stove or reaching carefully around An for something on the counter. Today she's focused on the cooking, looking intently into the pot when the shrimp are boiling, careful not to overcook them. She talks only when necessary, telling me just what I need to know about the food preparation—that she blanches the shrimp for a minute only or to show me the kind of beans she used to make the dipping sauce—and then continues about her work quietly.

It's Chee who's more gregarious. She chats freely as she helps in the kitchen, talking about Minh's school or raving about her sister-in-law's cooking, "She's really good," she says, explaining that the kids have been looking forward to Ha making the spring rolls today. I ask Chee whether there are any Vietnamese dishes that she likes to cook. She just shrugs.

"She's good at soup," Ha offers.

When it's time to begin assembling the spring rolls, Ha slips on her jacket and shoes to run to her house next door for more rice paper wrappers. While she's gone, Chee shows me a pitcher of deep burgundy liquid from the refrigerator. "It's special for our family," she explains, something she makes with beef bones and beets for her kids. "For their health." She says she sometimes worries that An, who doesn't eat a lot, isn't getting enough nutrients. "She loves it," Chee says, and then laughs when An asks for some.

When Ha returns, she makes sure I note the brand of wrappers she uses for her spring rolls. "OK is best," she tells me and slips one into the bowl of water on the counter. The rolling begins. Ha spreads a damp round of rice paper on a plate and carefully places two shrimp on this. "I want to see shrimp first," she says, her voice just a whisper. The cucumbers, lettuce, mint, chicken, and noodles are stacked carefully on top. Ha is precise and uses her chopsticks to portion the ingredients neatly in a mound on the rice paper and then rolls them to form delicate cylinders.

With Chee, Minh, and An helping, the large serving plate on the middle of the counter begins to take on a colorful pattern of pink and pale green, with the pieces of shrimp and cucumber still visible beneath the translucent paper rolls. "Look, I did a nice one," Chee smiles, holding hers up for us. We eat several each, dipping them into the slightly sweet sauce that Ha made earlier, then poured into individual bowls, and sprinkled with freshly ground peanuts. The sauce, a puree of beans and hoisin, is much lighter than that served in most Vietnamese restaurants, which is frequently made with peanut butter. Like Ha, this sauce is subtle and complements the delicate flavors in her spring rolls perfectly.

<hr />

I cook Vietnamese food almost every day, but sometimes I cook American foods, too, because we live in America. My daughter and son help me, especially when I make the Vietnamese noodles with chicken. That's the *pho,* and they love that in the winter. They can't cook it by themselves, but they know what goes in it. I also make the fresh spring rolls, and we serve them with our own sauce.

I learned these things from different people at home. I would go to their houses to eat, and, if I liked the food, I would ask what the secret was. I think everyone has their own way to cook. I grew up with my sister, and she influenced me a lot. She's fifteen years older, and, when I first came, I lived with her in Texas. She would cook, and I would help her. Now I repeat the pattern, because I cook with my family.

When I was in Vietnam, we lived close to the ocean and had lots of fresh fish. I loved the fish. I can make many of the same things here, but some things aren't as fresh. On the weekends, I bring my kids to the big Vietnamese market near my house, and we plan what we need to cook for the whole week. They like the food. They like the American things, too, but they always eat our Vietnamese food. I think it's the way I trained them when they were small. I always cooked our foods, so I think they're in the habit of eating that way. But I try to teach them to adapt to both cultures. So if it's an American holiday, like Thanksgiving, I'll cook the turkey, but I'll also make some Vietnamese food. I tell them that Thanksgiving is celebrated because the Puritans were thankful for their safety when they came here. And I explain that their parents are like Puritans, too, and they need to thank God because we made it here safely. So I teach them both ways.

For us, the important holiday is the New Year. In the past I've asked everybody to stay home for one day. The night before is very important. We have our special Vietnamese foods, like *bánh tét.* It's very traditional. They make it with sweet rice, yellow beans, and pork. They wrap everything in a banana leaf. This one I don't know how to do, so I go to the Vietnamese store. Every Vietnamese family must have that for New Year's because it's related to the story of the king. We also have special desserts, like the coconut ones that we buy or the watermelon seeds. And for the New Year, we always teach the children what they have to do. In our culture, they must go to the adults and wish them health. Then they must say sorry for the past if they did something that didn't please their parents so they will avoid that habit in the future.

In Vietnamese culture, we teach children to respect the adults. It's very, very traditional, but sometimes I think the kids are afraid to be close to their parents. They have to give so much respect, but it's hard for them to be open. So I like American culture. They teach kids respect, too, but it's different. I think American kids are more open with their parents: they can have eye contact when they talk. But in the Vietnamese tradition, no, you cannot even look at an adult; it's disrespectful. So the kids look down. And the way they talk, it's like you have to prepare to talk. If you want something, you don't say it straight; you have to talk soft and think about how to say it. I like the American way because the kids learn how to talk, not only with the family, but with society, and I think it helps them to be successful. If they get in trouble, they can stand up for themselves and explain things, but Vietnamese children don't feel confident to speak up in society. So I teach my kids both ways. For example, in the Vietnamese way, if I say something wrong to you, you can face me and talk, but you do it softly and ask in a nice way, respectfully. I remember one time my parents accused me of something. They thought I did something wrong, and they said, "You did that!" and I said, "No." But they just said, "No, we're right. When we say something, we're right, so don't talk back!" But I'm dif-

Ha's niece, An, helps out.

ferent. I let my children defend themselves, but in a nice way, a polite
way. And I listen.

Another thing I like about the United States is education. Anyone can
go to school, and you don't have to pay. Even in the public schools in
Vietnam, people still have to pay for certain things, so not everyone can
afford to go. And I like the relationships between the students and
teachers here. It's more open, and I think the students learn more. They
can ask questions, and that's very important, because the more you ask
questions, the more you understand. In Vietnam, kids still hesitate
when they're with the teachers. But things there are changing a little bit.
I think the kids are starting to be a little more open.

When I first came here, I didn't understand the education system. I
went to high school in Texas for three years. I wish they had had a bilingual program so I could have gotten more adapted. I think a bilingual
program for the first or second year helps you to feel confident. I got
completely lost. So I gave up and stayed home for three months and
didn't go to school. Every time I had to face school I started crying.

I didn't want to go because of the culture and the language. It was so different. I remember the first time I saw the students talking to the teacher. They were laughing, and it seemed like they had no respect. That was what I thought, because in Vietnam it was very different: you would go and sit quietly and bow your head to wait for the teacher. In class, we just listened. If we missed the homework or had bad behavior, the teacher could hit us. It was very strict.

Now I send my kids to Vietnamese school here so they can learn about our culture. They sing songs and learn how to write in the language. They like it. I bring them to Vietnam, too. I think they feel like it's their home. Sometimes they worry they will miss their friends here, but when they arrive in Vietnam, they're comfortable. The weather, the food, the environment, they feel like they're used to it, like they grew up there, even though they were born here. Even my husband's family was surprised about this. I think if you cook and you show them Vietnamese culture and speak the language with them, it makes it easier to go back.

My husband's family lives in Saigon, Ho Chi Minh City, and when we go my kids love to ride the motorcycles with their uncles. They go everywhere. It's fun because we go shopping. I buy fabric and bring it to the tailor. They can make the clothes very cheaply. But it's very, very crowded there because of all the motorcycles and people in the streets. My first time in Ho Chi Minh City, I was afraid because it was so crowded. Now it's okay, but I'm always happy to come back here.

But when I'm here, I miss the fresh food. In Vietnam, the market is always close, so you can get fresh things every day. We love the sugar-cane juice. My kids, too. That's always the first thing they run to buy. They just sell it out on the street. They make it with the fresh cane. The flavor is sweet and the drink is cool. In Vietnam, the weather is hot, so it is really delicious because it cools you down. That's something I'd like to have again.

Ha's Vietnamese *Goi Cuon* and *Tuong Ngot*

Spring Rolls with Dipping Sauce

Makes 20

This version of dipping sauce, which contains kidney beans, is something Ha and her sister created. Ha said the chicken and shrimp in the spring rolls can be replaced with tofu that has been cut into strips, steamed, and cooled.

6 cups plus 6 cups water, divided

1 teaspoon plus 1 teaspoon salt, divided

1 pound boneless, skinless chicken breast, trimmed

40 medium shrimp (about 1 pound), peeled and deveined

8 ounces rice vermicelli *(bun)**

20 rice paper spring roll wrappers *(bánh trang)**

1 cucumber, peeled, seeded, and sliced into thin strips approximately 2 inches long and ¼ inch wide

½ cup fresh mint leaves

10 lettuce leaves (green leaf, red leaf, or Boston), cut in half with stem ends removed

In a medium saucepan, bring 6 cups of water and 1 teaspoon of salt to a boil. Add the chicken breast and reduce the heat to a simmer. Cook until done, about 10 minutes. Reserving the water, remove the chicken from the pot and set it aside to cool on a plate. Slice it into thin strips, about ⅛ inch thick.

In the same pot, cook the shrimp until done, about 1 to 2 minutes. Cool in a cold-water bath to prevent further cooking. Drain well.

In a medium saucepan, bring 6 cups of water and 1 teaspoon of salt to a boil. Cook the noodles just until soft. Strain them and rinse under cold running water. Drain well.

To assemble the spring rolls: Have a large basin of warm water ready to soften spring roll wrappers. Soak a wrapper for several seconds (no longer) to soften it. Place this on a clean work surface. Place 2 shrimp across the bottom third of the wrapper. Place several slices of cucumber next to the shrimp. Place 2 or 3 tablespoons of noodles on top of this, followed by several mint leaves, a piece of lettuce, and finally 1 or 2 pieces of chicken. To roll the wrappers, fold the bottom third over the mound of ingredients and roll just until all are enclosed. Next, fold each side over this. Then gently roll into a cylinder to seal. Place the rolls on a plate covered with a damp towel to keep moist while you roll remaining wrappers.

Serve with the dipping sauce.

* Found in markets specializing in Asian products.

TUONG NGOT

One 15-ounce can dark kidney beans with liquid

½ cup hoisin sauce*

2 tablespoons sugar

½ teaspoon chili paste*

½ cup roasted peanuts, ground

In a blender, puree the kidney beans with their liquid, the hoisin sauce, sugar, and chili paste. Pour into individual dipping bowls and sprinkle with the ground peanuts.

* Found in markets specializing in Asian products.

Preserving Home

Sehin Mekuria, fifty-two, fled Ethiopia in 1979 and went to Kenya.
She made her way to the United States in 1981. Sehin works as an
accountant and lives in Jamaica Plain with her husband, who is also
from Ethiopia. The documentary film *Deluge,* which Sehin mentions
here, was produced by her sister, Salem Mekuria, a filmmaker living
in the United States. The film, which won numerous awards,
explores the revolution in Ethiopia that toppled the monarchy
of Haile Selassie in 1974.

ALTHOUGH SEHIN DOESN'T SEEM TO relish the task of preparing the
yebeg wot, a traditional lamb dish she will bring to her sister's tomorrow for
Easter, she leans over the twenty-five pounds of meat that is spread over
her kitchen table with an air of quiet resolve, occasionally putting her
knife down to explain the dish's complicated preparation to me. The des-
ignation of Sehin as food authority among her family here—a diaspora of
siblings forced to leave Ethiopia years ago—is something I imagine she's
slipped into with a sense of duty, her gesture at preserving the traditions of
a place far away, the memories of a brother long gone.

Standing in her kitchen now, she methodically picks up the long strips
of lamb from the pile stacked in front of her and scores them at half-inch
intervals as they dangle from her hand. The strips twist in the air as she
works her way upward, marking them with a large knife. Sehin isn't sure
why the meat is prepared in this manner; it's just the way it's always been

Opposite: Sehin butchers lamb for Easter dinner.

done, she explains. When I wonder aloud if it enables more of the sauce to be absorbed by the meat, she murmurs, "Yes, probably," the hint of a smile passing over her resolute face as she works through the pile.

On the stove, a large pot filled with a deep reddish brown liquid simmers away. This is the Ethiopian *wot,* the spicy sauce made with onions that have been cooked slowly for hours in clarified butter, and *berbere,* the classic spice mixture of red pepper, ginger, garlic, and coriander, which is ground by hand. In both of her freezers—there's one in the kitchen and another upstairs—Sehin has large glass jars of the *berbere* that her family sends from Ethiopia. These freezers are also packed with ziplock bags of the frozen sauce base made with spiced, clarified butter and onions. Containers of assorted herbs and coffee beans sent from home are also stored there.

Sehin talks about the huge amount of labor that goes into the sauces that are sent to her. Several pounds of chopped onions are cooked slowly in a large pan over a flame for hours. When she was young, it was her job to stir them. The meat preparation, she explained, was always done by several adults, so usually a group of women and children was involved in the cooking. Today, though, she cooks alone, working away at the meat while the sauce continues to cook into the afternoon. Hanging behind her on the wall is a large black-and-white photograph of a young Ethiopian girl in a traditional peasant dress carrying a jug of water and a bundle of wood. When I look at it now, I am reminded of Sehin. The girl gazes into the camera's lens with eyes that are direct and unwavering, yet suggest a faraway sadness, perhaps an attempt to mask something the viewer could never understand. When I ask Sehin if it is a photograph of herself, she laughs and explains that it's something she found in a shop when she was home. "I always liked that picture; I don't know why," she says.

She walks to the stove now with a handful of lamb pieces that she will cook for us to taste, placing them into a small pot filled with the simmering sauce. There's a package of *injera,* the Ethiopian flatbread, on the counter, and she pulls out several of the large disks, which are the consistency of a moist pancake, for us to spread onto our plates. The bread is used to scoop the *wot,* making forks and knives unnecessary at an Ethiopian table.

When we sit down to eat Sehin's delicious meal, she continues to stand, working away at her pile of meat and explaining that she'll have plenty tomorrow for Easter. The *yebeg wot* is extraordinary, the sauce rich with the sweet flavor of onion slowly cooked in spices sent from halfway around the world. *Wots* are also prepared with things other than lamb, including beef and chicken, sometimes fish. Sehin says that even tofu can be used. To me, it wouldn't matter, I realize as I wrap the *injera* around another piece of the lamb on my plate, which seems almost incidental. It's the sauce that is remarkable, a blending of flavors I'm certain I won't be able to re-create accurately in my own kitchen.

<hr />

We try to make the food here, but sometimes it just takes too much time. Our sauces need to cook for several hours, so we minimize the steps by bringing stuff from Ethiopia, like the sauce base, which they'll send to us. We get the spices from home, too, like the coriander, which is really similar to the Indian cardamom, the one that has the hard skin. And the butter, it's a clarified butter, and we flavor it with different things, depending upon which area in Ethiopia you're from. Usually it has garlic, ginger, coriander, and then maybe something else.

And then there's our bread, the *injera*. We can buy it here, but it's not really the same, because they can't always get the *teff;* that's the millet flour we use. So sometimes they'll just use wheat and mix it with barley or rice. You could get the *teff* before—we used to get it in Washington, D.C.—but it's become very scarce. There was a guy in Idaho or Texas who used to farm it and sell it to the restaurants, but I don't know what happened to him.

I've never really gone to Ethiopian restaurants here because I'd rather do it myself. We have someone living with us now, another Ethiopian woman, and she and I alternate with the cooking. So even if we don't have the *wot* every day, because that takes a long time, we do have things flavored with the spices. For our holidays, though, we make a lot of the traditional dishes. For Easter, we'll have lamb or chicken *wot.* If we decide to do it at my sister's, we might all go there and cook together. Sometimes, though, I'll just prepare something and bring it to someone's house. It takes a long time to cook anything, so we always share the responsibility. They sometimes make me do a lot of it because they say I'm a good cook. I don't know, though. My niece used to say, "Why can't you just tell them that they can cook for themselves?" And they do; they all cook, but they say that my food is like the real cooking.

Maybe it's because I always watched my mother. In Ethiopia, girls need to learn when they're about ten or so. You're told to sit and watch, so that's what you'd do. When I was little, my father was a governor out in one of the provinces, and there were special dinners he had to host. So there was always a lot of food being prepared, especially by the maids. There was one very, very good cook, and we were supposed to watch her. She would say, "Okay, do this, do that," and we did.

I can't do all the things now, but no matter what, coffee is the one thing that I will always keep. Whenever anyone goes home and asks what I'd like them to bring me, I always ask for coffee. Sometimes I try to do the whole ceremony when I have time. Back home, they do that outside in the grass with incense. They serve it with popped millet, which is kind of like popcorn. My mother and her friends used to do that every day. Here, whenever a guest comes, we'll serve the coffee. Sometimes my sister or sister-in-law will come on Sundays and we'll have it. But that's about it. During the week, I don't even make it at home because I don't have time. I'm always running around, making my lunch and doing other things, so I'll just have it at work. I bring my ground beans and make it in the percolator.

Back home, people can get together to have coffee. Here, we're just running all the time. There's so much you have to do in this country: work, pay the bills, worry about health insurance. It's like when I come home from work, there's still work. In Ethiopia, you don't worry as much. There aren't bills. If you have cash, you can buy something, and if you don't, you can't get it. Of course, you have more flexibility here, because you can get anything you need, but I also think you can do without so many things, that there are ways to substitute. And here, because you have all these things to think about, you don't really have time for friends. We still try to have our Ethiopian social life here: if someone dies, you have to go visit; if somebody is sick, you go; if someone has a baby, same thing. But that makes it very difficult because we want to live the life we had over there, but things are structured differently in America. I've seen a lot of conflict around that: the community wants things the way they were in Ethiopia, but it doesn't work here. Sometimes I think, oh, my God, how are we going to make it?

I look at families with kids, and I wonder how they do it. At home, even the neighbors would watch out for your kids. People don't have that here, and as a result, a lot of Ethiopian families have a hard time raising their children. Some of them actually send their kids back home and leave them with the grandparents until they're older.

I haven't been in a long time, almost ten years. Financially, it's hard. And then, once you don't go, maybe you don't think about it. Everybody there wonders when I'm coming. I haven't seen my mom in a long time.

I left in '79. I had to because of the military regime. They took control of the country when the monarchy ended. It was difficult for everybody then, not just the students involved in the movement, but really anybody who was young was a target. The military would screen houses looking for students, and if they came looking for your child, you would be subjected to many things. I think that happened to my parents. Some of us ended up in prison.

Then there was my oldest brother. He went to Russia for a while. The student movement had connections in other parts of the world. We asked him not to come back, but he said he couldn't stay away. He thought he had to contribute, to do whatever was necessary. When he did return, some of the people he had been in school with and who supported the military government knew that he had ties to the movement. So one day, he was taken from his office. He had been working as an electrical engineer. We don't know what happened. I know he must have died. That's like how many years ago—1978, '79? All we know is that they took him from his office, but we don't know anything that happened after that.

Most of the families found out about their loved ones, though. There were extensive records kept about the killings, and people used those to prosecute some of the officials. My sister tried to get information about my brother. She did the film *Deluge* about what happened. It explores the things that were going on at that time, a time when people just disappeared, when anybody who had power could just come and take you, and you wouldn't know where you were going. People were on different sides of the conflict, and there was so much confusion. You could just end up dead for nothing. If you read a certain paper, that might be considered a crime. Even kids, like fifteen or sixteen years old, maybe even younger, kids that didn't know anything, maybe they read something, something they didn't even understand, and then the same thing would happen to them.

There were so many things that were going on. Some people chose to write about it. My sister did the film. She interviewed me because I was involved in my own way with the movement. I worked for a social service agency, and it wasn't safe for me to be there after a while. I had to leave everything. Some friends helped me get through the border. My parents didn't know anything at the time. I didn't want to tell them, because it would be dangerous if they knew. I didn't call until I was in Kenya. My sister knew, though. She was the only one.

I think by now most of the people who were the leaders have been prosecuted. But still there are some who were involved in the regime, and even though everyone knows it, there's really no proof. I know the people who are responsible should go to jail, but you can't prosecute the whole country. It depends upon the extent of someone's involvement. Was it because he was forced to do it or was it that he purposely inflicted hardship and killing?

I know we can't become a democracy just like that. We need to learn that we can have differences but be together at the same time. A lot has changed, and we've been able to move away from some of it, but still, how much are we really willing to talk to each other? There are so many tribes, and sometimes there's mistrust between them: this tribe did this to us, another did that. For a while everybody was angry, and it created a lot of problems. I sometimes wonder when we will get to the point where we're all comfortable together. Because recently, with the election, it's clear there are still difficulties. People are trying, though. There are a lot of discussions going on, which is good, because we won't gain anything by continuing to fight, destroying everything we had. I'm hoping the more we learn about each other, the more that will all go away. And I think the younger generation can help the country change, because all of that isn't in their consciousness; they don't carry it with them. We do, though. Some of the people of my generation, they carry that baggage, and it gets us stuck.

So I don't think I'd go back there to live until maybe after I retired. I guess if I did go, I would like to do something that would be useful, and I'd like to not have to be afraid that I would end up in jail if I said something. Even though things have improved, we're still not there yet.

But I could visit. When you go back, everybody wants to invite you to their house. Something I would really love to have again is *kitfo*. It's a specialty from my region made with raw meat. They season it with clarified butter and spices. I would really love to have that. And then, if I went during the fasting period, there would be all the different dishes with vegetables, and the vegetables are so good there. You can get them fresh from the farmers at the markets.

So if I went to visit, one of the main things I could do is just go around and eat.

Sehin's Ethiopian *Yebeg Wot*

Ethiopian Lamb Stew

Serves 6

Although Sehin's family sends berbere, *the classic Ethiopian spice mixture, from home, it's not impossible to make here. Be certain that all the spices you use are fresh. The recipe can be increased and stored in the freezer for later use, as can the clarified butter, which is ideal for this dish, because the milk solids have been removed, allowing it to cook at a high temperature without burning. Because the* wot, *or stew, must cook for several hours, Sehin often makes the stew base ahead of time, reheating it to cook the lamb just before serving.*

According to Sehin, injera, *the Ethiopian flatbread made with* teff *flour, is difficult to prepare. She buys her* injera *at local markets specializing in Ethiopian goods. The pancakelike bread is used to scoop the* wot, *making utensils unnecessary. If you don't have* injera, *the* wot *can be served with rice.*

Finally, chicken can be substituted for lamb in this dish, in which case it would be called doro wot. *If using chicken, replace the lamb with 2½ pounds of skinless legs and thighs and cook a little longer than you would the lamb pieces, about 25 minutes total.*

¼ cup vegetable oil

2 pounds red onion, finely chopped (a food processor can be used)

½ cup clarified butter (recipe follows)

½ cup *berbere* spice mixture (recipe follows)

1 cup dry red wine

1 cup water

2 pounds lamb (from leg), cut into thin strips (¼ inch thick) and lightly scored along the edges

Salt and freshly ground black pepper

In a large, heavy saucepan, heat the oil over medium heat until shimmering. Add the onions and cook until caramelized to a deep golden-brown color, stirring frequently, about 30 to 40 minutes. Add the clarified butter and *berbere* spice mixture and continue to cook on low heat, stirring occasionally, for 30 minutes, adding a small amount of water if the onions begin to stick to the pan. Add the wine and 1 cup of water and continue to cook for 1½ to 2 hours, or until the onions are very soft. More water can be added if the onions begin to stick to the pan. (At this point the *wot* can be cooled and stored in the refrigerator for 2 to 3 days or in the freezer for up to 6 months.)

Season the lamb with salt and pepper. Add it to the pot and simmer, covered, until the meat is cooked through, about 15 minutes. Season the sauce with salt and pepper.

Serve with *injera* or rice.

CLARIFIED BUTTER

Makes about ¾ cup

2 sticks (½ pound) unsalted butter, cut into pieces

In a heavy saucepan over very low heat, melt the butter. Remove from the heat and let stand for 5 minutes.

Skim any foam from the top and discard. Pour the melted butter slowly into a container, discarding the milk solids at the bottom of the pan. Can be stored, tightly covered, in the refrigerator for up to 6 months.

BERBERE SPICE MIXTURE

Makes about 1 cup, or enough for two recipes

1 tablespoon cumin seed

4 whole cloves

½ teaspoon whole cardamom seed

½ teaspoon whole black peppercorns

½ teaspoon whole allspice

1 teaspoon fenugreek seed

2 tablespoons coriander seed

3 tablespoons sweet Hungarian paprika

1½ teaspoons cayenne pepper (or less if you prefer the sauce to be mild)

⅓ cup fresh ginger, peeled and grated

¼ cup garlic, minced

1 tablespoon salt

In a heavy saucepan over medium heat, toast the cumin seed, cloves, cardamom seed, black peppercorns, allspice, fenugreek, and coriander seed, stirring constantly until lightly browned, about 2 minutes. Cool.

With a mortar and pestle or in a spice grinder (a coffee grinder that has been thoroughly cleaned of coffee grounds will do), finely grind the toasted spices. Add the remaining ingredients and mix thoroughly, working the mixture to form a thick paste.

Can be stored, tightly covered, in the freezer for up to 6 months.

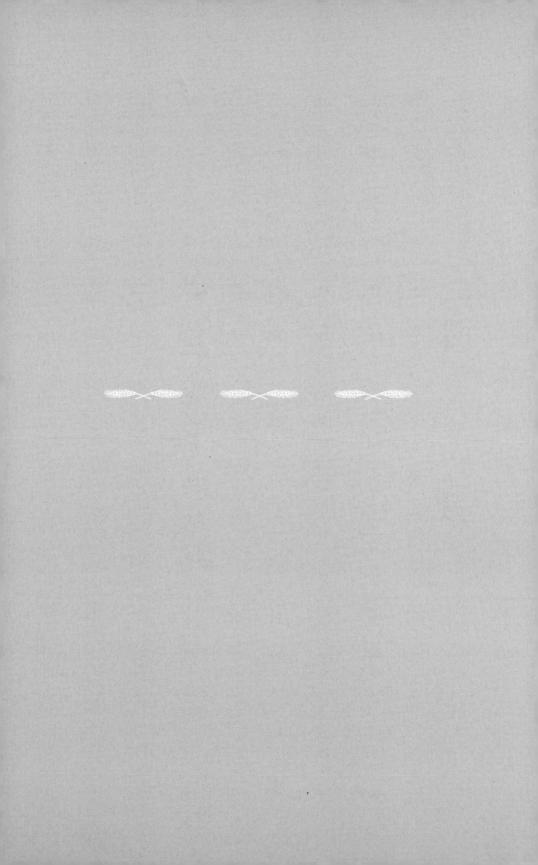

Less Conservative Now

Najia Pathan, twenty-six, is originally from Pakistan and came to the United States in 1999 with her parents and three brothers. When she first arrived, she studied at the University of Massachusetts in Boston, where she received her bachelor's degree. She now works as a fund accountant for a large bank in Boston.

———✕———

THE SMALL KITCHEN WHERE NAJIA and her mother, Perveen, cook their Pakistani foods is so filled with ingredients and cooking implements that hardly any surface is free for the women to work. Containers of yogurt and bowls filled with jalapeño peppers, garlic, and fresh ginger cover the table in the center of the room, and the counters are stacked with frying pans and piles of dinner plates. Perveen is preparing the tandoori chicken, working through a pile of legs and thighs by inserting a small knife several times into each before tossing them into a bowl to marinate. Her luminous black hair is pulled into a braid behind her, and the beige *dupata,* or head scarf, she wears falls loosely about her shoulders. She stops occasionally to comment about something Najia is doing or to tell us about her husband, at work now, who she says is a good cook and helpful around the house. Her face breaks into a broad smile when she lists some of the awards and scholarships her children, including Najia and her three sons, Adnan, twenty-three, Kamran, twenty-one, and Noman, fourteen, have received at their various high schools and universities.

"*Lakalakalakalaka!*" Perveen calls over to Najia now, shaking her head at her daughter. "Sometimes she puts too much," she explains, pointing to the

Opposite: Najia slices onions for salad.

container of cinnamon Najia has been pouring into a pot on the stove. Najia shrugs and returns the container to its spot on the counter. She picks up the mortar and pestle, brings them over to the table where her mother is, and begins to grind some ginger.

"At home, we'd get everything from our garden—the ginger, garlic, the mint, cilantro, and limes. We grow all of it fresh," Najia explains, adding that this ginger is store-bought. Najia speaks quickly in near-fluent English peppered with idiomatic expressions she's picked up in college and, recently, at work. She lists the ingredients that go into the marinade she is preparing for the chicken and turns to her mother occasionally to verify something in their language, Pashtu, before switching back to English. Najia radiates a carefree, natural beauty; her long dark hair and coffee-colored skin glow against the cool turquoise of her dress, and her nearly black eyes are thoughtful and curious. "There's a Pakistani restaurant near us, and you can get a lot of the dishes we're making today there. Sometimes I bring my American friends, and they really like it," she tells me.

While Najia describes the meal they are about to prepare, Perveen moves to the oven, a sleek unit somewhat incongruous in this well-worn kitchen. She bends down in front of it, adjusting the eyeglasses propped on the tip of her nose in order to read the settings. Najia explains that her father has just installed it because they were having a special on them at his work. Perveen, who understands English well but sometimes struggles to speak it, shakes her head and laments, "The old one was good," and then calls for Adnan to help her preheat the oven. Her oldest son programs the temperature, opens the oven door to help his mother put the tray of chicken on the rack, and returns to the next room, where his brothers are doing something on the computer.

Soon the heady scents of jalapeño and garlic fill the air when Najia begins to sauté them with some of the spices that are stored next to the stove. Unlike in many American kitchens, these are not kept in small containers in out-of-reach places. Rather, the counter is lined with commercial-sized containers of cardamom seed, cinnamon, clove, cumin, coriander, and turmeric, each left uncovered with a large spoon in it for easy and frequent access. The women are preparing the spice base for *palou,* a rice dish from the city of Peshawar, where they are from, and they begin to season the pot simultaneously, tossing in liberal amounts of spice. "Just use little bit," Perveen tells us, stepping in front of Najia to add a hefty spoonful of green cardamom seeds.

While Najia measures rice into a bowl, Perveen bends down to check the progress of the oven. She sticks her hand inside and makes a clicking sound with her tongue, shaking her head in frustration. The oven isn't preheating. Najia calls Adnan back into the kitchen and, after pushing some more buttons, removing the tray of chicken, rotating the oven racks, and finally placing the chicken back inside, he assures his mother that it's all set. Perveen raises her eyebrows, still skeptical, and wanders around aimlessly for several moments, half-heartedly wiping down the counter.

Najia, meanwhile, continues to chop, grind, mix, and sauté. She tosses a piece of ginger and several cloves of garlic into a small electric blender but stops when Perveen says something to her. Najia rolls her eyes and says, "My mom doesn't want me to use the electric mixer," and empties the contents into the mortar. "So I'm gonna use this."

Despite the overwhelming heat and humidity on this August day, the cooking continues into the afternoon, with Perveen and Najia turning out beautiful pots of spiced vegetables, scented meats, chutneys, and several kinds of bread. Najia uses the ends of her *dupata* to move pots from the stove to make room for Perveen to cook the flatbread. At one point, she steps around her mother—bent over a large bowl on the floor kneading dough—so that she can grab an onion from the counter.

When it's nearly time to eat, Adnan, Kamran, and Noman begin to move furniture from the living room into one of the bedrooms. Perveen spreads a batik cotton cloth onto the floor, and Najia places huge platters of food onto the center of it. Younis, Najia's father, who has just returned from work, joins the group. With a round frame and easy smile, he presents a jolly, carefree nature, laughing with his sons, who come out to greet him, and looking hungrily toward the food gliding by in Najia's hands. Perveen approaches the floor cloth with a stack of hot *paratha*, a type of flatbread, which smells almost sweet from browning on the pan; then she reaches for Younis's hand and lowers herself to the floor. "I'm tired now," she says. "When my husband is here, I sit."

<hr>

My mom and I cook all the same things now. We shop at Indian and Pakistani stores for the spices, and we cook our food every day. It's our food! When I come home after work, it's like I'm in Pakistan. It's comforting because it's the same smell.

The *chaplee kebab* is one of my favorite foods. It's made with beef and onions and tomatoes. If you go to Nowshera or Peshawar, that's what

Mother and daughter cooking.

you will have. They serve it over the naan, the flatbread. We have that at home a lot. And we eat *palou.* It's rice that you cook with beef or chicken. My favorite is *dal chaawal,* which is lentils over rice. The other night we had chicken *tikka,* roasted with spices. My mom makes the same things she did in Pakistan.

I started cooking when I was seventeen because my mom got sick. She was really, really sick, and my father was here in the U.S. After that, I would cook when we had guests because they liked my food. I'm a good cook. I learned from my mother. She taught me the basic things, like the spices you need for certain recipes. Most recipes start the same way: you fry the onions, add tomatoes and spices, and then whatever else you have, like the vegetables or the meat.

In the mornings, before we'd go to school, my brothers and I would be eating and we'd see my mother cooking. I watched so that when I grew up it was easy for me to learn how to do it. Sometimes my brothers like to cook now, but they only make simple things. In Pakistan, men usually don't cook. They go to their jobs, and when they come home, everything is ready for them.

I like American food, too, but I'm Muslim, so I can only eat halal meat. That makes it hard for me when I go out to restaurants. I usually order vegetable dishes, and actually my eating habits are changing because I'm starting to like vegetables more than beef or chicken. I don't really like the taste of the chicken over here. There's something different about it; it's hard to explain. Over there, it has more flavor. Here, it cooks a lot faster, and it just won't take the spice. And the fruit, that's different, too, like the mangoes. Over here, we have mangoes, yes, but I don't really like them. If you go to Pakistan in the summer, you will see mangoes everywhere. The moment you enter a shop, you'll smell them. You wouldn't believe the taste. The sweetness is incredible. It's awesome!

We have a lot of fruit there, and trust me, it's so much better because we don't use any fertilizers or chemicals to grow it. Like my grandmother, she has orange, lemon, and pomegranate trees. She lets the fruit take its own time. When the season comes and the fruit is ready, that's when we eat it. And the taste is good. I think it's because the foods in Pakistan are always local. When we cook now it tastes different. For example, in Pakistan the milk is completely different. You could boil it and see the butter and cream on top. We'd skim that off and put it in the fridge to eat for breakfast with bread and sugar. It's hard to get that here.

It took me a while to get used to the culture, too. Over there, you were always spending time with your relatives and neighbors, visiting them to eat and drink tea together. You don't have to make a call to tell them you're coming; there's always someone at home. And if you're not going to see your relatives, then you're going to your neighbor's house. You talk about your problems, and you just have a fun time and drink tea. Sometimes you live right next to your relatives. Actually, you are always somehow connected to your neighbors. If there are two Pashtuns or two Pathans in the same room, they will know that they are connected to each other somehow. You know every single person in your city. Over here, it's different. I still don't know my neighbors, and I've been living in the same apartment for six years. None of them! I don't even know who has moved in, who has moved out, or when people come and go in my building. I don't know anyone after six years.

I'm not sure why this is. Maybe because people over here are from so many different cultures, it's harder for them to get to know each other. Over there, you don't see that. I think that's really the beauty of the U.S. When I was in Pakistan, I didn't know anything about other countries. I didn't know about any other cultures, religions, or anything. I just knew about Pakistani people, Pakistani religion, and Pakistani culture. Whenever I saw Hollywood movies it seemed to me that the people were from another world. How they lived, what kind of food they ate, and how they dressed seemed so strange to me. I used to think about this stuff because over there you just see your own people.

I'm a more open person now. Maybe I'll say something to my friends back home and they might not understand. Like over here, gay and lesbian marriages are legal in some states, but over there, it's like a crime. I've begun to think about these things differently since I came here: maybe that's just the way some people want to live, and you should not try to force them to live another way. In Pakistan, if someone is gay, it would be considered a crime, like it's against nature or something. But here, if someone wants to marry someone from a different background or from a different religion or different ethnic group, it's okay because they fell in love. In Pakistan, it's hard to make people understand these things because our culture is kind of conservative, but here you have to be more open.

When I tell my friends these things, they tell me I'm Americanized, that I'm not a Pakistani girl anymore. I suppose my thinking has changed, but it doesn't mean that I'm Americanized. I'm just open to more cultures and different people. I'm still Pakistani, and actually I think I'm more connected to Pakistani culture than the people over there because I know how hard it is to live far from your people. Over there you really don't think about that. And the food, I'm really proud of the food now, too. I like to bring Pakistani dishes to parties or take my friends to the restaurant near my house. If I cook something for an American friend and they like my food, I just feel proud because they liked it. It's my food!

Sometimes I have to explain my culture, though. I have to explain Islam to some people. There's this guy at work who keeps asking me questions. He says, "Your religion is about violence." It makes me mad. I try to explain to him that it is not true, but he doesn't always understand.

So I'm proud of my culture, but I've also changed a lot. My brothers have, too. Over there, they were more conservative. Like my younger brother, Kamran, when he would have friends visit him over there, he wouldn't let me meet them, because he thought it wasn't right. Over here, it's different. I can meet his friends. He takes me to parties. He dances with me. And my other brother introduces me to his friends, and if I dance with some guy at a party, they won't mind. They will come and dance with me, too. We talk a lot now. They talk to me about my fiancé and they tell me when they like someone at school. They might compliment me if a dress looks good on me. Now whenever I go out, I ask them what I should wear. We've all changed a lot; we have a very close relationship.

I'm getting married next year. I have known for many years that my parents wanted me to marry him. They let me make the decision, though, and I'm happy about it. But going back to Pakistan will be hard for me. I'll miss my parents and my brothers a lot. I'll miss things about living here, like being able to do my own stuff. If I want something, I just go to a grocery store and I get it. If I want to buy some clothes, I can go alone; I don't have to wait for my brother to take me. Over there it will be hard because I can't really go out alone as a woman. If I did, the men would harass me. So, maybe my husband or a cousin will take me out.

I won't be able to work, either, and I'll really miss that. In the city where I'm from, it's difficult to find jobs because they're not open to women working. I guess it will be hard for me to stay home because I'm so used to working now and to being busy. I guess I'll try to do something else, like social work or something; I know it's going to be hard, but I'll try.

I have really gotten used to some American things. And yes, I'm less conservative now. It's not a bad thing. I want to teach that to my own kids someday. I think it makes your life easier, because if you're open to other people's cultures and to other people's feelings and to what they're doing with their lives, it really doesn't bother you. You're like, okay, this is their life. If that's how they want to spend it, just let them. It doesn't bother you. But if you think that all the things other people are doing is wrong, you'll spend your time thinking about how to stop them. When you don't feel like you have to do this, your life is really a lot easier.

Najia's Spicy Pakistani Dinner:
Tandoori Chicken, *Palou, Bhindi, Podina* Chutney, Salad, and *Paratha*

Roast Chicken with Spices; Spicy Rice; Fried Okra; Cilantro, Mint, and Yogurt Chutney; Salad; and Fried Bread

Serves 4 to 6 for dinner

Tandoori *refers to the cylindrical clay ovens called tandoors used in Pakistan, India, and Afghanistan for cooking and baking. Breads such as naan and chapati are cooked in tandoors. The dough is flattened by hand and stuck to the walls of the oven, which is heated to a very high temperature with wood or charcoal. Najia's tandoori chicken can be cooked in a conventional oven that's set on high heat. It's best to marinate the meat for at least a day for optimal flavor.*

TANDOORI CHICKEN

    1 whole chicken, about 2½ pounds, skin removed and
         cut into 8 serving pieces

    5 garlic cloves

One 2-inch piece of fresh ginger, peeled

    ½ jalapeño pepper, cored and seeded

    1 teaspoon chili powder

    1 teaspoon freshly ground black pepper

    2 tablespoons vegetable oil

    ½ teaspoon salt

Pat the chicken pieces completely dry with paper towels. With a small, sharp knife, cut slits about ½ inch deep and 1 inch long into the chicken pieces.

Using a mortar and pestle, grind the garlic, ginger, and jalapeño peppers, or puree them in a blender or food processor. (Remember to wash your hands immediately after handling hot peppers.) Transfer to a large bowl. Add the chili powder and black pepper. Add the chicken pieces and toss so that they are evenly coated with the marinade. Marinate in the refrigerator overnight.

Preheat the oven to 450°F. Brush the bottom and sides of a large baking dish with the oil. Arrange the chicken pieces in a single layer in the baking dish. Sprinkle with the salt and pour the remaining juices from the marinade over the chicken.

Roast, uncovered, in the middle of the oven for 15 minutes. Reduce heat to 350°F and continue to bake until the chicken is golden brown and cooked through, about 10 to 15 minutes. Arrange on a platter and serve.

PALOU

One 2-inch piece of tamarind*

1 cup warm water

3 tablespoons vegetable oil

1 small red onion, peeled, cut in half lengthwise, and sliced lengthwise into thin strips

2 garlic cloves, minced

1 tablespoon fresh ginger, peeled and finely chopped

2 plum tomatoes, chopped

¼ teaspoon ground chili pepper

1 teaspoon whole coriander seeds

½ teaspoon whole cloves

½ teaspoon whole cardamom seeds

1 cinnamon stick

2 cups basmati or long-grain white rice

3 cups beef stock (water can be substituted)

1 teaspoon salt

2 tablespoons fresh cilantro leaves, finely chopped

Soak the tamarind in 1 cup of warm water for 15 minutes. Strain by pressing the softened pulp and liquid through a strainer over a bowl. Discard the seeds and fibers.

Meanwhile, in a 2-quart pot, heat the oil over medium-high heat until shimmering. Add the onions and cook, stirring frequently, until golden brown but not burned, about 4 to 5 minutes. Add the garlic and ginger and continue to cook until they begin to soften, about 3 minutes. Add the tomatoes, chili pepper, coriander seeds, cloves, cardamom seeds, and cinnamon stick and continue to cook until the tomatoes are soft, about 3 minutes. Stir in the rice, and when the mixture is well combined, add the beef stock or water, 1 cup of tamarind water, and salt. (If your beef stock contains salt, decrease the amount you add to the rice.) Stirring frequently, bring the mixture to a boil. Reduce the heat to medium and cook the mixture, covered, until the rice is tender and all the liquid has been absorbed, about 20 minutes. Taste for seasoning.

To serve, transfer the rice mixture to a platter and sprinkle with the chopped cilantro.

* Found in markets specializing in Asian, Indian, and Afro-Caribbean products.

BHINDI

- 2 tablespoons vegetable oil
- 1 small red onion, peeled, cut in half lengthwise, and sliced lengthwise into thin strips
- 2 cloves garlic, minced
- One 1-inch piece fresh ginger, peeled and finely chopped
- ½ jalapeño pepper, cored, seeded, and finely chopped
- 2 plum tomatoes, chopped
- 1 teaspoon ground coriander
- ¼ teaspoon turmeric
- 1 pound okra, washed and stems removed
- ½ cup water
  Salt and freshly ground pepper

In a heavy 12-inch skillet, heat the oil over medium heat until shimmering. Add the onions and cook, stirring occasionally, until they are golden brown but not burned, about 5 minutes. Add the garlic and ginger and continue to cook until they begin to soften, about 2 minutes. Add the tomatoes, jalapeño pepper, coriander, and turmeric and continue to cook until the tomatoes are soft, about 3 minutes. Add the okra and ½ cup of water. Cook, covered, stirring occasionally, until the okra is tender, about 15 minutes. If the okra begins to stick to the pan, add more water.

Season with salt and pepper and serve.

PODINA CHUTNEY

½ cup strained or 1 cup unstrained plain yogurt

¼ cup fresh cilantro leaves and stems, finely chopped

¼ cup fresh mint leaves, finely chopped

¼ small jalapeño pepper, cored, seeded, and finely chopped

1 garlic clove, minced

Pinch of salt

If using unstrained yogurt, you will need to strain it. Do this by draping several thicknesses of cheesecloth over a strainer that has been placed over a large bowl. Pour the yogurt into this. Gather the ends of the cloth and twist to squeeze out the extra liquid. Allow the yogurt to drain for 1 to 2 hours.

In a medium bowl, mix the strained yogurt with the remaining ingredients. The chutney can be stored, tightly covered, in the refrigerator for 2 to 3 days.

2 cucumbers, peeled, seeded, and diced into ½-inch cubes

2 tomatoes, seeded and diced into ½-inch cubes

1 small red onion, diced into ½-inch cubes

¼ cup fresh cilantro leaves and some stems, chopped

1 tablespoon fresh lemon juice

Salt and freshly ground pepper

In a bowl, combine the cucumbers, tomatoes, onion, cilantro, and lemon juice. Season with salt and pepper.

PARATHA

- 2 cups flour plus additional flour for working dough
- ½ teaspoon salt
- 1 cup water
- 1 tablespoon vegetable oil, plus more for frying

In a bowl, combine the flour and salt. Slowly add the water and oil, and, using your fingers, mix the dough until it can be gathered into a ball. If the dough crumbles, add more water. If it is too wet, add flour. Knead the dough by folding it end to end and then, with the heel of your hand, pressing it down and folding it forward. Repeat until the dough is smooth and elastic, about 7 to 8 minutes. Gather the dough into a ball, place it in a lightly greased bowl, cover with a cloth, and let rest for 30 minutes.

Divide the dough into 8 pieces. Using your hands, shape each piece into a ball. On a very lightly floured surface, using a rolling pin, roll each ball into an 8-inch disk, approximately ⅟₁₆ inch thick.

Heat 1 tablespoon of oil in a heavy-bottomed skillet or a cast-iron pan over medium-high heat until shimmering. When the pan is very hot, add one of the *paratha*. Shake the pan back and forth to prevent the *paratha* from sticking. Cook until bubbles begin to appear and the bread is lightly browned, about 1 minute. Turn the *paratha* over and cook it for another minute, allowing it to puff up slightly. Cook the remaining *paratha* in the same manner, adding oil to the skillet each time. Arrange them on a plate and serve immediately.

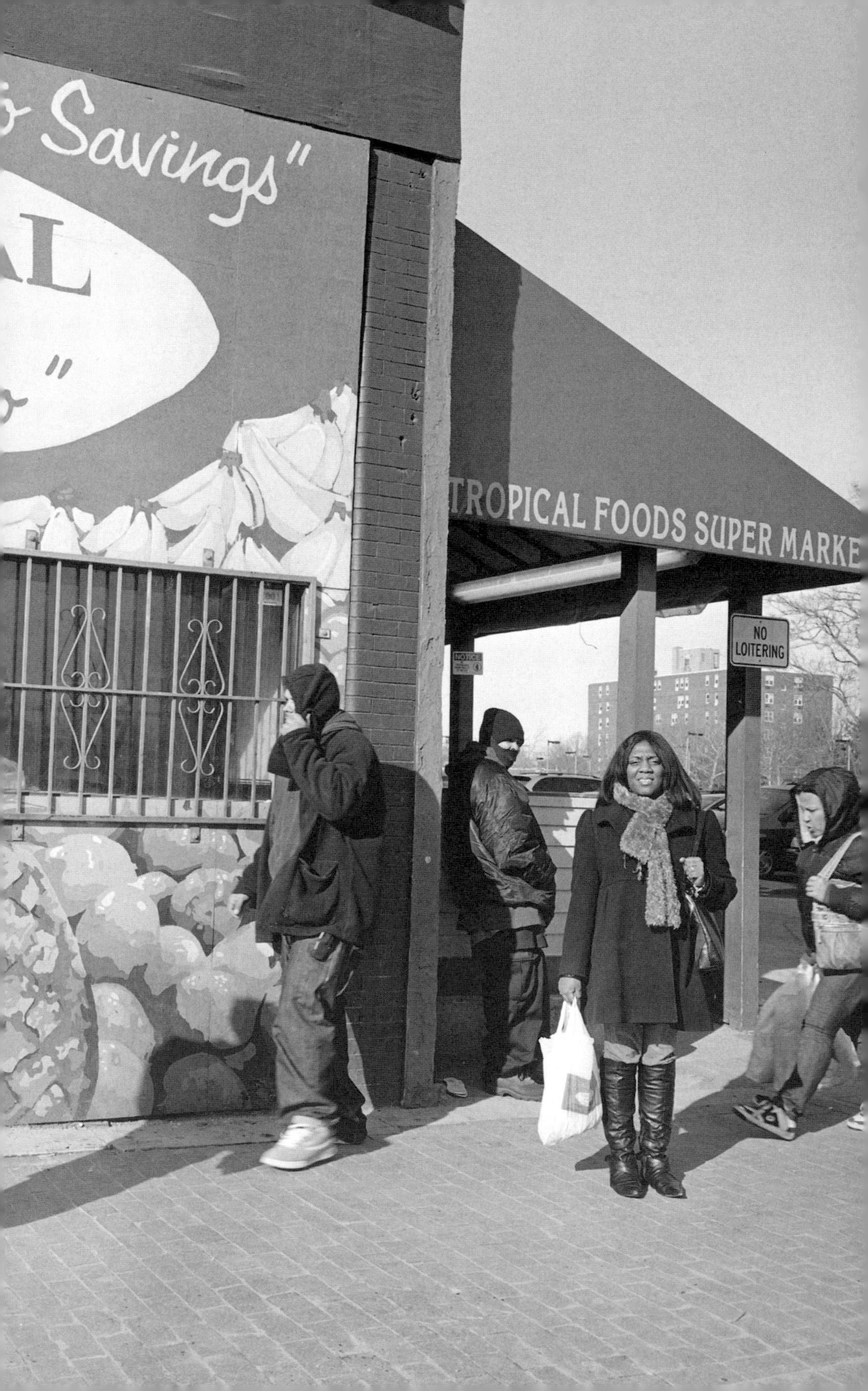
"Savings"
TROPICAL FOODS SUPER MARKE
NO LOITERING

It's Okay to Be Different

Tanisha Cooper, thirty, was born in the United States but moved to
Panama at the age of two months to stay with her grandmother for
several years. When she was five, she returned to the United States
and lived with her parents in Virginia, where her father was stationed
in the army. Today, Tanisha lives in Boston with her husband and
works as a kindergarten teacher at the Neighborhood House
Charter School in Dorchester. Her mother, Marcia Ngadi, fifty-five,
lives nearby.

※✕※

THE CORNER IN DUDLEY SQUARE where Tropical Foods is located pulses
with activity on this cold Saturday morning in January. Several men in over-
sized coats and sweatshirts linger in a patch of sunshine outside the Afro-
Caribbean market, where shoppers who come from places like Jamaica,
Trinidad, Panama, Brazil, and Ghana can find the *fufu* flour, plantains,
and fresh tamarind they need for their favorite dishes.

A mural, spanning the side of the building in seven large panels, is radiant
in the sharp winter sunlight. Its bold colors depict scenes from inside the
store, giving the area a lively, artsy feel. This part of Boston, known as Roxbury, has seen many changes since it was first settled by wealthy clergymen
and merchants in the seventeenth century. Some of the earliest buildings
in the city can be found nearby, including a former governor's mansion. The
Italianate-style brick structure across the street gestures to a more affluent

Opposite: Tanisha pauses with her groceries in Dudley Square, Roxbury, Massachusetts.

time, but it is abandoned now and plastered with peeling advertisements for rock concerts. In the past sixty years, the area has become a center of African-American culture, with Latino, West Indian, and African immigrants moving into the outlying neighborhoods and the furniture businesses of decades past giving way to hair-braiding salons, money transfer offices, even a strip club.

There's a steady stream of people moving up the ramp that leads to the supermarket entrance. Most walk quickly, their heads bent to protect their faces from the frigid air. One middle-aged woman, clearly uncomfortable, has the sleeves of her down jacket pulled over her hands so that the arms dangle loosely by her side. Over the roar of buses and cars traveling toward the nearby expressway, the disparate rhythms of English, Spanish, and languages I don't recognize can be heard in the parking lot adjacent to the store. There's a line of cars waiting to park; a woman wearing a red and purple African head wrap turns around to say something to three kids in the back seat of her minivan while the driver behind beeps his horn, signaling a parking spot ahead has opened up.

Inside the store it is warm: the yellow walls and bright prints depicting island life are another world from the winter scene outside. This is a busy place on a Saturday morning: families, women, and a surprising number of men shopping on their own push carts or carry baskets in their arms as they roam the aisles. "The chicken gravy, where's the chicken gravy at?" I hear one man mutter to himself as he scans a shelf of canned squid, octopus, and sardines. The meat section, which wraps around the rear and one side of the store, is filled with cuts not readily available in most American markets: turkey gizzards and tails, chicken backs, necks, and feet. For pork, there's anything from chops to chitterlings, smoked jowl, and stomach. A large package of burnt beef feet looks like nothing I've ever seen, and the size of the deep brown beef liver spread on a tray reminds me just how big a cow really is.

When someone stumbles near the front entrance, several shoppers turn. It's a large woman who, in her rush to push through the thick plastic panels hanging in the doorway to keep the heat in, has tripped over the rug on the floor. She regains her balance just before knocking into a display of coconut soda. "I'm six months pregnant," she announces angrily, looking around for a manager and warning anyone who will listen that she might just sue the place.

Tanisha arrives, breezing into the market with a warm smile and an air of self-possessed calm. She moves the way I'd imagine someone from the

Caribbean might, as if she has all the time in the world for you, unbothered by the chaos around her. This may be one of the reasons she's so well liked by her kindergarten students. I've observed her on several occasions guiding a group of twenty or more five-year-olds back to their spots on the carpet or bringing their attention to something she's written on the board. She does this without ever losing her patience, enticing them with her calm, soothing voice, her generous smile. Today she takes us down the aisles of one of her favorite markets, a place where she first began shopping with her grandmother years ago. Tanisha doesn't get here so much these days, just for holidays and special occasions or when she needs to stock up on hard-to-find ingredients. "I'm a Stop and Shop girl now," she laughs, pointing to some of the things she and the other women in her family use to cook their Panamanian dishes. We stop in the medicinal herb section, where there's a colorful display of powders, seeds, and leaves that are all unfamiliar to me. She reaches for a package filled with what looks to be deep red flower petals, explaining, "We use it for sorrel, a drink we make with ginger. It's so refreshing!" I put the package in my basket so I can try the drink at home.

Tanisha lists the benefits of the other items on display: chaney root, "Used for bellyaches," she says; senna, "Like a laxative"; and finally, isinglass, which is made from the bladders of fish and sometimes used in beer and wine making. "Men use this sometimes," Tanisha lowers her voice with a smile, "when they're having problems."

We move to the produce section, where long stalks of sugarcane are stacked in a pile. "We like to chew on it," she says, "but it's not as good as the ones in Panama." The yam aisle is next. African, Brazilian, and yellow yams are displayed next to several different kinds of yucca, their gnarly appearance probably not so appetizing to the uneducated cook. Tanisha describes the different soups her family makes with these. Then there's the yucca they deep-fry and press much like a plantain chip. "I did that with the kids this year." She often cooks with the kindergartners, drawing on the Panamanian foods her grandmother first taught her to make as well as recipes like fish cakes.

We wind our way toward the rice section, an area about fifteen by fifteen feet and packed with every size bag imaginable—anything from one to fifty pounds—stacked nearly to the ceiling. "This is the only kind we use for the arroz con pollo," Tanisha tells us, pointing to one of the numerous brands on display. Her cousin, whose daughter is in Tanisha's class, made several huge platters of it for the harvest festival at the school this year. "It was a hit," Tanisha smiles. "I know someone who had five platefuls, but then I'm not mentioning names," she giggles, turning toward the curry powder display. The store carries her favorite West Indian brand, one that she uses to make curried goat, a Jamaican-style dish made with rice and peas. She tosses the largest bag she can find into the basket.

Wandering through the crowded aisles, we brush past a man who seems out of place in his large white cowboy hat and an older woman who struggles with her basket, which contains only two small items. She shuffles in tiny steps down the aisle, trying hard not to get too close to anyone. Another woman wheels a large travel bag by us purposefully, and I wonder if she's just returning from somewhere or is on her way out of town. Besides food, the store sells phone cards, artwork, suitcases, paddles used for making *buss-up-shot,* a bread similar to *roti,* and even machetes. When I ask Tanisha about this, she smiles. "Yeah, Caribbeans love their machetes." She tells me that even her grandmother, who's eighty-nine, has one. "She's never used it, though. She just waves it around when she's mad at the neighbors." I ask Tanisha if she, too, has one. She just shakes her head and laughs.

Earlier, when I met Tanisha's mother, Marcia, she told me her daughter was more American than Panamanian. Maybe she's right.

⊰⊱ ✕ ⊰⊱

Tanisha: In our culture, every Sunday is like Thanksgiving. You cook a lot of food—meat, vegetables, everything. We have a lot of family here and everyone cooks. So we'll all get together and eat, usually at my grandmother's, but sometimes we'll do it at my mom's.

Marcia: When they come to my house, there will always be a bunch of us—the ladies—cooking the favorites. We make the arroz con pollo a lot. That's the rice with chicken, one of our national dishes. We also make the empanadas, the tortillas, the tamales. And then there's the *carimaño-las;* they're made with cassava, what you call yucca. It's the same as the empanada, but instead of the dough being made with corn, you use the cassava. You boil it and then mash it with flour and put meat inside. Back home, lunch is the big dinner, and everyone eats together. We'd have rice, beans, chicken, fish, vegetables, anything. If you have time, you have a little siesta after the meal and then you go back to work.

Tanisha: I just love it there. It's such a different culture. It's so laid back, and the people, they're so charming. They'll be walking in the street and everyone says hello or good morning to you. People are always socializing: after work everyone's outside, sitting on their porches and talking.

Christmas is like a whole other world there. Everyone goes to church and after that we eat. There are lots of special breads and cakes and things we make for the holiday, like the souse. It's made with pig's feet and peppers and cucumbers and onions. Even the markets, where we'd go to get everything, they're so interesting. I love them! They're outside and they'll have chickens running around. They have goat, fresh eggs. And the rice, you buy it right from the container. No cans or plastic. Even the bread, nobody buys Wonder Bread there; everything is always fresh; the food is natural. People really make time to prepare healthy, homemade food. Here, I think people eat at McDonald's too much, but over there, it's different; we only do it sometimes. We eat at home; like for breakfast we'll have porridge: plantain porridge or coconut porridge. The plantain porridge is one of my favorite things. You mash the plantains—green or yellow—cook them, and then add a little butter.

But Christmas, that's the time when we really cook. All the neighbors will make something, and we'll just go from house to house and talk and eat. The kids play outside and get to stay up until midnight. Sometimes we go to the beach. And on New Year's, that's another celebration where we visit with the neighbors and eat a lot.

Marcia: Like here, I don't even know my neighbors to do that. People keep to themselves. When I first came to this country it was hard, because I wasn't used to this. In Panama, no matter who's next to you or behind you, you always communicate. It doesn't matter if you don't know them. Here, no. When I first came and it was Christmastime, it was so hard. That first Christmas I was in my house and I didn't know anyone. Even on New Year's, nothing. Over there, everyone knocks on your door.

But I don't regret coming. I had to because Tanisha's father was in the army, so I came as a wife. I've gotten used to things now. There, it's a little more traditional. I tried to raise the kids with our customs. The most important thing for me was that they respect our elders. I always said, "Don't disrespect anybody! At school, don't ever curse the teachers; don't hit anybody." I try to teach her the values. She's American, though, like the way she acts. At eighteen, they think they're grown, but in Panama, they stay with their families longer. My kids can stay with me as long as they want, as long as they follow the rules.

Tanisha: In that respect, the cultures are different. Like the way people think about school, it's very different in Panama. My uncle, he's an engineering professor, and he's revered there. Everybody loves teachers. Here it's a little different. I think it's because, in Panama, parents are so much more involved in their child's education. Even the poorest person is involved. Here, I think with the different social classes, it makes it hard, and some families don't have what they need to help their kids. Over there, no matter where you are at the economic level, everybody wants to be involved. The dream is to have your child educated. Here, parents are lazy about it, or they don't have the resources to do it, or they're frightened. I think many of them just don't know how to do it. I've noticed that a lot of American kids are way behind the children there.

Marcia: Yeah, we're both teachers, and what I've found is that when parents disrespect you, the kids disrespect you. I saw it in the preschool where I was. It's different. It's a difference of culture. In Panama, you don't disrespect your elders no matter what. You don't do that. You don't curse at your teacher. I've had little ones that wanted to hit me. So I always tried to teach my kids our values.

Tanisha: My grandmother is even more traditional than my mother. After I graduated from college, I got my own apartment. Well, it took her about a year to get over that! In our culture, women don't do that. They come back home and stay until they get married. I'm different. And then women in our culture are supposed to have kids by now, and I don't; I keep going to school. They all think something is wrong with me. Yeah, they do. All the women in my family are married and have children already. I'm the only one this age who doesn't have kids. I'm the weird one. I guess they think I'm kind of Americanized because I believe in schooling and working before marriage. I have to keep explaining myself all the time: "Yeah, but I value my education first. Then I can commit to have children," I'm always telling them. My mom is fine with it, but my grandmother still has a hard time.

Actually, I'd like to raise my kids in Panama. My husband, though, he's from Trinidad, and he'd probably prefer to be there. I like the education system in Panama, the culture, the people, the manners. Not everyone has manners here. And respect for elderly people, you can't always get that here. I want my kids to have that. And the way of life is so different. It's much more laid back and not as fast and crazy. Over there, we have a strong sense of community. If you work, it's like a community. And when you stop for lunch, it could be two hours. You go home and relax. Even as a teacher, because schools have a break in the middle of the day, I'd go home and relax with my family.

Marcia: When I first got here—oh, my God, this rushing, rushing everywhere—my life was completely different. It took me a while. I just wanted to go back, but my mother kept saying, "No, you have your husband. That's where you belong." But the rushing—oh, Americans rush around a lot. They rush for everything. You don't do that there. You just relax. You take your time with things. You take your time to go to the bus, then you come home and you take your time with your kids. Over here, you're always thinking, what do I have to do tomorrow?

And now I've started to rush around! Like when I go to New York, I get off the bus and rush to my mother's house. I rush to the bus, rush to get to the train, rush to get groceries. Sometimes, when I go to Panama now, I start to get annoyed because I feel like they're too slow. I think, come on, let's get into the bus, let's get going on the train. But they take their time.

Tanisha: Me, too! It annoys me sometimes. Just to get from point A to point B, you have to stop and talk to everybody. It takes like fifteen extra minutes just to get down the street. When I'm there, I try to walk really fast, because that's what I'm used to, but I can't. People try to stop me. And even if they don't know me, they know I'm not from there. They think I'm kind of strange because I'm walking so fast. Also because I use the ATM. Even going to the ATM is like a huge thing for people over there. It takes me not even two minutes to use it, but for them, it's a weird thing to go to a machine instead of talking to someone at the bank.

Marcia: Panamanians are just very social. And they tend to welcome whoever. Anybody. For example, with music, Panamanians will dance to any music from any part of the world. We don't discriminate. And with race, I never thought about different races until I came to America. The first time I was called a nigger, it was in Virginia when Tanisha was small. They said, "Take your banana boat and go back." I started laughing because I thought it was a joke. I didn't come on a boat. I came on Bryant International Airlines! And a nigger, I didn't know what that was. I had to ask my husband.

The race problem in Virginia was kind of hard, because I've always been a friendly person. We had a lot of white neighbors there, and I think it took them maybe three years to talk to us. One of them later told me they were testing us to see what kind of people we were, to make sure I wasn't one of those black people who liked to fight or whatever. I thought, what's the difference? I'm a person just like you. It never bothered me, though, and it never will. And I raised my kids to think the same: "Don't worry about it; it's our color," I always told them.

Tanisha: Yeah, Virginia was hard, because it was kind of a closed, conservative place. Moving to New York was totally different, because it opened my eyes to other cultures. In Virginia, I was the only black kid sitting in the classroom, but in New York, I could identify with people more. There were Panamanian restaurants on every corner and there was the West Indian–American Day Parade. So it was kind of a relief, because, before that, no one even knew where Panama was. They had no clue. Or they had never really met black people who spoke Spanish. It was just not normal for them. But in New York, everybody understood. And now, in Boston, it's in between.

Going to college was a little hard, too. I went to a predominantly Caucasian school, and so I was again one of the only black students. It was like I had gone back to my earlier years, like I was reliving it all again, because I was in school with a lot of people who weren't used to seeing people like me. It was hard to deal with that. I think I experienced racism at that point. I remember when I was a freshman, it was one of my first days of school, and we were reading about Audre Lorde, a black poet, and they were all shocked that I didn't know a lot about her. They said, "Well, you're black, you should know about Audre Lorde!" I was like, no, in my school we never really focused on that.

I don't tolerate that kind of thing in my classroom. I remember when coming from another culture wasn't cool. But in our class, we try to create an atmosphere where it's okay to be different, where different cultures are celebrated. We've done fish cakes from Barbados because that's where one of the teachers is from. Or, if there's a child from another culture, we try to get the parent in to share. We've had a mom from Cuba who's come in to read and Vietnamese parents who taught us songs and talked about the lucky money for Asian New Year. The kids really liked the lucky money!

So, I think if you can expose children early on to different cultures, it's important. Some people never get a chance to experience that.

TANISHA'S PANAMANIAN SORREL DRINK

Serves 4 to 6

This drink, deep burgundy in color, is made from the sepals of the roselle flower, a species of hibiscus bearing no relation to the green European sorrel. Besides the drink's popularity in the West Indies, variations of it are popular in Mexico, Central America, Southeast Asia, and Africa, where the plant also grows. Tanisha says it's the perfect thing on a hot Panamanian day.

6 cups water

2 ounces dried sorrel,* about 1½ cups

1 piece orange peel, approximately 3 inches by 1 inch

One 2-inch piece of fresh ginger, peeled and sliced

2 cinnamon sticks

6 whole cloves

1⅓ cups sugar

¼ cup rum, optional

In a nonreactive pot, boil the water. Add all the remaining ingredients except the optional rum, stirring continuously for 1 minute.

Cool and let steep, covered, at room temperature for at least 2 hours. (It can steep overnight for up to 8 hours for a stronger flavor.) Strain the liquid through a fine sieve into a glass jar or pitcher. (Note: sorrel will stain plastic.) Discard sorrel, orange peel, ginger, and spices. Taste for strength and sweetness. If it is too strong, add water. If it is too tart, more sugar can be added. If using rum, add before serving.

Pour over ice.

---

*Found in markets specializing in Afro-Caribbean, Latino, Middle Eastern, or Asian products.

Cooking Every Day

Limya Ibrahem, thirty-eight, lives in Everett, Massachusetts, with her husband and three children. Originally from Sudan, she came to the United States in 1998. She studies English as a second language at Bunker Hill Community College in Boston.

✻

LIMYA IS A QUIET COOK. She floats soundlessly about her kitchen in a red and black *toab,* a large sheet of light cotton fabric that she drapes over her head and wraps around her body. Occasionally a corner of it catches on a kitchen chair or the edge of the stove, and she'll stop what she's doing, sigh softly, and unsnag it. When she wraps it around her waist again now, she knots it tightly and then turns back to the mortar and pestle on the counter. This is filled with garlic cloves she's been pounding throughout the morning. She works the garlic to a paste and spoons it into the various pots on the stove, refilling the mortar whenever it gets low.

Limya is preparing *mulukhiyah* this morning, something she ate nearly every day when she lived in Sudan. It's a stew made of lamb and the *mulukhiyah* leaf, also known as mallow, popular in Middle Eastern cooking. When cooked, the leaves resemble spinach but are slightly bitter in taste. In another pot, she's frying some lamb with spices. "This one I make for my husband," she tells me, adding several heaping tablespoons of coriander.

Her children, Leena, Ayman, and Luddan, who are nine, seven, and five, watch a children's program on television in the next room. Although it's midmorning, the room is dark because the heavy drapes have been

Opposite: Limya uses a mortar and pestle to pound garlic for *mulukhiyah.*

pulled across the windows. The fabric is a deep wine color, which matches the sofas and Persian-style rug displayed in the center of this immaculately kept room. Ayman, Limya's son, sits between his two sisters on the sofa and bounces up and down when things on the large flat-screen TV get exciting. His little sister seems bored and begins to wander about the room until he and Leena complain, asking her to sit down so they can see. The children bicker quietly in English until Luddan finally moves, poking a shy face through the doorway to check on the cooking.

The kitchen takes on an otherworldly quality, disconnected from anything beyond the confines of the tiny room, with several pressure cookers hissing away loudly on the stove, the pungent smell of garlic, coriander, and lamb becoming almost overwhelming, and Limya covered from head to foot in fabric that billows around her when she moves. She reaches toward the one small window above the refrigerator and opens it. "Strong," she says, referring to the scents filling the room. When she calls to Leena, loudly now because of all the noise in the kitchen, her older daughter comes right away, and Limya directs her in Arabic to the task of pounding garlic. The little girl works the pestle quietly for several minutes until Limya tells her she may return to her TV program.

The *mulukhiyah* leaves are added to the stew when the meat is nearly cooked. Limya buys these frozen at the halal market nearby and uses a *mufraka,* a long wooden mixing implement, she brought back with her from Sudan. "We do it like this," she says, clasping the handle between the palms of her hands and rolling it back and forth to break the leaves into tiny pieces and distribute them evenly throughout the stew. Limya works the *mufraka* for several minutes, her gaze lost in the deep green stew in the pot, a tangible reminder of her life in Sudan, where she helped her mother prepare this same dish. Limya's mother passed away recently. She told me she thinks about her mother especially when she cooks, trying to remember all the things she learned at the stove. When she talks about her mother now, her voice trails off. She turns back to the pot and twirls the *mufraka* again.

Something about the way this quiet Sudanese woman moves around her tiny American kitchen makes her actions seem temporary, almost fleeting, a presence not fully complete. When I ask why the *mufraka* has a crack running down its middle, she considers the question for a moment and then laughs. "Oh, my kids, they were playing one day and it broke." Limya has a subtle, wistful beauty, and when she smiles, it comes at you full force, her black eyes darting about playfully and her laughter revealing teeth that are white against skin the color of walnut. The smile lasts for only a moment, though, and she quickly tucks the dark curls that have fallen into her face back under her *toab* and resumes mixing.

While we wait for the stew to cook, Limya brings out a tray with a pitcher of pineapple juice and some glasses that she's placed on paper doilies. "In Sudan, if a guest comes to your house, you must give them something." She looks at her children in the next room and tells us about her dreams of moving to Dubai one day, when her kids are teenagers, she says, because she's worried about them growing older here. When I ask how they feel about leaving, she tells me she's certain they'll like it. I wonder, though, as I listen to the three of them laughing together at American television.

At noon, the stew is done. This will be served with *kissrah,* a Sudanese flatbread Limya buys at the market. They'll eat later, she explains, when her husband, who is sleeping now because he works the night shift, can join them. "I'm bored," one of the kids announces from the other room, their program having ended.

"Maybe we'll go out for lunch today, to the buffet," Limya sighs. "I need a break from cooking."

<hr>

When I was younger, my mother used to tell me, "You must learn to cook," but I didn't want to. She began to teach me when I was twelve, maybe thirteen. Now, it's different. I have a family; I have my children. I have to cook. Every day. Maybe two or three hours every day I cook. Sometimes my kids like it, but a lot of times they want American food, like chicken nuggets from McDonald's. I don't like this stuff, and I feel so sad when they ask for that. It's boring. I don't really like American food. But I like Chinese; it's hot! Our stuff is hot, too. Sometimes my kids like to eat with me; like my son, he likes my cooking still. He likes it when I make the *maschi.* I stuff green pepper with spices and beef and cook it. You can eat it with rice.

They're like American kids now. Sometimes I play the Sudanese channel on TV, and they don't understand because of the Arabic. I'll start to explain it to them, but sometimes they'll say, "I don't like this. I hate Sudan!" My small daughter, Luddan, says, "Oh, I hate Sudan!" I'll ask her, "Why? It's your country. It's your people," but she just says, "No, I'm American, from Boston!"

I just watch. I don't say anything. If I push them a lot, maybe they'll have bad feelings. They're still young. Maybe when they're grown up, they'll understand. I try to talk to them about our traditions. I like the marriage celebration: we make hennas for our hands and wear special dresses when we get married—white first and then, after the marriage, a red one. Some girls, when they come here, they still do this. I think my daughters will, too.

We celebrate our holidays here, like Ramadan. We find a place for one day, and all the Sudanese come together. Sometimes there are other Muslims there, too, like people from Morocco, Egypt, Lebanon, and Pakistan. We're all together. It's good for the kids because they learn what Ramadan means, and we have all the special foods. I have to go to the Arab store sometimes for the things I need, especially for the holiday. They have a special kind of *jibna*, it's like a soft cheese, and they have the halal meat. I bring things back from Sudan with me, too. Like dried okra—we need this for Ramadan, so I have to bring it back because I can't get the right kind here. We use it to make *aseeda;* it's like a custard, and it's special for the holiday.

And for Ramadan, I wear the *hijab* [head scarf]. I don't always wear it at other times, though. Oh, I feel like everybody looks at me when I have it on, like maybe they have bad feelings about me. I think it's because of September 11th. Before that, nobody cared. Once on the train, this woman, she was with her daughter, and they walked up to me. I remember the woman put her face right next to mine, very angry, and shook her head at me. I couldn't understand what she said, so I just walked away. I don't want trouble with anybody. Not all people are like that, but still I don't wear it all the time. And my girls, just for Arabic school they wear the *hijab,* because they cannot pray without it.

Some things are different here. When the kids are teenagers, they have girlfriends and boyfriends. Maybe that's hard for us because we're Muslim. I don't know what I'll do when my girls get older. I'm thinking about a special school, like a Catholic school, because they're more strict. I'm afraid of public schools here, of boys and girls together. We don't do that in Sudan.

Another thing that's different is the way people talk to each other. I think it's too strong sometimes. People can say anything they want. It makes me shocked because I've never been able to just say anything. Even women do this here! They are not shy. In my country, it's different. You can't say anything you want, unless maybe it's just girls or women together. But sometimes, it's hard there, too. There are a lot of things you can't do in Sudan. If you're a woman, you cannot stay out late. If you're divorced, maybe people will talk about you. Women have more freedom in the United States. We change here. Even the men, they are closer to their women here. In my country, the man, he goes from work to see his friends. He's not there when you have a baby; it's your mother, your sisters that help you with that. Here, he's the only one that can help you, so he stays with you. When I had a baby, they gave my husband some vacation from work, and he stayed with me for maybe one month. He changed when he came here.

I left after I married. Everybody wants to come to America. It's a big dream. They all think there are dollars everywhere, that anybody who comes will be rich. But this is not true! You work hard. They don't understand that in Sudan. When you go back, they'll ask you for money. They'll say, "Give me a thousand dollars," and I'll think, oh, really? You really think I can give you a thousand dollars? I don't even have two! Then I have to explain that what they are thinking about America is not true, but they don't believe me. They think I'm saying that because I don't want them to come. All they want is to be rich. "Come and try it!" I tell them. They'll be disappointed. It's a hard life. In Sudan, it's not easy, but it's not like here. In Sudan, at least you can relax. You can take your time. Here, you can't. Here, it's do this and do that, always something.

I feel like I'm American now. It's been ten years, and I feel like I'm not really Sudanese anymore. Maybe if I went back to my country, somebody might say, "Why do you do that?" Like if I wear blue jeans, people will say, "Why? She is married now. She is old. She has kids. Why does she wear jeans?" When I went, I wore pants, not jeans, but pants. After that, they talked about me. I remember my mother said, "She went to America, and now she wears pants. Is she American?"

I miss my mother a lot. When I cook, I think about her. Sometimes I cry. I'm okay now, but right after she died, I was so bad. I dreamed about her all the time because she passed away just like that. We would cook together and make traditional things, like the Sudanese perfume. I spent a long time with her learning how to do it. We use sandalwood; we soak it with clove and then boil it to make incense. We do that for marriage ceremonies. You burn the incense in the fire, and the bride gets the smell all over her body. All Sudanese women, they are supposed to show their daughters how to do this. And because I was going to travel away to America, my mother needed to teach me this.

Someday I'll show my daughters these things and tell them to not be strong with their husbands, to speak nicely, to take care of the house and family and to cook. I'll tell them they need to cook every day and that they need to take care of themselves, to never be dirty, to always line their eyes before they go out. My mother taught me everything, but after she died, I left it all. I stopped lining my eyes, I stopped doing a lot of things. I don't know why. I couldn't do it. I felt like I was forgetting my mother. People would say, "That's not good," and I'd say, "I know, but I can't do it." Now, I'm trying again.

Sometimes in my dreams I hear her talk to me: "Remember to do the henna. Remember the incense. Remember the cooking." Then she'll ask me things: "Why do you do this? Why are you doing that?" When I hear her at night, I can't sleep. It's hard, because my kids don't know anything about her. When I talk about my mother, they just look at me like they're confused. So when I cook now, I try to talk about her. When I do the *hodra,* I talk about how my mother would prepare it, how she'd cook the meat and onions with it, and how we'd all eat it together.

I think especially Leena will know how to do all of these things one day. She likes to know about everything I do. When I wear some gold or a special dress, she likes it. "Mama, I like this," she'll say, and ask to try it on. She helps me in the kitchen, too. She prepared something with me this morning. And someday, my little one, Luddan, she'll help, too. But my son, no. He doesn't always help. He just likes to fill his stomach with my food.

LIMYA'S SUDANESE *MULUKHIYAH*

Lamb and Mallow Stew

Serves 6

Jew's mallow, also called mulukhiyah *or* molochiya, *is a mucilaginous vegetable, which means it possesses a natural thickening agent, making it the perfect addition for this stew by the same name. Different versions of the dish are popular throughout the Middle East. This is Limya's mother's recipe.*

2   pounds lamb stewing meat, trimmed and cut into 1-inch pieces

    Salt and freshly ground black pepper

2   tablespoons vegetable oil

2   medium onions, chopped

6   cloves garlic, minced

2   tablespoons ground coriander

1   teaspoon cardamom seed

4   plum tomatoes, chopped

One   15-ounce can ground tomatoes

3   tablespoons tomato paste

Two   16-ounce packages frozen jew's mallow* (one 16-ounce package of frozen spinach and one 16-ounce package of frozen okra can be substituted)

Season the meat with salt and pepper. In a large pot, heat the oil over medium-high heat until shimmering. Add the meat, onions, garlic, coriander, and cardamom and cook until the meat and onions become lightly browned, about 8 to 10 minutes. Add the plum tomatoes, canned tomatoes, tomato paste, and enough water to cover the ingredients. Bring to a slow simmer.

Cover and cook until the lamb is tender, about 1½ hours. Add the frozen jew's mallow (or spinach and okra) and continue to cook for 10 minutes. Season with salt and pepper.

Serve with rice.

* Found in markets specializing in Arabic and Asian products.

Why Not Teach Them to Cook?

Ana Beatriz Chacón, thirty-six, lives in the Jamaica Plain section of
Boston with her husband, Tony, and their two sons, Juan Antonio,
four, and Alejandro, twenty-one months. She has lived in the United
States since 1990 and has yet to return to her native country,
Guatemala, because of legal restrictions.

BEATRIZ BRUSHES ASIDE A STRAND of her dark, wavy hair that has fallen
into her face and reaches for a ceramic bowl on a shelf near the floor. This is
the one she uses for tortillas, something she learned to make as a child when
she cooked with her mother and siblings in Guatemala. "It was harder there,
because we had to make a fire, so we'd all take turns getting the wood," she
says. They prepared these and *chuchitos,* a type of tamale, every morning
and then accompanied her mother to the market, where they'd sell all the
food.

Today, four-year-old Juan Antonio is clearly interested in the cooking
going on in his own kitchen; he checks in and out, holding a plastic shark
in one hand and pointing excitedly with the other, questioning his mother
about the meal in a mixture of Spanish and English. His little brother,
Alejandro, scampers about in diapers, following the bowl of tortilla dough
Beatriz carries across the room. When some of it falls onto the table, he
stands on tiptoe to reach for it with a triumphant smile.

Beatriz chats freely, stepping over a pile of plastic animals on the
floor to stir the beans cooking on the stove, and then slips an arm around

Opposite: Making the tortillas.

Alejandro, who is balanced precariously on a chair. She deposits him gently onto the floor in front of the toys and tells us about the market in her village, one of her favorite places, where the foods and people she longs for in this country can still be found. She brings the bowl of tortilla dough over to the sink to add more water, working it into the corn mixture with her hands. "I could probably make tortillas with my eyes closed," she laughs.

When it's time to shape the dough, Juan Antonio, smiling proudly, saddles up to the table on a stool. He's an expert tortilla maker, Beatriz has told me, and he demonstrates with flair how to pat the dough quickly between his hands to shape the disks that will be cooked on the griddle. It's the fourth day this week Beatriz has cooked these, and when Juan Antonio has friends over, they always make tortillas. I can see why: manipulating the soft golden *masa* into edible disks of rich corn would be the perfect activity for a playdate.

Soon the only sound in the kitchen is the gentle clapping of hands, Beatriz and her older son turning out tortillas, while little Alejandro sits patiently next to them, waiting for dough to fall in his direction.

⋇

Certain times were more difficult at first, like Christmas, because I didn't have my family, and I really missed all the food. When I first came here I had to learn everything—the language, the weather, everything! I was like a newborn. Even the food was new; it was really hard.

For us, holidays are about food, and that's when we cooked the most. Every Christmas we made tamales and this special drink called *ponche*. It's made with raisins, coconut, plantain, and pineapple, and it's so delicious. When I first came here, I knew I had to have those at Christmas. Now, when I make them, it makes being here easier. I like to cook with my kids so they can see what we did in Guatemala. It's hard because they haven't been there, so they don't know a lot. But the food, that's one thing that I can do with them.

I try to do other things, but it's difficult sometimes. Like the language; Juan Antonio speaks a lot of English now. The other day my friend from Guatemala said to me, "Oh, you should make him talk in Spanish!" How do I make him? I can't! I try to remind him, but he'll just start the sentence with Spanish and then he finishes it with English. But he understands everything. When my sister was here, they had no problem communicating because she'd talk to him in Spanish and he'd answer in English. She'd understand what he said. It was different with my mother, though. He had to point to things or ask me.

When I get my papers, I want them to visit Guatemala with me every summer. Just for them to speak in Spanish for a whole day with my family would be wonderful. We have so many beautiful things that I want them to know about, like the Mayan culture. It's so sad for me to be saying this, but it took me coming to this country to understand what we have there—not that my mother didn't give it any value—but because we were there, maybe we didn't think about it.

They do know about the food, though, like the tortillas. When I was really little we always cooked tortillas with my mother. We were very poor then because she wasn't working and she had to take care of five of us, so I don't have a lot of memories of cooking different kinds of foods at that time, just the tortillas. It makes me sad to talk about it. I probably never realized before that we didn't cook a lot of different things because we didn't really have anything to eat. I do remember on birthdays my mother would do whatever she could to make it special. And of course the tortillas and the beans and the cheese were always the main things we ate then. Beans and tortillas and cheese.

We cooked with my mother a lot. When we were a little bit older, she used to have this little corner at the *mercado,* the market, where she would sell coffee and *chuchitos.* These are like little tamales, with corn dough and meat wrapped in a corn husk and steamed. I made them for Juan Antonio's birthday this year. We would make them at home and then we'd all take them to the *mercado* with her. She'd be selling the stuff there and we'd play with the other kids. It was really fun, because we knew everyone. I remember there were these people who would come with a blender and a bunch of fruit, and they'd make you a *licuado.* It's like a cold drink. Then there would be another woman with hot drinks. There's this one drink, *atol blanco,* that I just dream about now. It's made out of the same corn flour that you use for the tortillas. You cook it with a lot of water, so it's like a liquid. When you go there, they put it in a clay bowl and they put black beans, chili powder, lime, and salt in it. I'm just dying to go and have that. I can almost taste the beans in my mouth. That's the one thing that I really crave.

Oh, I miss going to the *mercado,* because that's a thing you do every day, not like going to the supermarket once a week, like here. People still do that because food is a big thing for us Guatemalans, especially on the weekends. That's when we'd make special things like chiles rellenos or *paches*. Those are tamales made out of potato. Every weekend, my mother would always ask us, "What should I make today?" We'd love to think about what to cook, even if we couldn't always make all the things we wanted.

Now I like to do that with Juan Antonio and Alejandro, and I just hope that someday they will have nice memories of the times that we are spending together now. I hope that when they grow up they will want to come back and ask me to cook something for them. I've seen kids here that, when they grow up, don't even see their parents, and months go by and they don't call them. I think that in this country we are so busy doing so many things that we don't spend time together. I don't want to say it the wrong way, but for a lot of families, going to McDonald's, that's spending time together. Well, it *is* spending time together, but there is a better way to do it. I don't need to go to McDonald's to have a good time with the kids. I'd rather go to the playground with them. Or make tortillas.

Why not teach them to cook? They love to make the tortillas. Last week, there was one day when I didn't make them, and Juan Antonio said, "Aren't we going to make the tortillas today?" I'm glad he knows about that part of the culture. I always tell him things about Guatemala, and he tells the stories to other people and about how, one day, we are going to go there. I want them to go. For them to know Guatemala is very important to me. I want them to know where they came from and to learn something from it.

Where I lived, we just knew everybody, and people looked out for you. I want the boys to have that experience. When I was little, we had this friend, Doña Zoila. She was like a mother to me. I could talk to her about anything. She would always give us something when we went to her. Maybe she'd just give us an orange, but it was always something. I remember people would come to her with their kids and ask if they could leave them for a while. She'd always say yes, and the baby would be running around, no problem. Here you have to make appointments and set up everything because people get aggravated if you just show up. But there, it's different. People do those things there.

I remember this other woman, Doña Bertita. She had a store near the *mercado,* and she used to cook a lot. She was very good to us. She would say, "I'll just cook up a pot of chicken soup for you." We'd go to her and she'd feed us. We couldn't care less about the soup; we just wanted the chicken because we never ate that. We were poor, and when I think about it, I realize now that some people didn't want to have a relationship with us. She was different. She used to call me Beatrizita, little Beatriz. She was the only one that called me that way.

Oh, the *mercado!* It was just like that! All those people. And the food. It's probably different now, but the way it used to be, wow! It was just a street, but we knew everybody. It's hard not to miss that. It was such a part of us growing up for so long. So my first thing I want to do when I bring the boys to Guatemala is walk to the *mercado,* just to remember all that.

BEATRIZ'S GUATEMALAN *TORTILLAS CON FRIJOLES Y QUESO*

Corn Tortillas with Beans and Cheese

Serves 4

Beatriz says that her mother always served her tortillas so that la cara, *the face, would be seen when it was eaten. This is the first side that's cooked and, Beatriz says, is the most visually appealing. The tortilla is served with this side placed down on the plate, topped with beans and cheese, and then folded.*

BEANS

1 tablespoon vegetable oil

½ onion, finely chopped (about ½ cup)

3 cloves garlic, minced

Two 15-ounce cans of black beans

Salt and pepper

TORTILLAS

Makes 10 to 12

2 cups *masa harina** (corn flour)

½ teaspoon salt

1¾ cups water

1½ cups grated mozzarella, Monterey jack, or other mild, melting cheese for serving

In a medium-sized pot, heat the oil over medium heat until shimmering. Add the onions and garlic and cook, stirring frequently, until soft, about 5 minutes. Add the beans with their liquid, cover, reduce the heat to low, and simmer until the beans are soft, about 30 minutes. Season with salt and pepper.

Meanwhile, preheat a large, heavy-bottomed skillet or electric griddle to medium-high. Combine the *masa harina* and salt in a large mixing bowl. Add the water and mix with your hands until the dough comes together. Knead for 2 to 3 minutes by pressing the heel of your hand into the ball of

---

* Found in large supermarkets and markets specializing in Latino and Afro-Caribbean products.

dough and folding it over onto itself in the bowl. (The dough should be moist and slightly sticky. Add more water if necessary.)

To shape tortillas, wet your hands to prevent the dough from sticking to them. (A small bowl of water nearby is helpful.) Pinch off a piece of dough about the size of a golf ball and roll it between your palms until round. Pat this between your palms and fingers in quick, gentle clapping motions, passing it back and forth from one hand to the other to flatten it. Continue until you have formed a disk approximately 4 inches in diameter and ¼ inch thick.

Place the tortilla onto the ungreased griddle or skillet and cook until golden, about 3 to 5 minutes on each side, using a spatula to flip. Stack the tortillas on a plate and cover with a cloth to keep warm until serving.

To serve, pour a spoonful of hot beans over each tortilla. Sprinkle with 1 to 2 tablespoons of the grated cheese. The tortillas can be folded in half and eaten with your hands.

CALIFORNIA STUDIES IN FOOD AND CULTURE

Darra Goldstein, Editor

Text: 11.25/13.5 Adobe Garamond
Display: Adobe Garamond, Adobe Woodtype Ornaments
Compositor: Westchester Book Group
Printer and Binder: Thomson-Shore, Inc.